KATHERINE MANSFIELD

Auckland International Airport Limited

"The longer I live the more I turn to New Zealand. A young country is a real heritage though it takes one time to recognise it. But New Zealand is in my very bones"

Katherine Mansfield 1922

Wishing you a most memorable stay in New Zealand!

Managing Director
Auckland International Airport Limited

KATHERINE MANSFIELD

new zealand STORIES

SELECTED BY
VINCENT O'SULLIVAN

Auckland

OXFORD UNIVERSITY PRESS

Oxford   Melbourne   New York

OXFORD UNIVERSITY PRESS NEW ZEALAND
Oxford New York
Athens Auckland Bangkok Bogotá
Buenos Aires Calcutta Cape Town Chennai
Dar es Salaam Delhi Florence Hong Kong
Istanbul Karachi Kuala Lumpur Madrid
Melbourne Mexico City Mumbai Nairobi
Paris Port Moresby São Paulo Singapore
Taipei Tokyo Toronto Warsaw
and associated companies in Berlin Ibadan

OXFORD is a trade mark of Oxford University Press

ISBN 0 19 558404 X

Edited by Cathryn Game
Typesetting and text and cover design by Steve Randles
Cover photograph of Katherine Mansfield from
Alexander Turnbull Library, National Library of New
Zealand; background photograph by Lyn Pool
Printed through Bookpac Production Services, Singapore
Published by Oxford University Press
540 Great South Road, Greenlane, PO Box 11-149
Auckland, New Zealand

Contents

INTRODUCTION

'Then you are an Englishwoman?'
'Well, hardly — '

'The Luftbad', 1910.

Kathleen Mansfield Beauchamp was born into a family, and a country, constantly checking themselves in a mirror. So much of their reality had to do with how 'Britain' was reflected in their values and assumptions, with how they gave back, at times in aggressive miniature, features defined on the other side of the world.

If, like the youngish, kindly, and mildly pompous Harold Beauchamp, you had made a fist of commerce through hard work and acumen, were infused with public zeal, and had a sharp eye for the main chance, then you knew very well that you played an important role in the vast enterprise of Empire. Didn't Wellington like to call itself 'the Empire city'? Weren't you part and parcel of what Joseph Chamberlain had called, mid-way through the 1890s, 'the greatest governing race the world had ever seen'? If you had four daughters and only one son — well, you still gave the girls the best, which meant, to top it off, the polish of a ladies' college in London. And although the paradox might never have struck you, the further you lived from the imperial centre, the more you deserved a share of its fruits; the more loyalty you had to 'Home', the more you believed yourself a New Zealander. But if your cleverest daughter was inclined to size you up with a beady intelligence, and was volatile to a fault, then the verities could be in for a challenge. It was a challenge, in one form or another, that defined her writing for the next twenty-five years, under a name she preferred to take from her maternal grandmother.

The early stories in this collection show something of the same imitative drive that was the mark of her city and her class, yet the pull towards what was local and at hand. 'About Pat', written as a schoolgirl in London, is a simple enough anecdote from life in distant Karori. Her early 'prose poems', as she saw them, surfaced from her immersion in *fin-de-siècle* fashions, and were written once she was back in Wellington at the end of her teens.

The first Mansfield stories to attract wider attention were the ones she wrote soon after the months she spent in Bavaria, during her pregnancy in 1909. Collected as *In a German Pension* in 1911, they are mostly blunt satiric lunges at the provoking targets of foreignness, love, and social conventions. As with much of her later work, the best of them take their force from quick dashes of mood, the swerve from calm, and perhaps suppression, to moments in which rage or unexpected truth buckle the surface of apparent normality. One, however, is quite different in its tone, different in its intentions. Although the characters have German names, the setting of 'The Birthday' is indisputably Wellington, the subject that interplay of personality in a family which, under different guises, will dominate so much of her mature work.

Commentary on Mansfield seldom picks up on just how much of her writing is primarily satirical. Of the stories set in England or Europe — more than half of what she wrote — at least two-thirds of those are satiric in intent or form. And within those again, the greater part of the satire is directed at the exacting, deceptive and self-deceiving intricacies of sexual exchange. 'Europe', if constructed from Mansfield's fiction, is above all the site of sexual complexity, a complexity that rings the changes on naivety, ethnic resonances, the obsessiveness inseparable from emotional rapport. Many of the stories move within the perspective of 'adventure', a synonym perhaps for the constantly fluid sense of the outsider. As the novelist Elizabeth

Bowen put it, 'Amid the etherealities of Bloomsbury she was more than half hostile, a dark-eyed tramp'.[1] So much in those stories derives from alert, imposed detachment. It is a position particularly congenial to the satirist, even as it implies that ease or intimacy are hardly at her command. Yet satire is a mode of reinforcing oneself, a protection on the principle of the pre-emptive strike. To focus from the margins can also be a particularly fruitful procedure for a temperament that demands an almost photographic fixing of momentary patterns, a declared affinity with impressionism.

> It is such strange delight to observe people and to try to understand them [she told Bertrand Russell], to arrive late at night in strange cities or to come into little harbours just at pink of dawn when it's cold with a high wind blowing somewhere *up* in the air, to push through the heavy door into little cafés and to watch the pattern people make among tables & bottles and glasses, to watch women when they are off their guard ... To air oneself among these things, to seek them out, to explore them and then to go apart and detach oneself from them — and to write — after the ferment has subsided.[2]

This, it seems, was the particular gift of isolation, the habitual condition of those *femmes seules* who appear in so much of her fiction. To be so 'ecstatically aware of the surface of things', in her friend Conrad Aiken's words, her mastery of 'twinkling circumstance',[3] helped to bring such conviction to her edgy, febrile young women, to her adolescents and children, for that too was how they received the world. Mansfield herself knew the limitations of this vivid alertness. In a review in 1919, she remarked how 'It is not enough to be comforted with colours, to finger bright shawls, to watch the fireworks, to wonder what those strange men are shouting down at the wharves ... our curiosity is roused as to what lies beneath these strange rich surfaces.'[4]

How, then, do her New Zealand stories relate to those set on the other side of the world? Stories in which there was far less call for satiric defence, for defensive attack; where she does not need to articulate so pressingly that '*cry against corruption*'[5] which she claimed was one of her compelling reasons for writing, and which is there, in one form or another, in practically everything set in London or on the Continent.

It is useful first to think of that broad frame of Empire which in a sense coerces a great deal of what she wrote. Almost all her fiction comes from a decade bracketed by the heyday of Edwardian imperial certainties and by the altered perceptions that followed World War I. Examples might be taken more or less at random. 'Stay-laces' is a story she wrote in 1915, 'the audacity of whose satire', Antony Alpers supposed, 'can only be explained by a savage reaction to the war's destruction of her brother'.[6] The sketch begins as though it is to be a dialogue between two London women out for a day's shopping but becomes the monologue of one of them. It is a collage of triteness while the country is at war, with the merest of throw-away remarks on the uniforms of those invalided back from the Front. 'I can't *think* who thought of that bright red tie against that bright blue. It's such a note, isn't it?' The piece's message is laboured enough — frivolity continues as ever, shopping proceeds unchanged, while carnage goes on a few hundred miles south. And the sketch's final lines carry it to a conclusion that might seem almost accidental, its effect unlikely to be quite as Mansfield intended. Yet for a present-day reader, it places the story squarely within its political frame. As the woman prattles on about lunch at Selfridges and fashions in corsets, she is distracted by a figure in military dress. 'Look at that enormous

Indian creature in khaki ... Do you think you could ever be attracted to a dark man? I mean. Oh, you know.'

The reader does know, of course. Here is the sexual stir that is sometimes supposed to be part of the glamour of war, as well as of the black as forbidden lover. But the event is more than that. Is it not insisting how beyond Selfridges, beyond London and the trenches, there is something which sustains it all — the Empire? That 'Indian creature in khaki', the exotic trigger to fantasy, is also a figure of tributary loyalty. Like the recently dead 21-year-old from Thorndon Road, he keeps the enterprise of King and Country, the shopping of Mrs Busk and Mrs Bone, afloat.

There is another story that offers a kind of antipodean equivalent to the distortions of 'Stay-laces'. In 1917, soon after acting as an extra in an American-produced movie, Mansfield wrote what was published as a sketch but is in fact a film script. The parentheses in 'A Pic-nic' are actually instructions for the camera, the visual images we are to have in mind as the dialogue proceeds.

Where in the earlier story we heard the chatter of London, with Empire present in the detached satiric observer as much as in the colonial soldier, we now overhear an English painter visiting Wellington, as he takes in the charms of a local housewife. 'She's such an amazing type to find in a place like this. Awfully primitive. Extraordinarily barbaric.' And the implied camera moves to what his words evoke. *'He sees himself in a strange country, dressed as a hunter, striding back to the camp fire of evening. A woman crouches over the fireglow.'* Rather than such wild colonial expectations, the reality of the picnic at Days Bay is a muddle of suburban trivia and skimmed emotion. But if this is how the English take in New Zealand, doesn't the story at least raise the possibility that a reverse misreading might also occur? The exchange of perspectives between the heart of Empire, and Empire's furthest reaches, is a rather more tricky business than the balance of trade.

With a touch of staged moroseness, Mansfield once imagined herself as 'the little colonial' being shouted at for 'pretending this is her garden … She is a stranger — an alien'.[7] She did not always believe that, nor worry about it for long. But Elizabeth Bowen's remark is pertinent: 'In London she lived, as strangers are wont to do, in a largely self-fabricated world.'[8] Many of her stories are delicate calibrations on quite what belonging does mean.

The New Zealand fiction is a different matter. It might now seem odd that the most impressive of her early stories set in her own country were written to meet the editorial agenda of *Rhythm*, a magazine established by the young John Middleton Murry. Determined to be Modern above all else, the journal was committed to challenging convention, and carried the slogan it took from the Irish playwright, J.M. Synge: 'Before art can be human again it must learn to be brutal.'[9]

What Mansfield provided in answer to that call has variously been dismissed as untypical of her work, or taken to suggest that she might have become a predominantly regionalist writer. In a sense her *Rhythm* stories come out of the blue. They go far beyond the backblock sketches and colonial yarns that preceded them in New Zealand writing, and there is nothing to make one think she drew on her Australian contemporary, Henry Lawson. The probing rawness as much as the melodramatic psychology of 'The Woman at the Store' and 'Millie' seem vividly her own. Yet when she turned to middle-class Wellington in 'The Wind Blows' a few years later, she moved not only closer to home but also towards a quite different conception of narrative. In the form she now devised, with its deft switches in time levels, the merging of mood and image in ways more usually found in poetry, the discarding of anything like conventional plot, she attempts something much further from what was usually meant by the short story. When Mansfield reviewed Jane Mander's *Story of a New Zealand River* in 1920, she took her compatriot to task for leaning too hard on English models, for not trusting herself more to those 'moments when we catch a bewilderingly vivid glimpse of what she really felt and knew about the small settlement of people'. At such moments, 'her characters move quickly, almost violently'. The new material of colonial fiction, she insists, must find its own form, 'the new sketch, the new story'.[10]

Within weeks of 'The Wind Blows', the death of her brother in Belgium directed Mansfield even more towards 'recollections of my own country. ... But all must be told with a sense of mystery, a radiance, an afterglow. ... Almost certainly in a kind of special prose'.[11] That dual prompting to commemorate, and to find a new aesthetic form, now define Mansfield as both a Modernist and as a specifically New Zealand writer. First in *Prelude* in 1917, then in 'At the Bay' four years later, she hit on the narrative form she was after when she spoke of that 'kind of special prose'. As she wrote to a painter friend about the first of these stories, 'As far as I know it's more or less my own invention.' As she thinks back to Wellington,

> I always remember feeling that this little island had dipped back into the dark blue sea during the night only to rise again at beam of day, all hung with bright spangles and glittering drops ... I tried to catch that moment — with something of its sparkle and its flavour. And just as on those mornings white milky mists rise and uncover some beauty, then smother it again and then again disclose it, I tried to lift that mist from my people and let them be seen and then to hide them again.[12]

In arriving at what was 'more or less my own invention', Mansfield had learned from her interest in film. In those two long stories as much as in cinema, narrative proceeds not in

linear completeness but in setting its images, its discrete
episodes, in relation to each other, one scene cutting against
another in mid action. Mansfield was writing of a painting, but
might well have been describing each single section of these
stories, when she described 'the sudden arrest, poise, *moment
captured* ... in a flowing shade and sunlight world'.[13] Both *Prelude*
and 'At the Bay' are written in sections whose apparent random-
ness works towards the overarching revelation of one family. Its
members are seen in their public and private roles, in their
shared identity, and their diverse fragmentary selves. In 'At the
Bay' we are shown not just a single day, although that is what the
movement from dawn to night suggests. But that one day is part
too of a process of life, a rhythmic fragment of a much larger
rhythm. Through apparently trivial incidents, we have seen the
cycle of women's lives from childhood to old age, and something
of a male cycle as well.

Frank O'Connor, the Irish short story writer, and the
sharpest of Mansfield's critics, said of these stories that their
'manner has something in common with that of the fairy tale'.
They are set where 'speechless things talk like anyone else',
where there is a Garden of Eden-like suspension from good and
evil. A lost world is indeed restored by 'an act of pure creation'.[14]
But O'Connor argues too that, although they deserve to be
placed with Proust and Joyce, the social world they represent is
insubstantial, divorced from context and history. Yet take these
stories as they should be taken, with Mansfield's other New
Zealand fiction, and that reservation loses its force.

There are times when the reading of Mansfield in her own
country has meant fairly persistent simplifying. The almost innate
belief in most New Zealanders that theirs is a classless community, that the social hierarchies of an older world, if not quite
shucked off, are certainly less constraining, has perhaps led to
odd distortions. 'The Garden Party', understandably a classroom

favourite, is usually read as a story about growing up, one in which there might indeed be an element of social criticism, but where most of all we see a 17-year-old girl face the impenetrable reality of death and mature before its disturbing wonder. The story is read too in terms of its lingering colonial charm, a further and older glimpse, under another name, of the engaging Kezia, her conventional sisters, delicate Mother again drifting off in the background, Father still footing the bills. We tend to assume that because Mansfield clearly enjoyed writing her Wellington stories, because 'the memory game' (as she called it) was a consoling recovery of a kind, then there is an implied approval of a family so evidently similar to her own. The text defies such an easy assumption. Unless we are swamped by a particular biographical wash, the narrative will not allow us to regard the Sheridans as other than pampered, conventional, smugly riddled with the certainties of a class for whom the rest of society exists in a tributary role. Laura's early amazement at a workman's delighting in the scent of lavender is merely a novice's version of her mother's fully fledged snobbery, her self-sustaining remark that 'People like that don't expect sacrifices from us', as one side of Tinakori Road looks across at the other. 'The very smoke out of their chimneys was poverty-stricken. Little rags and shreds of smoke, so unlike the great silvery plumes that uncurled from the Sheridans' chimneys.'

If Laura's sensitivity is read as the story's commanding focus, then surely such politically insistent images are to be taken up and modified by the teenager's growing wisdom. For doesn't the girl from the big house come to realise that such otherness as poverty, and such total otherness as death, assume their place in a finer, more encompassing view of life? That to see the working-man's corpse, so peaceful and handsome, takes her quite beyond her sisters who did not cross the road with the garden party's left-overs? After all, hadn't she been unable to realise, even a few hours before, that death was actually *there*? 'Why couldn't she [realise]? She stopped a minute. And it seemed to her that kisses, voices, tinkling spoons, laughter, the smell of crushed grass, were somehow inside her. She had no room for anything else.'

Against the reality and gaiety of her own afternoon, poverty at close quarters is suitably melodramatic. It smells, it talks funny, it stares, it is obsequious, it is stagily 'lighted by a smoky lamp'. But the dead man atones for all this, as it were. He is 'wonderful, beautiful ... All is well, said that sleeping face'. The point, of course, is that all seems well *because* the man is dead. The fact of his total absence means that quite rightly she might think, 'What did garden parties matter to him? He was far from all those things', just as his working-class reality is no longer a trouble to her. Everything, for the moment, is transcended — Laura's own earlier sense of guilt, the nastiness of the poor, that intimation that there was 'no room in her' for anything beyond the privileges of her class.

But the story does not stop there. Laura hurries back past 'all those dark people', cherishing her *frisson*, her vision of death-as-provided-by-a-handsome-workingman, to a brother who asks, as she herself might have asked a few minutes before, 'Was it awful?' When she can only stammer, 'Isn't life ... isn't life?' he 'quite understood'. Which he did not, in the least. He has no idea what she is speaking of, how a man's death has been aesthetic-ally transformed to her moment of vague, comforting enlight-enment. 'This is just as it should be, I am content', she had supposed the dead man, with his five young fatherless children and his new widow, as conveying to her. The experience is deeply, egotistically, about Laura and nothing else. But the work-man's corpse sustains it, a final service from poor to rich, the final appropriation by the wealthy from the impoverished.

Yet for all that, one does take Laura's experience as instruc-tive and enlightening. Hers is a genuine moment of fulfilment, even as it does not alter in the least the limiting rigidity of her class. The reader is directed to acknowledge both. The play of one against the other is where the pathos of the story lies.

This dimension in Mansfield's fiction, this sharp and particular scoring of social demarcations, like the psychological ploys through which one class engages with another, is more usually picked up in the English stories than in the New Zealand ones. But in both there are few narratives that do not trace out the exercise of authority, and at least the opportunities for happiness, along economic lines. This underwrites other aspects of the stories. Whether Mansfield depicts the sexual manoeuvres that corral single women, or the experiences of the solitary and the bereft, the economic framing of her characters almost always is apparent. The events of a story are primarily the consequence of that.

'The Doll's House', that equally celebrated story Mansfield wrote just after 'The Garden Party', extends her critique of the New Zealand middle class and its rather smudged carbon copy of how the English do things. Again, here is a story that usually is admired for its 'sympathy' with the way Kezia eludes the starchy social postures of her family and, even more, for that final image of 'our Else', daughter of a washerwoman and a convict, delighting in the little lamp she was never meant to see. It has become an iconic moment in Mansfield fiction, the child sitting in her ecstasy of achieved desire, which 'the world' has conspired to deny her. The impact of that final image, the narrative's pace as it draws towards the diminishment of anything but the light of Else's illumination, has perhaps prevented our taking the story for what it also does. After the Kelveys are driven off by Aunt Beryl who so 'frightened those little rats', the outcast sisters, rodent-like still, huddle together on a drainpipe. Earlier in the story, when one of the schoolchildren had bawled out in front of the playground that the Kelveys' father was in prison, the rest of the children 'rushed away in a body, deeply, deeply excited, wild with joy'. The language, the veering and welter of emotional release, is close to that scene in *Prelude* when Pat the handyman beheads the duck and the children move from fear to hysterical delight. In 'The Doll's House' it is again the excitement of the kill, but as well as that, it is the social ritual of the scapegoat, a stoning of the pests. And set against this malevolence, the tiny defiant flare of what an individual cannot be deprived of. In her own country, the reading of Mansfield has been so loaded with a kind of cosiness, an assumed final endorsement on her part not just of her family but also the *kind* of family her fiction returns to, that her hard clarity in depicting its limitations is often obscured.

It is true that her family stories were a considered attempt to propose a particular kind of love, 'warm, vivid, intimate — not "made up" — not *self conscious*',[15] and to carry the enchantment that memory and distance gave her childhood. They were also, in the last years of her life, predominant among the stories where she achieved those 'new moulds for our new thoughts & feelings'[16] that a post-war, modern consciousness demanded. It is the richness of those stories that they do precisely that, as they offer a critique of her own country, her own social *milieu*; that they convey expansive family warmth so convincingly, even as the ferocity of individual drives is tempered by the roles community sets in place.

The insincerity Aunt Beryl detects in herself in both *Prelude* and 'At the Bay', her tacking between a troubled questing self and a fabricated display, is the status of settler society writ small. One remembers the fractious teenage Mansfield saying after her trip to the Ureweras, 'Give me the tourist and the Maori but nothing in-between'.[17] That 'in-between', however, is where her New Zealand fiction is placed, while her characters shuttle between performance and authentic selves. This is a process, should one care to trace it out, in Mansfield's own considered observations of herself. Her 'shedding false selves' was a deeply personal challenge. It was as much a pressing factor in the society in which she was raised, where values tended to accrue about the colonial 'fault-line', as one might call it, with its sense of regretted severance and persistent mimicry, and yet an insistence on local worth, on achieved difference.

The stories in this collection demand that we read them with an eye to both. At the gentler end of the spectrum, Kezia winningly refuses to think or behave quite as siblings or parents would expect, while her mother's fey sexual revolt takes her no further than a dreamy, enfolding egotism. At the other end of that spectrum, an unbalanced child — the incipient artist? — draws the forbidden pictures that give the family away; a pakeha child must be rescued from the encompassing attraction and threat of Maori *aroha*; the poor are savaged in an implacable class war. Even in the best known anthology pieces, where the fiction moves in the warm tidal affection that family evokes, there are those other currents as well. In their sublimated violence and incipient rebellion, their drift of sexual recklessness, there move the refined filaments of that 'bloodiness and guts' the editor of *Rhythm* asked for and drew from Mansfield in her early local stories. And so often, in the shaping of individual experience, there is a presence like that of the warning fat man in 'Her First Ball', his shadow for the moment put aside in 'the beautiful flying wheel of the dance'. Yet that very word *wheel* tells us that his time will come again.

These hovering intimations are not so much ranged against the patterned ringing immediacy of the fiction as set in counterpoint. Each is given its due, while it is the living moment, always, which for the space of the story at least wins out. Yet this alertness to what threatens, to what troubles the borders, helps to place the stories so firmly as historical occasions, to define their period and place; at the same time as their first attraction is somewhere else, in their total freshness within the genre of the short story, in their accomplishment as art.

This is the first time Katherine Mansfield's stories about her own country have been brought together in the order in which she wrote them. To take them in sequence and as a group defines, rather more acutely than we might have thought, how emphases fall differently than in her other fiction. Certainly it presents, with a more insistent local accent, her quest for that 'new story' she believed was called for to put forward a new world.

1 Elizabeth Bowen, 'A Living Writer', *Cornhill Magazine*, Winter 1956–57, p. 128.
2 *The Collected Letters of Katherine Mansfield*, Vincent O'Sullivan and Margaret Scott, Clarendon Press, Oxford, Vol. 1, 1984, pp. 287–8.
3 Conrad Aiken, 'The Short Story as Colour', *The Freeman*, 21 June 1922, p. 357.
4 'Glancing Light', a review of *Java Head* by Joseph Hergesheimer, *Athenaeum*, 13 June 1919, in *Novels and Novelists*, 1930, p. 40.
5 *Collected Letters*, Vol. 2, 1987, p. 54.
6 Antony Alpers, *The Stories of Katherine Mansfield*, Oxford University Press, 1984, p. 555.
7 *The Journal of Katherine Mansfield*, ed. John Middleton Murry, Constable, London, 1962, p. 157.
8 Elizabeth Bowen, 'A Living Writer', p. 128.
9 Antony Alpers, *The Life of Katherine Mansfield*, Penguin Books, 1982, p. 134.
10 'First Novels', *Athenaeum*, 9 July 1920, in *Novels and Novelists*, pp. 217–20.
11 *Journal*, pp. 93–4.
12 *Collected Letters*, Vol. 1, p. 331.
13 *Collected Letters*, Vol. 4, 1996, p. 354.
14 Frank O'Connor, *The Lonely Voice: A Study of the Short Story*, Macmillan, London, 1963, p. 141.
15 *Collected Letters*, Vol. 4, p. 242.
16 *Collected Letters*, Vol. 3, 1993, p. 82.
17 *The Urewera Notebook*, ed. Ian A. Gordon, Oxford University Press, 1978, p. 61.

About Pat

A day or two ago I was in a train. A small child sat opposite with her brother and asked questions as to 'Why the train didn't run backwards, and if the engine turned topsy-turvy.' What next?

I found myself wondering whether I had said and done such things in just the same manner. I suppose that we all have.

In the days of our childhood we lived in a great old rambling house planted lonesomely in the midst of huge gardens, orchards and paddocks. We had few toys, but — far better — plenty of good, strong mud and a flight of concrete steps that grew hot in the heat of the sun and became dreams of ovens.

The feeling of making a mud pie with all due seriousness, is one of the most delicious feelings that we experience; you sit with your mixture in the doll's saucepan, or if it is soup, in the doll's hand-wash basin, and stir and stir, and thicken and 'whip', and become more deliciously grimy each minute; whilst the sense of utter wickedness you have if it happens to be on clean pinafore days thrills me to this hour.

Well I remember one occasion when we made pies with real flour, stole some water from the dish by the dog's kennel, baked them and ate them.

Very soon after three crushed, subdued little girls wended their way quietly up to bed, and the blind was pulled down.

At that period our old Irish gardener was our hero. His name was Patrick Sheehan. On Sunday he wore gloves with real 'kid backs', and a tie pin made out of a boar's tusk. Every morning I went across to the feed room where he cleaned father's boots, and always at a certain stage of the proceedings, I would say, 'Please, Pat, don't.' He as invariably replied that 'nothing else at all gave them such a fine gloss'. He used to hoist me up on to the table, and recount long tales of the Dukes of Ireland whom he had seen and even conversed with. We were most proud of our gardener having rubbed shoulders with Ireland's aristocracy, and in the evening when Pat was at tea in the kitchen we would steal out and beg him to show us the manners of the people in Ireland. Standing in a row, hand in hand, we would watch while Pat put some salt on his knife, tapped it off with his fork, the little finger of his right hand well curled, in a manner which seemed to us ingenious enough for the first Lords of the land.

Pat was never very fond of me. I am afraid he did not think my character at all desirable. I professed no joy in having a bird in a cage; and one day committed the unpardonable offence of picking a pumpkin flower. He never recovered from the shock occasioned by that last act of barbarism. I can see him now, whenever I came near, nodding his head and saying, 'Well now, to think. It might have become the finest vegetable of the season, and given us food for weeks.'

Pat's birthdays occurred with alarming frequency. We always gave him the same presents — three sticks of Juno tobacco and three cakes of hokey-pokey. The presentation took place in the back-yard, and he sang us a wonderful Irish song, of which we never guessed any more than the phrase 'I threw up me hat.' It seemed to be the one definite remark throughout.

He considered it a duty to propose to each cook who came to the house, making them the offer of himself, the gloves with the 'kid backs', and the boar-tusk tie pin whenever the occasion demanded. They never by any chance accepted him, and I am sure that he never expected them to do so.

Every afternoon he used to brush his old brown bowler hat, harness the mare and start for town, and every evening when he had come home it was my delight to wait till he had unharnessed the mare, then to be lifted on to her back, and start at a jogging trot through the big white gates, down the quiet road and into the paddock. There I waited until Pat came swinging along with the milk pails.

On those late evenings he had wonderful stories to tell of a little old man no bigger than his thumb with a hat as high as the barb-wired fence, who, in the night, crept out of the creek, climbed up the blue gum tree, picked some leaves from the top-most branches and then crept down again.

'You see,' Pat would say, his dear weather-beaten face as grave as possible, 'it's from blue gums that you get eucalyptus, and the old man suffered from cold, living in such dampness.'

On those evenings, too, I had my first lesson in the mysteri-ous art of milking, but try as I would I could never obtain more than a teacup full. On several occasions the ignominy of this reduced me to tears, but Pat would say, 'You see, she's such a keen old cow, is Daisy. Having had children of her own, she knows how much you ought to have, and how much more would give you indigestion.' I was always much comforted. Pat had a wonderfully young heart. He entered into our pleasures with as much zest as we did ourselves. I played a game which had no ending or beginning, but was called 'Beyond the Blue Mountains'. The scene was generally placed near the rhubarb beds, and Pat officiated as the villain, the hero, and even the vil-lainess, with unfailing charm.

Sometimes, to make it more real, we had lunch together, sit-ting on the wheel-barrow turned upside down, and sharing the slice of German sausage and a bath bun with loaf sugar in it.

On Sunday mornings Pat, in the full glory of a clean blue shirt and corduroy trousers, took us for a walk in the great pine plantation.

He, childishly, used to collect gum and carry it in a corner of his handkerchief. For years afterwards I believed that those trees just grew for the old witches of the woods, who used their needles in making the big, big umbrella over our heads, and all the dresses of the flowers, basting their nice, fine, blue sky cali-co with the gum thoughtfully provided for them …

When we left that house in the country and went to live in town, Pat left us to try his luck on the goldfields. We parted with bitter tears. He presented each of my sisters with a goldfinch, and me with a pair of white china vases cheerfully embroidered with forget-me-nots and pink roses. His parting advice to us was to look after ourselves in this world and never to pick flowers out of the vegetable garden because we liked the colour.

From that day to this I have never heard of him.

I should dearly love to show him the sights of London, and take him to the 'Carlton' for a slice of German sausage and a bath bun, and see once again the way in which the Dukes of Ireland balanced their salt on their knives.

In the Botanical Gardens

They are such a subtle combination of the artificial and the natural — that is, partly, the secret of their charm.

From the entrance gate down the broad central walk, with the orthodox banality of carpet bedding on either side, stroll men and women and children — a great many children, who call to each other lustily, and jump up and down on the green wooden seats. They seem as meaningless, as lacking in individuality, as the little figures in an impressionist landscape.

Above the carpet bedding, on one hand, there is a green hedge, and above the hedge a long row of cabbage trees. I stare up at them, and suddenly the green hedge is a stave, and the cabbage trees, now high, now low, have become an arrangement of notes — a curious, pattering, native melody.

In the enclosure the spring flowers are almost too beautiful — a great stretch of foam-like cowslips. As I bend over them, the air is heavy and sweet with their scent, like hay and new milk and the kisses of children, and, further on, a sunlit wonder of chiming daffodils.

Before me two great rhododendron bushes. Against the dark, broad leaves the blossoms rise, flame-like, tremulous in the still air, and the pearl rose loving-cup of a magnolia hangs delicately on the grey bough.

Everywhere there are clusters of china blue pansies, a mist of forget-me-nots, a tangle of anemones. Strange that these anemones — scarlet, and amethyst, and purple — vibrant with colour, always appear to me a trifle dangerous, sinister, seductive, but poisonous.

And, leaving the enclosure, I pass a little gully, filled with tree ferns, and lit with pale virgin lamps of arum lilies.

I turn from the smooth swept paths, and climb up a steep track, where the knotted tree roots have seared a rude pattern in the yellow clay. And suddenly, it disappears — all the pretty, carefully tended surface of gravel and sward and blossom, and there is bush, silent and splendid. On the green moss, on the brown earth, a wide splashing of yellow sunlight. And everywhere that strange indefinable scent. As I breathe it, it seems to absorb, to become part of me — and I am old with the age of centuries, strong with the strength of savagery.

Somewhere I hear the soft rhythmic flowing of water, and I follow the path down and down until I come to a little stream idly, dreamily floating past. I fling myself down, and put my hands in the water. An inexplicable, persistent feeling seizes me that I must become one with it all. Remembrance has gone — this is the Lotus Land — the green trees stir languorously, sleepily — there is the silver sound of a bird's call. Bending down, I drink a little of the water, Oh! is it magic? Shall I, looking intently, see vague forms lurking in the shadow staring at me malevolently, wildly, the thief of their birthright? Shall I, down the hillside, through the bush, ever in the shadow, see a great company moving towards me, their faces averted, wreathed with green garlands, passing, passing, following the little stream in silence until it is sucked into the wide sea …

There is a sudden, restless movement, a pressure of the trees — they sway against one another — it is like the sound of weeping …

I pass down the central walk towards the entrance gates. The men and women and children are crowding the pathway, looking reverently, admiringly, at the carpet bedding, spelling aloud the Latin names of the flowers.

Here is laughter and movement and bright sunlight — but behind me — is it near, or miles and miles away? — the bush lies hidden in the shadow.

Leves Amores

I can never forget the Thistle Hotel. I can never forget that strange Winter night.

I had asked her to dine with me, and then go to the Opera. My room was opposite hers. She said she would come, but — could I do up her evening bodice, it was hooks at the back. Very well.

It was still daylight when I knocked at the door and entered. In her petticoat bodice and a full silk petticoat she was washing, sponging her face and neck. She said she was finished, and I might sit on the bed and wait for her. So I looked around at the dreary room. The one filthy window faced the street. She could see the choked, dust-grimed window of a wash-house opposite. For furniture, the room contained a low bed, draped with revolting, yellow, vine-patterned curtains, a chair, a wardrobe with a piece of cracked mirror attached, a washstand. But the wall paper hurt me physically. It hung in tattered strips from the wall.

In its less discoloured and faded patches I could trace the pattern of roses — buds and flowers — and the frieze was a conventional design of birds, of what genus the good God alone knows.

And this was where she lived. I watched her curiously. She was pulling on long, thin stockings, and saying 'damn' when she could not find her suspenders. And I felt within me a certainty that nothing beautiful could ever happen in that room, and for her I felt, contempt, a little tolerance, and very little pity.

A dull, grey light hovered over everything; it seemed to accentuate the thin tawdriness of her clothes, the squalor of her life. She, too, looked dull and grey and tired. And I sat on the bed, and thought: 'Come, this Old Age. I have forgotten passion. I have been left behind in the beautiful golden procession of Youth. Now I am seeing life in the dressing-room of the theatre.'

So we dined somewhere and went to the Opera. It was late when we came out into the crowded night street, late and cold. She gathered up her long skirts. Silently we walked back to the Thistle Hotel, down the white pathway fringed with beautiful golden lilies, up the amethyst shadowed staircase.

Was Youth dead? ... *Was* Youth dead?

She told me as we walked along the corridor to her room that she was glad the night had come. I did not ask why. I was glad, too. It seemed a secret between us. So I went with her into her room to undo those troublesome hooks. She lit a little candle on an enamel bracket. The light filled the room with darkness. Like a sleepy child she slipped out of her frock, and then, suddenly, turned to me and flung her arms round my neck. Lo every bird upon the bulging frieze broke into song. Lo every rose upon the tattered paper budded and formed into blossom. Yes, even the green vine upon the bed curtains wreathed itself into strange chaplets and garlands, twined round us in a leafy embrace, held us with a thousand clinging tendrils.

And Youth was not dead.

A Birthday

Andreas Binzer woke slowly. He turned over on the narrow bed and stretched himself — yawned — opening his mouth as widely as possible and bringing his teeth together afterwards with a sharp 'click'. The sound of that click fascinated him; he repeated it quickly several times, with a snapping movement of the jaws. What teeth! he thought. Sound as a bell, every man jack of them. Never had one out, never had one stopped. That comes of no tomfoolery in eating, and a good, regular brushing night and morning. He raised himself on his left elbow and waved his right arm over the side of the bed to feel for the chair where he put his watch and chain overnight. No chair was there — of course, he'd forgotten, there wasn't a chair in this wretched spare room. Had to put the confounded thing under his pillow. 'Half-past eight, Sunday, breakfast at nine — time for the bath' — his brain ticked to the watch. He sprang out of bed and went over to the window. The venetian blind was broken, hung fan-shaped over the upper pane ... 'That blind must be mended. I'll get the office boy to drop in and fix it on his way home to-morrow — he's a good hand at blinds. Give him twopence and he'll do it as well as a carpenter ... Anna could do it herself if she was all right. So would I, for the matter of that, but I don't like to trust myself on rickety step-ladders.' He looked up at the sky: it shone, strangely white, unflecked with cloud; he looked down at the row of garden strips and backyards. The fence of these gardens was built along the edge of a gully, spanned by an iron suspension bridge, and the people had a wretched habit of throwing their empty tins over the fence into the gully. Just like them, of course! Andreas started counting the tins, and decided, viciously, to write a letter to the papers about it and sign it — sign it in full.

The servant girl came out of their back door into the yard, carrying his boots. She threw one down on the ground, thrust her hand into the other, and stared at it, sucking in her cheeks. Suddenly she bent forward, spat on the toecap, and started polishing with a brush rooted out of her apron pocket ... 'Slut of a girl! Heaven knows what infectious disease may be breeding now in that boot. Anna must get rid of that girl — even if she has to do without one for a bit — as soon as she's up and about again. The way she chucked one boot down and then spat upon the other! She didn't care whose boots she'd got hold of. *She* had no false notions of the respect due to the master of the house.' He turned away from the window and switched his bath towel from the washstand rail, sick at heart. 'I'm too sensitive for a man — that's what's the matter with me. Have been from the beginning, and will be to the end.'

There was a gentle knock at the door and his mother came in. She closed the door after her and leant against it. Andreas noticed that her cap was crooked, and a long tail of hair hung over her shoulder. He went forward and kissed her.

'Good-morning, mother; how's Anna?'

The old woman spoke quickly, clasping and unclasping her hands.

'Andreas, please go to Doctor Erb as soon as you are dressed.'

'Why,' he said, 'is she bad?'

Frau Binzer nodded, and Andreas, watching her, saw her face suddenly change; a fine network of wrinkles seemed to pull over it from under the skin surface.

'Sit down on the bed a moment,' he said. 'Been up all night?'

'Yes. No, I won't sit down. I must go back to her. Anna has been in pain all night. She wouldn't have you disturbed before because she said you looked so run down yesterday. You told her you had caught a cold and been very worried.'

Straightaway Andreas felt that he was being accused.

'Well, she made me tell her, worried it out of me; you know the way she does.'

Again Frau Binzer nodded.

'Oh yes, I know. She says, is your cold better, and there's a warm under-vest for you in the left-hand corner of the big drawer.'

Quite automatically Andreas cleared his throat twice.

'Yes,' he answered. 'Tell her my throat certainly feels looser. I suppose I'd better not disturb her?'

'No, and besides, *time*, Andreas.'

'I'll be ready in five minutes.'

They went into the passage. As Frau Binzer opened the door of the front bedroom, a long wail came from the room.

That shocked and terrified Andreas. He dashed into the bathroom, turned on both taps as far as they would go, cleaned his teeth and pared his nails while the water was running.

'Frightful business, frightful business,' he heard himself whispering. 'And I can't understand it. It isn't as though it were her first — it's her third. Old Shäfer told me, yesterday, his wife simply "dropped" her fourth. Anna ought to have had a qualified nurse. Mother gives way to her. Mother spoils her. I wonder what she meant by saying I'd worried Anna yesterday. Nice remark to make to a husband at a time like this. Unstrung, I suppose — and my sensitiveness again.'

When he went into the kitchen for his boots, the servant girl was bent over the stove, cooking breakfast. 'Breathing into that, now, I suppose,' thought Andreas, and was very short with the servant girl. She did not notice. She was full of terrified joy and importance in the goings on upstairs. She felt she was learning the secrets of life with every breath she drew. Had laid the table that morning saying, 'Boy', as she put down the first dish, 'Girl', as she placed the second — it had worked out with the saltspoon to 'Boy'. 'For two pins I'd tell the master that, to comfort him, like,' she decided. But the master gave her no opening.

'Put an extra cup and saucer on the table,' he said; 'the doctor may want some coffee.'

'The doctor, sir?' The servant girl whipped a spoon out of a pan, and spilt two drops of grease on the stove. 'Shall I fry something extra?' But the master had gone, slamming the door after him. He walked down the street — there was nobody about at all — dead and alive this place on a Sunday morning. As he crossed the suspension bridge a strong stench of fennel and decayed refuse streamed from the gully, and again Andreas began concocting a letter. He turned into the main road. The shutters were still up before the shops. Scraps of newspaper, hay, and fruit skins strewed the pavement; the gutters were choked with the leavings of Saturday night. Two dogs sprawled in the middle of the road, scuffling and biting. Only the public-house at the corner was open; a young barman slopped water over the doorstep.

Fastidiously, his lips curling, Andreas picked his way through the water. 'Extraordinary how I am noticing things this morning. It's partly the effect of Sunday. I loathe a Sunday when Anna's tied by the leg and the children are away. On Sunday a man has the right to expect his family. Everything here's filthy, the whole place might be down with the plague, and will be, too, if this street's not swept away. I'd like to have a hand on the government ropes.' He braced his shoulders. 'Now for this doctor.'

'Doctor Erb is at breakfast,' the maid informed him. She showed him into the waiting-room, a dark and musty place, with some ferns under a glass-case by the window. 'He says he won't be a minute, please, sir, and there is a paper on the table.'

'Unhealthy hole,' thought Binzer, walking over to the window and drumming his fingers on the glass fern-shade. 'At breakfast, is he? That's the mistake I made: turning out early on an empty stomach.'

A milk cart rattled down the street, the driver standing at the back, cracking a whip; he wore an immense geranium flower stuck in the lapel of his coat. Firm as a rock he stood, bending back a little in the swaying cart. Andreas craned his neck to watch him all the way down the road, even after he had gone, listening for the sharp sound of those rattling cans.

'H'm, not much wrong with him,' he reflected. 'Wouldn't mind a taste of that life myself. Up early, work all over by eleven o'clock, nothing to do but loaf about all day until milking time.' Which he knew was an exaggeration, but he wanted to pity himself.

The maid opened the door, and stood aside for Doctor Erb. Andreas wheeled round; the two men shook hands.

'Well, Binzer,' said the doctor jovially, brushing some crumbs from a pearl-coloured waistcoat, 'son and heir becoming importunate?'

Up went Binzer's spirits with a bound. Son and heir, by Jove! He was glad to have to deal with a man again. And a sane fellow this, who came across this sort of thing every day of the week.

'That's about the measure of it, Doctor,' he answered, smiling and picking up his hat. 'Mother dragged me out of bed this morning with imperative orders to bring you along.'

'Gig will be round in a minute. Drive back with me, won't you? Extraordinary, sultry day; you're as red as a beetroot already.'

Andreas affected to laugh. The doctor had one annoying habit — imagined he had the right to poke fun at everybody simply because he was a doctor. 'The man's riddled with conceit, like all these professionals,' Andreas decided.

'What sort of a night did Frau Binzer have?' asked the doctor. 'Ah, here's the gig. Tell me on the way up. Sit as near the middle as you can, will you, Binzer? Your weight tilts it over a bit one side — that's the worst of you successful business men.'

'Two stone heavier than I, if he's a pound,' thought Andreas. 'The man may be all right in his profession — but heaven preserve me.'

'Off you go, my beauty.' Doctor Erb flicked the little brown mare. 'Did your wife get any sleep last night?'

'No; I don't think she did,' answered Andreas shortly. 'To tell you the truth, I'm not satisfied that she hasn't a nurse.'

'Oh, your mother's worth a dozen nurses,' cried the doctor, with immense gusto. 'To tell you the truth, I'm not keen on nurses — too raw — raw as rump-steak. They wrestle for a baby as though they were wrestling with Death for the body of Patroculus ... Ever seen that picture by an English artist. Leighton? Wonderful thing — full of sinew!'

'There he goes again,' thought Andreas, 'airing off his knowledge to make a fool of me.'

'Now your mother — she's firm — she's capable. Does what she's told with a fund of sympathy. Look at these shops we're passing — they're festering sores. How on earth this government can tolerate — '

'They're not so bad — sound enough — only want a coat of paint.'

The doctor whistled a little tune and flicked the mare again.

'Well, I hope the young shaver won't give his mother too much trouble,' he said. 'Here we are.'

A skinny little boy, who had been sliding up and down the back seat of the gig, sprang out and held the horse's head. Andreas went straight into the dining-room and left the servant girl to take the doctor upstairs. He sat down, poured out some coffee, and bit through half a roll before helping himself to fish. Then he noticed there was no hot plate for the fish — the whole house was at sixes and sevens. He rang the bell, but the servant girl came in with a tray holding a bowl of soup and a hot plate.

'I've been keeping them on the stove,' she simpered.

'Ah, thanks, that's very kind of you.' As he swallowed the soup his heart warmed to this fool of a girl.

'Oh, it's a good thing Doctor Erb has come,' volunteered the servant girl, who was bursting for want of sympathy.

'H'm, h'm,' said Andreas.

She waited a moment, expectantly, rolling her eyes, then in full loathing of menkind went back to the kitchen and vowed herself to sterility.

Andreas cleared the soup bowl, and cleared the fish. As he ate, the room slowly darkened. A faint wind sprang up and beat the tree branches against the window. The dining-room looked over the breakwater of the harbour, and the sea swung heavily in rolling waves. Wind crept round the house, moaning drearily.

'We're in for a storm. That means I'm boxed up here all day. Well, there's one blessing; it'll clear the air.' He heard the servant girl rushing importantly round the house, slamming windows. Then he caught a glimpse of her in the garden, unpegging tea towels from the line across the lawn. She was a worker, there was no doubt about that. He took up a book, and wheeled his armchair over to the window. But it was useless. Too dark to read; he didn't believe in straining his eyes, and gas at ten o'clock in the morning seemed absurd. So he slipped down in the chair, leaned his elbows on the padded arms and gave himself up, for once, to idle dreaming. 'A boy? Yes, it was bound to be a boy this time ... ' 'What's your family, Binzer?' 'Oh, I've two girls and a boy!' A very nice little number. Of course he was the last man to have a favourite child, but a man needed a son. 'I'm working up the business for my son! Binzer & Son! It would mean living very tight for the next ten years, cutting expenses as fine as possible; and then — '

A tremendous gust of wind sprang upon the house, seized it, shook it, dropped, only to grip the more tightly. The waves swelled up along the breakwater and were shipped with broken foam. Over the white sky flew tattered streamers of grey cloud.

Andreas felt quite relieved to hear Doctor Erb coming down the stairs; he got up and lit the gas.

'Mind if I smoke in here?' asked Doctor Erb, lighting a cigarette before Andreas had time to answer. 'You don't smoke, do you? No time to indulge in pernicious little habits!'

'How is she now?' asked Andreas, loathing the man.

'Oh, well as can be expected, poor little soul. She begged me to come down and have a look at you. Said she knew you were worrying.' With laughing eyes the doctor looked at the breakfast-table. 'Managed to peck a bit, I see, eh?'

'Hoo-wih!' shouted the wind, shaking the window-sashes.

'Pity, this weather,' said Doctor Erb.

'Yes, it gets on Anna's nerves, and it's just nerve she wants.'

'Eh, what's that?' retorted the doctor. 'Nerve! Man alive! She's got twice the nerve of you and me rolled into one. Nerve! she's nothing but nerve. A woman who works as she does about the house and has three children in four years thrown in with the dusting, so to speak!'

He pitched his half-smoked cigarette into the fireplace and frowned at the window.

'Now *he's* accusing me,' thought Andreas. 'That's the second time this morning — first mother and now this man taking advantage of my sensitiveness.' He could not trust himself to speak, and rang the bell for the servant girl.

'Clear away the breakfast things,' he ordered. 'I can't have them messing about on the table till dinner!'

'Don't be hard on the girl,' coaxed Doctor Erb. 'She's got twice the work to do to-day.'

At that Binzer's anger blazed out.

'I'll trouble you, Doctor, not to interfere between me and my servants!' And he felt a fool at the same moment for not saying 'servant'.

Doctor Erb was not perturbed. He shook his head, thrust his hands into his pockets, and began balancing himself on toe and heel.

'You're jagged by the weather,' he said wryly, 'nothing else. A great pity — this storm. You know climate has an immense effect upon birth. A fine day perks a woman — gives her heart for her business. Good weather is as necessary to a confinement as it is to a washing day. Not bad — that last remark of mine — for a professional fossil, eh?'

Andreas made no reply.

'Well, I'll be getting back to my patient. Why don't you take a walk, and clear your head? That's the idea for you.'

'No,' he answered, 'I won't do that; it's too rough.'

He went back to his chair by the window. While the servant girl cleared away he pretended to read ... then his dreams! It seemed years since he had had the time to himself to dream like that — he never had a breathing space. Saddled with work all day, and couldn't shake it off in the evening, like other men. Besides, Anna was interested — they talked of practically nothing else together. Excellent mother she'd make for a boy; she had a grip of things.

Church bells started ringing through the windy air, now sounding as though from very far away, then again as though all the churches in the town had been suddenly transplanted into their street. They stirred something in him, those bells, something vague and tender. Just about that time Anna would call him from the hall. 'Andreas, come and have your coat brushed. I'm ready.' Then off they would go, she hanging on his arm, and looking up at him. She certainly was a little thing. He remembered once saying when they were engaged, 'Just as high as my heart,' and she had jumped on to a stool and pulled his head down, laughing. A kid in those days, younger than her children in nature, brighter, more 'go' and 'spirit' in her. The way she'd run down the road to meet him after business! And the way she laughed when they were looking for a house. By Jove! that laugh of hers! At the memory he grinned, then grew suddenly grave. Marriage certainly changed a woman far more than it did a man. Talk about sobering down. She had lost all her go in two months! Well, once this boy business was over she'd get stronger. He began to plan a little trip for them. He'd take her away and they'd loaf about together somewhere. After all, dash it, they were young still. She'd got into a groove; he'd have to force her out of it, that's all.

He got up and went into the drawing-room, carefully shut the door and took Anna's photograph from the top of the piano. She wore a white dress with a big bow of some soft stuff under the chin, and stood, a little stiffly, holding a sheaf of artificial poppies and corn in her hands. Delicate she looked even then; her masses of hair gave her that look. She seemed to droop under the heavy braids of it, and yet she was smiling. Andreas caught his breath sharply. She was his wife — that girl. Posh! it had only been taken four years ago. He held it close to him, bent forward and kissed it. Then rubbed the glass with the back of his hand. At that moment, fainter than he had heard it in the passage, more terrifying, Andreas heard again that wailing cry. The wind caught it up in mocking echo, blew it over the house-tops, down the street, far away from him. He flung out his arms, 'I'm so damnably helpless,' he said, and then to the picture, 'Perhaps it's not as bad as it sounds; perhaps it is just my sensitiveness.' In the half light of the drawing-room the smile seemed to deepen in Anna's portrait, and to become secret, even cruel. 'No', he reflected, 'that smile is not at all her happiest expression — it was a mistake to let her have it taken smiling like that. She doesn't look like my wife — like the mother of my son.' Yes, that was it, she did not look like the mother of a son who was going to be a partner in the firm. The picture got on his nerves; he held it in different lights, looked at it from a distance, sideways, spent, it seemed to Andreas afterwards, a whole lifetime trying to fit it in. The more he played with it the deeper grew his dislike of it. Thrice he carried it over to the fire-place and decided to chuck it behind the Japanese umbrella in the grate; then he thought it absurd to waste an expensive frame. There was no good in beating about the bush. Anna looked like a stranger — abnormal, a freak — it might be a picture taken just before or after death.

Suddenly he realised that the wind had dropped, that the whole house was still, terribly still. Cold and pale, with a disgusting feeling that spiders were creeping up his spine and across his face, he stood in the centre of the drawing-room, hearing Doctor Erb's footsteps descending the stairs.

He saw Doctor Erb come into the room; the room seemed to change into a great glass bowl towards him, like a goldfish in a pearl-coloured waistcoat.

'My beloved wife has passed away!' He wanted to shout it out before the doctor spoke.

'Well, she's hooked a boy this time!' said Doctor Erb. Andreas staggered forward.

'Look out. Keep on your pins,' said Doctor Erb, catching Binzer's arm, and murmuring, as he felt it, 'Flabby as butter.'

A glow spread all over Andreas. He was exultant.

'Well, by God! Nobody can accuse *me* of not knowing what suffering is,' he said.

Love-Lies-Bleeding

At half-past two the servant girl stumped along the narrow passage from the kitchen to the dining-room, thrust her head in at the door and shouted in her loud, impudent voice: 'Well, I'm off, Mrs Eichelbaum. I'll be here to-morrow, Mrs Eichelbaum.' Muffi waited until she heard the servant's steps crunch down the gravel path, heard the gate creak and slam, listened until those steps died away quite, and silence like a watchful spider began to spin its web over the little house. Everything changed. The white curtains bulged and blew out as though to the first breath of a mysterious breeze, blowing from nowhere; the dark furniture swelled with rich important life; all the plates on the sideboard, the pictures and ornaments, gleamed as though they shone through water; even the lilies, the faded lilies flung all over the green wallpaper, solemnly uncurled again, and she could hear the clock, ticking away, trotting away, galloping away — a rider with a dark plume round his hat riding on a white horse down a lonely road in the moonlight.

Stealthy as a little cat Muffi crept into the kitchen, up the stairs into their bedroom and the children's room, down again and into the study, to make sure that nobody was there, and then she came back to the dining-room and folded herself upon the shabby sofa before the window, her feet tucked under her, her hands shut in her lap.

The window of the dining-room looked out on to a paddock covered with long grass and ragged bushes. In one corner lay a heap of bricks, in another a load of timber was tumbled. Round three sides of the paddock there reared up three new houses, white, unsubstantial, puffed up in the air like half-baked meringues. A fourth was being built; only the walls and criss-cross beams showed. Everything that afternoon was blurred with a thick sea mist, and somewhere in the paddock, out of sight, a man was playing the cornet. He must have been walking about while he played, for sometimes the notes sounded loud and harsh, full of despair and threatening anger, sometimes they came from far away, bubbles of melancholy sound floating on the swaying mist.

> Ta-ta-ta
> Tiddle-um tiddle-um
> Ta tiddly-um tum ta.

There was nobody to be seen and nothing to be heard except that cornet and the tap of hammers in the hollow house.

'It's autumn,' thought Muffi. Her lips trembled, tasting the mist and the cold air. 'Yes, it's autumn.'

Not that she felt sad. No, she merely responded, just as she held up her face to the sun and wrapped herself together against the rain. It was not Muffi's nature to rebel against anything.

Why should she? What good would it do? She accepted life with cowlike female stupidity, as Max put it.

'And you are like all women,' he would sneer. 'You love to make men believe that you are rarer beings, more delicately attuned than they ... Nothing surprises me,' Max would squeak in a mincing voice, flirting his fat hand, 'nothing alarms me, I knew that it was going to rain, I knew that we were going to miss the train, I knew that my children would catch cold. I have my celestial messengers. But any man old enough to shave himself knows that divine calm is simply your lack of imagination, and that no woman ever feels anything — once she is out of bed.'

The children loved their father when he began to talk like that. He would walk up and down the room, holding up his coat-tails for a skirt, laughing and jeering at women and at their imbecile unbelievable vanity ... The children used to sit at the table and bang with their fists and clap their hands and jump up and down. 'Ah, Papa! Ah, my Papa! My darling clever little Papa!' Rudi would cry; but Katerina, who was eleven years old and quite a woman, realised that Papa really meant Muffi when he tiptoed and squeaked, and therein lay her joy.

Muffi smiled too, and when Rudi, quite overcome, would fling himself upon her, crying breathlessly: 'Isn't it wonderful, my Papa?' she would answer: 'Yes, he is wonderful.' What did it matter?

Ta-ta-ta
Tiddle-um tiddle-um
Ta tiddley-um tum ta

went the cornet. She had never heard it before. She hoped it was not going to be there every afternoon. Perhaps it was the sea mist that had brought it. What was the player like? He was an old man wearing a peaked cap and his grey beard was hung with a web of bright drops. She smiled; he stood before her, the cornet under his arm, wiping his face with a coloured handkerchief that smelt of tar ... Tell me, why do you play the cornet? ... Now he was gone again, sitting perhaps behind the heap of timber, far away, and playing more forlornly than ever ...

She stirred and sighed and stretched herself.

'What am I going to do this afternoon?' thought Muffi. Every day she asked herself that question, and every day it ended in her doing just the same thing — nothing at all. In the winter she lay in front of the fire, staring at the bright dazzle; in summer she sat at the open window and watched the breeze skim through the long gleaming grass, and then those ragged bushes were covered with tiny cream flowers; and in autumn and winter she sat there too, only then the window was shut. Some days a sea mist covered everything, and other days the wild hooting south wind blew as if it meant to tear everything off the earth, tear everything up by the roots and send it spinning. She did not even think or dream. No, as she sat there, ever so faintly smiling, with something mocking in the way her eyelids lay upon her eyes, she looked like a person waiting for a train that she knew would not come, never would by any chance carry her away, did not even exist ...

During the afternoon the baker's boy came and left a loaf on the kitchen window sill. The round basket on his back always reminded her of a snail's shell. 'Here comes the snail,' she would say. Three times a week an awful butcher, a man so raw and red and willing to oblige that she always felt if he hadn't the pound and a half of steak she wanted he'd be quite willing to cut it off his own person and never notice the difference ... And very, very rarely, two shabby old nuns wheeling a perambulator knocked at the door and asked her if she had any scraps or bits of things for the orphan children at Lyall Bay ... No, she never had, but she liked very much seeing them at her door, smiling so gently, their hands tucked in their sleeves. They made her feel so small somehow, so like an orphan child herself. One of them always did the talking, and the other kept silent.

'You're not married, are you?' asked the talkative nun on one occasion.

'Oh, yes,' said Muffi.

'Glory be!' cried the old nun, and seemed positively to wring her hidden hands in horror.

'You've no children?' she asked, her old mouth falling open.

'Yes, I've a little boy of seven.'

'Mother of God!' cried the old nun, and that day they went away pushing the perambulator very slowly, as though it were heavy with the incredible news.

Any time after five o'clock the children came home from school ...

Five o'clock struck. Muffi got up from the sofa to put the kettle on for their tea. She was bending over the kitchen stove when someone tapped on the window. Rudi. Yes, there he was tapping on the window, smiling and nodding. Ah, the darling. He was home early. She flew to the back door and just had time to open it ... to hold out her arms and in he tumbled.

'You're early. You darling. You're so beautifully early,' she stammered, kissing and hugging him. How wet and cold his cheeks were; and his fingers, even his fringe was damp. For a moment he could not speak. He might have been a little boy picked out of the sea, so breathless and exhausted was he. At last he swallowed twice and gave a final gasping sigh.

'I'm simply sopping from this mist,' he panted. 'Feel my cap, Muffi. Drenched!'

'Drenched,' said she, kneeling down to take off his reefer jacket.

'Oh, I'm still so out of breath,' he cried, stamping and wriggling his way out of the sleeves. 'I simply flew home.'

'Let me jump you on the table and take off your boots, my precious.'

'Oh, no!' He had got back his self-contained deliberate little voice. 'I can take off my own boots, Muffi, I always do.'

'Ah, no! Let me,' she pleaded. 'Just this once. Just for a treat.'

At that he threw back his head and looked at her, his eyes dancing.

'Well, you have got funny ideas of a treat.'

'Yes,' said she. 'I know I have. Awfully funny ideas. Now the other foot, old man.'

When she had finished, he sat on the table edge and swung his leg, pouting and frowning, and showing off just a tiny bit. He knew, as he sat there, that he was the most loved little boy in the world, the most admired, the most cherished. And Muffi let him know it. They were alone together so seldom; they could not afford to pretend, to waste a moment. He seemed to realise that. He said: 'Katerina will be home in a minute. I passed her on my way, dawdling along with that Lily Tar. I can't stand Lily Tar, Muffi. She's always got her arm round someone and she's always whispering.'

'Don't bother about her,' said Muffi, as much as to say: 'If Lily Tar dares to get in your way I shall see that she is destroyed instantly.' Lily Tar was gone. He looked down at his little red paws.

'My fingers are so stiff,' he said. 'I'll never be able to practise.'

'Sit down on the hassock here before the fire and give them a good warm.'

'It's very nice down here,' he decided after a moment. 'I love being down low and looking up at things — don't you? At people moving and the legs of chairs and tables and the shadows on the floor.' His voice tailed off, dreamy and absorbed. She let him be. She thought: 'He is getting back to himself after that horrible rowdy school.' But a moment later the front door slammed and Katerina came into the kitchen.

'Hullo!' said she, very airy. 'Why did you tear home so, Rudi? Lily and I could not help screaming at the way you were rushing along.'

'I heard you,' said Rudi. 'I knew you meant me to hear, didn't you?' At that she opened her big velvety eyes at him and laughed.

'What a baby you are!'

'But you did, didn't you?' he protested.

'Of course not,' she jeered. 'We were laughing at something quite different.'

'But you just said you were laughing at me, Katerina.'

'Oh, only in a way,' she drawled.

Rudi jumped up. 'Oh, Katerina,' he wailed, 'why do you tell such awful stories?'

Muffi's back was turned, so Katerina made a hideous face at him and sat down at the table. All the while she was eating her tea Katerina could not helping smiling her strange little cat smile. The lids fell over her eyes as though she were basking before some mysterious warm secret that she would never share with a baby boy. When she helped herself to jam, holding the jam spoon high up in the air and letting the jam fall in red blobs on her bread, Rudi hated her so much he gave a great shudder of horror and pushed back his chair. Again she opened those big pansy velvet eyes and again the wide surprised stare.

'What is the matter, now?' asked Katerina.

But that was too much for Rudi. He couldn't understand it, no, he couldn't. 'Muffi, why does she do it? How can she?'

But Muffi gave barely a sign. 'Don't tease him so, Katerina!' she said. She poured some warm water into a basin and gave Rudi a thin shave of soap. And as he washed his hands he turned to her ...

The Woman at the Store

All that day the heat was terrible. The wind blew close to the ground — it rooted among the tussock grass — slithered along the road, so that the white pumice dust swirled in our faces — settled and sifted over us and was like a dry skin itching for growth on our bodies. The horses stumbled along, coughing and chuffing. The pack horse was sick — with a big, open sore rubbed under the belly. Now and again she stopped short, threw back her head, looked at us as though she were going to cry, and whinnied. Hundreds of larks shrilled — the sky was slate colour, and the sound of the larks reminded me of slate pencils scraping over its surface. There was nothing to be seen but wave after wave of tussock grass — patched with purple orchids and manuka bushes covered with thick spider webs.

Jo rode ahead. He wore a blue galatea shirt, corduroy trousers and riding boots. A white handkerchief, spotted with red — it looked as though his nose had been bleeding on it — knotted round his throat. Wisps of white hair straggled from under his wideawake — his moustache and eyebrows were called white — he slouched in the saddle — grunting. Not once that day had he sung 'I don't care, for don't you see, my wife's mother was in front of me!' ... It was the first day we had been without it for a month, and now there seemed something uncanny in his silence. Hin rode beside me — white as a clown, his black eyes glittered, and he kept shooting out his tongue and moistening his lips. He was dressed in a Jaeger vest — a pair of blue duck trousers, fastened round the waist with a plaited leather belt. We had hardly spoken since dawn. At noon we had lunched off fly biscuits and apricots by the side of a swampy creek.

'My stomach feels like the crop of a hen,' said Jo. 'Now then, Hin, you're the bright boy of the party — where's this 'ere store you kep' on talking about. "Oh, yes," you says, "I know a fine store, with a paddock for the horses an' a creek runnin' through, owned by a friend of mine who'll give yer a bottle of whisky before 'e shakes hands with yer." I'd like ter see that place — merely as a matter of curiosity — not that I'd ever doubt yer word — as yer know very well — *but …* '

Hin laughed. 'Don't forget there's a woman too, Jo, with blue eyes and yellow hair, who'll promise you something else before she shakes hands with you. Put that in your pipe and smoke it.'

'The heat's making you balmy,' said Jo. But he dug his knees into his horse. We shambled on. I half fell asleep, and had a sort of uneasy dream that the horses were not moving forward at all — then that I was on a rocking-horse, and my old mother was scolding me for raising such a fearful dust from the drawing-room carpet. 'You've entirely worn off the pattern of the carpet,' I heard her saying, and she gave the reins a tug. I snivelled and woke to find Hin leaning over me, maliciously smiling.

'That was a case of all but,' said he, 'I just caught you. What's up, been bye-bye?'

'No!' I raised my head. 'Thank the Lord we're arriving somewhere.'

We were on the brow of the hill, and below us there was a whare roofed in with corrugated iron. It stood in a garden, rather far back from the road — a big paddock opposite, and a creek and a clump of young willow trees. A thin line of blue smoke stood up straight from the chimney of the whare, and as I looked, a woman came out, followed by a child and a sheep dog — the woman carrying what appeared to me a black stick. She made frantic gestures at us. The horses put on a final spurt, Jo took off his wideawake, shouted, threw out his chest, and began singing, 'I don't care, for don't you see … ' The sun pushed through the pale clouds and shed a vivid light over the scene. It gleamed on the woman's yellow hair, over her flapping pinafore and the rifle she was carrying. The child hid behind her, and the yellow dog, a mangy beast, scuttled back into the whare, his tail between his legs. We drew rein and dismounted.

'Hallo,' screamed the woman. 'I thought you was three 'awks. My kid comes runnin' in ter me. "Mumma," says she, "there's three brown things comin' over the 'ill," says she. An' I comes out smart, I can tell yer. They'll be 'awks, I says to her. Oh, the 'awks about 'ere, yer wouldn't believe.'

The 'kid' gave us the benefit of one eye from behind the woman's pinafore — then retired again.

'Where's your old man,' asked Hin.

The woman blinked rapidly, screwing up her face.

'Away shearin'. Bin away a month. I suppose yer not goin' to stop, are yer? There's a storm comin' up.'

'You bet we are,' said Jo. 'So, you're on your lonely, missis?'

She stood, pleating the frills of her pinafore, and glancing from one to the other of us, like a hungry bird. I smiled at the thought of how Hin had pulled Jo's leg about her. Certainly her eyes were blue, and what hair she had was yellow, but ugly. She was a figure of fun. Looking at her, you felt there was nothing but sticks and wires under that pinafore — her front teeth were knocked out, she had red pulpy hands, and she wore on her feet a pair of dirty 'Bluchers'.

'I'll go and turn out the horses,' said Hin. 'Got any embrocation? Poi's rubbed herself to hell!'

'Arf a mo!' The woman stood silent a moment, her nostrils expanding as she breathed. Then she shouted violently, 'I'd rather you didn't stop — you *can't* and there's the end of it. I don't let out that paddock any more. You'll have to go on; I ain't got nothing!'

'Well, I'm blest!' said Jo, heavily. He pulled me aside. 'Gone a bit off 'er dot,' he whispered, 'too much alone, *you know*,' very significantly. 'Turn the sympathetic tap on 'er, she'll come round all right.'

But there was no need — she had come round by herself.

'Stop if yer like!' she muttered, shrugging her shoulders. To me — 'I'll give yer the embrocation if yer come along.'

'Right-o, I'll take it down to them.' We walked together up the garden path. It was planted on both sides with cabbages. They smelled like stale dishwater. Of flowers there were double poppies and sweet-williams. One little patch was divided off by pawa shells — presumably it belonged to the child — for she ran from her mother and began to grub in it with a broken clothes peg. The yellow dog lay across the doorstep, biting fleas; the woman kicked him away.

'Gar-r, get away, you beast ... the place ain't tidy. I 'aven't 'ad time ter fix things to-day — been ironing. Come right in.'

It was a large room, the walls plastered with old pages of English periodicals. Queen Victoria's Jubilee appeared to be the most recent number — a table with an ironing board and wash tub on it — some wooden forms — a black horsehair sofa, and some broken cane chairs against the walls. The mantelpiece above the stove was draped in pink paper, further ornamented with dried grasses and ferns and a coloured print of Richard Seddon. There were four doors — one, judging from the smell, led into the 'Store', one on to the 'backyard', through the third I saw the bedroom. Flies buzzed in circles round the ceiling, and treacle papers and bundles of dried clover were pinned to the window curtains. I was alone in the room — she had gone into the store for the embrocation. I heard her stamping about and muttering to herself: 'I got some, now where did I put that bottle? ... It's behind the pickles ... no, it ain't.' I cleared a place on the table and sat there, swinging my legs. Down in the paddock I could hear Jo singing and the sound of hammer strokes as Hin drove in the tent poles. It was sunset. There is no twilight in our New Zealand days, but a curious half-hour when everything appears grotesque — it frightens — as though the savage spirit of the country walked abroad and sneered at what it saw. Sitting alone in the hideous room I grew afraid. The woman next door was a long time finding that stuff. What was she doing in there? Once I thought I heard her bang her hands down on the counter, and once she half moaned, turning it into a cough and clearing her throat. I wanted to shout 'Buck up,' but I kept silent.

'Good Lord, what a life!' I thought. 'Imagine being here day in, day out, with that rat of a child and a mangy dog. Imagine bothering about ironing — *mad*, of course she's mad! Wonder how long she's been here — wonder if I could get her to talk.'

At that moment she poked her head round the door.

'Wot was it yer wanted,' she asked.

'Embrocation.'

'Oh, I forgot. I got it, it was in front of the pickle jars.'

She handed me the bottle.

'My, you do look tired, you do! Shall I knock yer up a few scones for supper? There's some tongue in the store, too, and I'll cook yer a cabbage if you fancy it.'

'Right-o.' I smiled at her. 'Come down to the paddock and bring the kid for tea.'

She shook her head, pursing up her mouth.

'Oh no. I don't fancy it. I'll send the kid down with the things and a billy of milk. Shall I knock up a few extry scones to take with you ter-morrow?'

'Thanks.'

She came and stood by the door.

'How old is the kid?'

'Six — come next Christmas. I 'ad a bit of trouble with 'er one way an' another. I 'adn't any milk till a month after she was born and she sickened like a cow.'

'She's not like you — takes after her father?'

Just as the woman had shouted her refusal at us before, she shouted at me then.

'No, she don't; she's the dead spit of me. Any fool could see that. Come on in now, Els, you stop messing in the dirt.'

I met Jo climbing over the paddock fence.

'What's the old bitch got in the store?' he asked.

'Don't know — didn't look.'

'Well, of all the fools. Hin's slanging you. What have you been doing all the time?'

'She couldn't find this stuff. Oh, my shakes, you are smart!'

Jo had washed, combed his wet hair in a line across his fore-head, and buttoned a coat over his shirt. He grinned.

Hin snatched the embrocation from me. I went to the end of the paddock where the willows grew and bathed in the creek. The water was clear and soft as oil. Along the edges held by the grass and rushes, white foam tumbled and bubbled. I lay in the water and looked up at the trees that were still a moment, then quivered lightly, and again were still. The air smelt of rain. I for-got about the woman and the kid until I came back to the tent. Hin lay by the fire, watching the billy boil.

I asked where Jo was and if the kid had brought our supper.

'Pooh,' said Hin, rolling over and looking up at the sky. 'Didn't you see how Jo had been tittivating — he said to me before he went up to the whare, "Dang it! she'll look better by night light — at any rate, my buck, she's female flesh!" '

'You had Jo about her looks — you had me, too.'

'No — look here. I can't make it out. It's four years since I came past this way, and I stopped here two days. The husband was a pal of mine once, down the West Coast — a fine, big chap, with a voice on him like a trombone. She'd been barmaid down the Coast — as pretty as a wax doll. The coach used to come this way then once a fortnight, that was before they opened the rail-way up Napier way, and she had no end of a time! Told me once in a confidential moment that she knew one hundred and twenty-five different ways of kissing!'

'Oh, go on, Hin! She isn't the same woman!'

'Course she is ... I can't make it out. What I think is the old man's cleared out and left her: that's all my eye about shearing. Sweet life! The only people who come through now are Maoris and sundowners!'

Through the dark we saw the gleam of the kid's pinafore. She trailed over to us with a basket in her hand, the milk billy in the other. I unpacked the basket, the child standing by.

'Come over here,' said Hin, snapping his fingers at her.

She went, the lamp from the inside of the tent cast a bright light over her. A mean, undersized brat, with whitish hair, and weak eyes. She stood, legs wide apart and her stomach protruding.

'What do you do all day?' asked Hin.

She scraped out one ear with her little finger, looked at the result and said — 'Draw.'

'Huh! What do you draw? — leave your ears alone.'

'Pictures.'

'What on?'

'Bits of butter paper an' a pencil of my Mumma's.'

'Boh! What a lot of words at one time!' Hin rolled his eyes at her. 'Baa-lambs and moo-cows?'

'No, everything. I'll draw all of you when you're gone, and your horses and the tent, and that one' — she pointed to me — 'with no clothes on in the creek. I looked at her where she wouldn't see me from.'

'Thanks very much! How ripping of you,' said Hin. 'Where's Dad?'

The kid pouted. 'I won't tell you because I don't like yer face!' She started operations on the other ear.

'Here,' I said. 'Take the basket, get along home and tell the other man supper's ready.'

'I don't want to.'

'I'll give you a box on the ear if you don't,' said Hin, savagely.

'Hie! I'll tell Mumma. I'll tell Mumma' — the kid fled.

We ate until we were full and had arrived at the smoke stage before Jo came back, very flushed and jaunty, a whisky bottle in his hand.

' 'Ave a drink — you two!' he shouted, carrying off matters with a high hand. ' 'Ere, shove along the cups.'

'One hundred and twenty-five different ways,' I murmured to Hin.

'What's that? Oh! stow it!' said Jo. 'Why 'ave you always got your knife into me. You gas like a kid at a Sunday School beano. She wants us to go up there to-night, and have a comfortable chat. I' — he waved his hand airily — 'I got 'er round.'

'Trust you for that,' laughed Hin. 'But did she tell you where the old man's got to?'

Jo looked up. 'Shearing! You 'eard 'er, you fool!'

The woman had fixed up the room, even to a light bouquet of sweet-williams on the table. She and I sat one side of the table, Jo and Hin the other. An oil lamp was set between us, the whisky bottle and glasses, and a jug of water. The kid knelt against one of the forms, drawing on butter paper. I wondered, grimly, if she was attempting the creek episode. But Jo had been right about night time. The woman's hair was tumbled — two red spots burned in her cheeks — her eyes shone — and we knew that they were kissing feet under the table. She had changed the blue pinafore for a white calico dressing jacket and a black skirt — the kid was decorated to the extent of a blue sateen hair ribbon. In the stifling room with the flies buzzing against the ceiling and dropping on to the table — we got slowly drunk.

'Now listen to me,' shouted the woman, banging her fist on the table. 'It's six years since I was married, and four miscarriages. I says to 'im, I says, what do you think I'm doin' up 'ere?' If you was back at the Coast, I'd 'ave you lynched for child murder. Over and over I tells 'im — you've broken my spirit and spoiled my looks, and wot for — that's wot I'm driving at.' She clutched her head with her hands and stared round at us. Speaking rapidly, 'Oh, some days — an' months of them I 'ear them two words knockin' inside me all the time — "Wot for," but sometimes I'll be cooking the spuds an' I lifts the lid off to give 'em a prong and I 'ears, quite sudden again, "Wot for." Oh! I don't mean only the spuds and the kid — I mean — I mean,' she hiccoughed — 'you know what I mean, Mr Jo.'

'I know,' said Jo, scratching his head.

'Trouble with me is,' she leaned across the table, 'he left me too much alone. When the coach stopped coming, sometimes he'd go away days, sometimes he'd go away weeks, and leave me ter look after the store. Back 'e'd come — pleased as Punch. "Oh, 'allo," 'e'd say. "Ow are you gettin' on. Come and give us a kiss." Sometimes I'd turn a bit nasty, and then 'e'd go off again, and if I took it all right, 'e'd wait till 'e could twist me round 'is finger, then 'e'd say, "Well, so long, I'm off," and do you think I could keep 'im? — not me!'

'Mumma,' bleated the kid, 'I made a picture of them on the 'ill, an' you an' me, an' the dog down below.'

'Shut your mouth,' said the woman.

A vivid flash of lightning played over the room — we heard the mutter of thunder.

'Good thing that's broke loose,' said Jo. 'I've 'ad it in me 'ead for three days.'

'Where's your old man now?' asked Hin slowly.

The woman blubbered and dropped her head on to the table. 'Hin, 'e's gone shearin' and left me alone again,' she wailed.

' 'Ere, look out for the glasses,' said Jo. 'Cheer-o, 'ave another drop. No good cryin' over spilt 'usbands! You Hin, you blasted cuckoo!'

'Mr Jo,' said the woman, drying her eyes on her jacket frill, 'you're a gent, an' if I was a secret woman, I'd place any confidence in your 'ands. I won't mind if I do 'ave a glass on that.'

Every moment the lightning grew more vivid and the thunder sounded nearer. Hin and I were silent — the kid never moved from her bench. She poked her tongue out and blew on it as she drew.

'It's the loneliness,' said the woman, addressing Jo — he made sheep's eyes at her — 'and bein' shut up 'ere like a broody 'en.' He reached his hand across the table and held hers, and though the position looked most uncomfortable when they wanted to pass the water and whisky, their hands stuck together as though glued. I pushed back my chair and went over to the kid, who immediately sat flat down on her artistic achievements and made a face at me.

'You're not to look,' said she.

'Oh, come on, don't be so nasty!' Hin came over to us, and we were just drunk enough to wheedle the kid into showing us. And those drawings of hers were extraordinary and repulsively vulgar. The creations of a lunatic with a lunatic's cleverness. There was no doubt about it, the kid's mind was diseased. While she showed them to us, she worked herself up into a mad excitement, laughing and trembling, and shooting out her arms.

'Mumma,' she yelled. 'Now I'm going to draw them what you told me I never was to — now I am.'

The woman rushed from the table and beat the child's head with the flat of her hand.

'I'll smack you with yer clothes turned up if yer dare say that again,' she bawled.

Jo was too drunk to notice, but Hin caught her by the arm. The kid did not utter a cry. She drifted over to the window and began picking flies from the treacle paper.

We returned to the table — Hin and I sitting one side, the woman and Jo, touching shoulders, the other. We listened to the thunder, saying stupidly, 'That was a near one,' 'There it goes again,' and Jo, with a heavy hit, 'Now we're off,' 'Steady on the brake,' until rain began to fall, sharp as cannon shot on the iron roof.

'You'd better doss here for the night,' said the woman.

'That's right,' assented Jo, evidently in the know about this move.

'Bring up yer things from the tent. You two can doss in the store along with the kid — she's used to sleep in there and won't mind you.'

'O, Mumma, I never did,' interrupted the kid.

'Shut yer lies! An' Mr Jo can 'ave this room.'

It sounded a ridiculous arrangement, but it was useless to attempt to cross them, they were too far gone. While the woman sketched the plan of action, Jo sat, abnormally solemn and red, his eyes bulging, and pulled at his moustache.

'Give us a lantern,' said Hin. 'I'll go down to the paddock.' We two went together. Rain whipped in our faces, the land was as light as though a bush fire was raging — we behaved like two children let loose in the thick of an adventure — laughed and shouted to each other, and came back to the whare to find the kid already bedded in the counter of the store. The woman brought us a lamp. Jo took his bundle from Hin, the door was shut.

'Good-night all,' shouted Jo.

Hin and I sat on two sacks of potatoes. For the life of us we could not stop laughing. Strings of onions and half-hams dangled from the ceiling — wherever we looked there were advertisements for 'Camp Coffee' and tinned meats. We pointed at them, tried to read them aloud — overcome with laughter and hiccoughs. The kid in the counter stared at us. She threw off her blanket and scrambled to the floor where she stood in her grey flannel night gown, rubbing one leg against the other. We paid no attention to her.

'Wot are you laughing at,' she said, uneasily.

'You!' shouted Hin, 'the red tribe of you, my child.'

She flew into a rage and beat herself with her hands. 'I won't be laughed at, you curs — you.' He swooped down upon the child and swung her on to the counter.

'Go to sleep, Miss Smarty — or make a drawing — here's a pencil — you can use Mumma's account book.'

Through the rain we heard Jo creak over the boarding of the next room — the sound of a door being opened — then shut to.

'It's the loneliness,' whispered Hin.

'One hundred and twenty-five different ways — alas! my poor brother!'

The kid tore out a page and flung it at me.

'There you are,' she said. 'Now I done it ter spite Mumma for shutting me up 'ere with you two. I done the one she told me I never ought to. I done the one she told me she'd shoot me if I did. Don't care! Don't care!'

The kid had drawn the picture of the woman shooting at a man with a rook rifle and then digging a hole to bury him in.

She jumped off the counter and squirmed about on the floor biting her nails.

Hin and I sat till dawn with the drawing beside us. The rain ceased, the little kid fell asleep, breathing loudly. We got up, stole out of the whare, down into the paddock. White clouds floated over a pink sky — a chill wind blew; the air smelled of wet grass. Just as we swung into the saddle, Jo came out of the whare — he motioned us to ride on.

'I'll pick you up later,' he shouted.

A bend in the road, and the whole place disappeared.

How Pearl Button was
Kidnapped

Pearl Button swung on the little gate in front of the House of Boxes. It was the early afternoon of a sunshiny day with little winds playing hide-and-seek in it. They blew Pearl Button's pinafore frill into her mouth and they blew the street dust all over the House of Boxes. Pearl watched it — like a cloud — like when mother peppered her fish and the top of the pepper-pot came off. She swung on the little gate, all alone, and she sang a small song. Two big women came walking down the street. One was dressed in red and the other was dressed in yellow and green. They had pink handkerchiefs over their heads, and both of them carried a big flax basket of ferns. They had no shoes and stockings on and they came walking along, slowly, because they were so fat, and talking to each other and always smiling. Pearl stopped swinging and when they saw her they stopped walking. They looked and looked at her and then they talked to each other waving their arms and clapping their hands together. Pearl began to laugh. The two women came up to her, keeping close to the hedge and looking in a frightened way towards the House of Boxes. 'Hallo, little girl!' said one. Pearl said, 'Hallo!' 'You all alone by yourself?' Pearl nodded. 'Where's your mother?' 'In the kitching, ironing-because-it's-Tuesday.' The woman smiled at her and Pearl smiled back. 'Oh,' she said, 'haven't you got very white teeth indeed! Do it again.' The dark woman laughed and again they talked to each other with funny words and wavings of the hands. 'What's your name?' they asked her. 'Pearl Button.' 'You coming with us, Pearl Button? We got beautiful things to show you,' whispered one of the women. So Pearl got down from the gate and she slipped out into the road. And she walked between the two dark women down the windy road, taking little running steps to keep up and wondering what they had in their House of Boxes.

They walked a long way. 'You tired?' asked one of the women, bending down to Pearl. Pearl shook her head. They walked much further. 'You not tired?' asked the other woman. And Pearl shook her head again, but tears shook from her eyes at the same time and her lips trembled. One of the women gave over her flax basket of ferns and caught Pearl Button up in her arms and walked with Pearl Button's head against her shoulder and her dusty little legs dangling. She was softer than a bed and she had a nice smell — a smell that made you bury your head and breathe and breathe it. . . . They set Pearl Button down in a long room full of other people the same colour as they were — and all these people came close to her and looked at her, nodding and laughing and throwing up their eyes. The woman who had carried Pearl took off her hair ribbon and shook her curls loose. There was a cry from the other women and they crowded close and some of them ran a finger through Pearl's yellow curls, very gently, and one of them, a young one, lifted all Pearl's hair and kissed the back of her little white neck. Pearl felt shy but happy at the same time. There were some men on the floor, smoking, with rugs and feather mats round their shoulders. One of them made a funny face at her and he pulled a great big peach out of his pocket and set it on the floor, and flicked it with his finger as though it were a marble. It rolled right over to her. Pearl picked it up. 'Please can I eat it?' she asked. At that they all laughed and clapped their hands and the man with the funny face made another at her and pulled a pear out of his pocket and sent it bobbling over the floor. Pearl laughed. The women sat on the floor and Pearl sat down too. The floor was very dusty. She carefully pulled up her pinafore and dress and sat on her petticoat as she had been taught to sit in dusty places, and she ate the fruit, the juice running all down her front. 'Oh,' she said, in a very fright-ened voice to one of the women, 'I've spilt all the juice!' 'That doesn't matter at all,' said the woman, patting her cheek. A man came into the room with a long whip in his hand. He shouted something. They all got up, shouting, laughing, wrapping themselves up in rugs and blankets and feather mats. Pearl was carried again, this time into a great cart, and she sat on the lap of one of her women with the driver beside her. It was a green cart with a red pony and a black pony. It went very fast out of the town. The driver stood up and waved the whip round his head. Pearl peered over the shoulder of her woman. Other carts were behind like a procession. She waved at them. Then the country came. First fields of short grass with sheep on them and little bushes of white flowers and pink briar rose baskets — then big trees on both sides of the road — and nothing to be seen except big trees. Pearl tried to look through them but it was quite dark. Birds were singing. She nestled closer in the big lap. The woman was warm as a cat and she moved up and down when she breathed, just like purring. Pearl played with a green ornament round her neck and the woman took the little hand and kissed each of her fingers and then turned it over and kissed the dimples. Pearl had never been happy like this before. On the top of a big hill they stopped. The driving man turned to Pearl and said, 'Look, look!' and pointed with his whip. And down at the bottom of the hill was something perfectly different — a great big piece of blue water was creeping over the land. She screamed and clutched at the big woman. 'What is it, what is it?' 'Why,' said the woman, 'it's the sea.' 'Will it hurt us — is it coming?' 'Ai-e, no, it doesn't come to us. It's very beautiful. You look again.' Pearl looked. 'You're sure it can't come,' she said. 'Ai-e, no. It stays in its place,' said the big woman. Waves with white tops came leaping over the blue. Pearl watched them break on a long piece of land covered with garden-path shells. They drove round a corner. There were some little houses down close to the sea, with wood fences round them and gardens inside. They comforted her. Pink and red and blue washing hung over the

fences and as they came near more people came out and five yellow dogs with long thin tails. All the people were fat and laughing,
with little naked babies holding on to them or rolling about in the
gardens like puppies. Pearl was lifted down and taken into a tiny
house with only one room and a veranda. There was a girl there
with two pieces of black hair down to her feet. She was setting the
dinner on the floor. 'It *is* a funny place,' said Pearl, watching the
pretty girl while the woman unbuttoned her little drawers for her.
She was very hungry. She ate meat and vegetables and fruit and the
woman gave her milk out of a green cup. And it was quite silent
except for the sea outside and the laughs of the two women watching her. 'Haven't you got any Houses in Boxes?' she said. 'Don't
you all live in a row? Don't the men go to offices? Aren't there any
nasty things?'

They took off her shoes and stockings, her pinafore and
dress. She walked about in her petticoat and then she walked
outside with the grass pushing between her toes. The two
women came out with different sorts of baskets. They took her
hands. Over a little paddock, through a fence, and then on warm
sand with brown grass in it they went down to the sea. Pearl held
back when the sand grew wet, but the women coaxed. 'Nothing
to hurt, very beautiful. You come.' They dug in the sand and
found some shells which they threw into the baskets. The sand
was wet as mud pies. Pearl forgot her fright and began digging
too. She got hot and wet and suddenly over her feet broke a
little line of foam. 'Oo, oo!' she shrieked, dabbling with her feet,
'Lovely, lovely!' She paddled in the shallow water. It was warm.
She made a cup of her hands and caught some of it. But it
stopped being blue in her hands. She was so excited that she
rushed over to her woman and flung her little thin arms round
the woman's neck, hugging her, kissing ... Suddenly the girl gave
a frightful scream. The woman raised herself and Pearl slipped
down on the sand and looked towards the land. Little men in

blue coats — little blue men came running, running towards her with shouts and whistlings — a crowd of little blue men to carry her back to the House of Boxes.

The Little Girl

To the little girl he was a figure to be feared and avoided. Every morning before going to business he came into the nursery and gave her a perfunctory kiss to which she responded with 'Good-bye, Father'. And oh, the glad sense of relief when she heard the noise of the buggy growing fainter and fainter down the long road!

In the evening, leaning over the banisters at his home-coming, she heard his loud voice in the hall. 'Bring my tea into the smoking room ... Hasn't the paper come yet? Have they taken it into the kitchen again? Mother, go and see if my paper's out there — and bring me my slippers.'

'Kass,' mother would call to her, 'if you're a good girl you can come down and take off Father's boots.' Slowly the little girl would slip down the stairs, holding tightly to the banisters with one hand — more slowly still, across the hall and push open the smoking-room door.

By that time he had his spectacles on and looked at her over them in a way that was terrifying to the little girl.

'Well, Kass, get a move on and pull off these boots and take them outside. Been a good girl to-day?'

'I d-d-don't know, Father.'

'You d-d-don't know? If you stutter like that Mother will have to take you to the doctor.'

She never stuttered with other people — had quite given it up — only with Father because then she was trying so hard to say the words properly.

'What's the matter? What are you looking so wretched about? Mother, I wish you would teach this child not to appear on the brink of suicide … Here, Kass, carry my teacup back to the table — carefully; your hands jog like an old lady. And try to keep your handkerchief in your pocket, *not* up your sleeve.'

'Y-y-yes, Father.'

On Sundays she sat in the same pew with him in church, listening while he sang in a loud, clear voice, watching while he made little notes during the sermon with the stump of a blue pencil on the back of an envelope — his eyes narrowed to a slit — one hand beating a silent tattoo on the pew ledge. He said his prayers so loudly that she was certain God heard him above the clergyman.

He was so big — that was what frightened the little girl — his hands and his neck — especially his mouth when he yawned. Thinking about him alone in the nursery was like thinking about a giant.

On Sunday afternoons Grandmother sent her down to the drawing-room, dressed in her 'brown velvet', to have a 'nice talk with Mother and Father'. But the little girl always found Mother reading the *Sketch* and Father stretched out on the couch, his handkerchief on his face, feet propped on one of the best sofa pillows, and so soundly sleeping that he snored.

She, perched on the piano stool, gravely watched him until he woke and stretched, and asked the time — then looked round at her.

'Don't stare so, Kass. You look like a little brown owl.'

One day, when she was kept indoors with a cold, the Grandmother told her that Father's birthday was next week and suggested she should make him a pincushion for a present out of a beautiful piece of yellow silk.

Laboriously, with a double cotton, the little girl stitched three sides. But what to fill it with? That was the question. The

Grandmother was out in the garden, and she wandered into Mother's bedroom to look for 'scraps'. On the bed table she discovered a great many sheets of fine paper, gathered them up, shredded them into tiny pieces and stuffed her case, then sewed up the fourth side.

That night there was a hue and cry over the house. Father's great speech for the Harbour Board had been lost. Rooms were ransacked — servants questioned. Finally Mother came into the nursery.

'Kass, I suppose you didn't see some papers on a table in our room?'

'Oh, yes,' she said. 'I tore them up for my s'prise.'

'*What*!' screamed Mother. 'Come straight down to the dining-room this instant.'

And she was dragged down to where Father was pacing to and fro, hands behind his back.

'Well?' sharply.

Mother explained.

He stopped and stared in a stupefied manner at the child.

'Did you do that?'

'N-n-no,' she whispered.

'Mother, go up to the nursery and fetch down the damned thing — see that the child's put to bed this instant.'

Crying too much to explain she lay in the shadowed room watching the evening light sift through the venetian blinds and trace a sad little pattern on the floor.

Then Father came into the room with a ruler in his hands.

'I am going to whip you for this,' he said.

'Oh, no, no,' she screamed, cowering down under the bed-clothes.

He pulled them aside.

'Sit up,' he commanded, 'and hold out your hands. You must be taught once and for all not to touch what does not belong to you.'

'But it was for your b-b-birthday.' ...

Down came the ruler on her little, pink palms.

Hours later, when the Grandmother had wrapped her in a shawl and rocked her in the rocking chair the child cuddled close to her soft body.

'Why did Jesus make Fathers for?' she snivelled.

'Here's a clean "hanky", darling, with some of my lavender water on it. Go to sleep, pet, you'll forget all about it in the morning. I tried to explain to Father but he was too upset to listen to-night.'

But the child never forgot. Next time she saw him she whipped both her hands behind her back, and a red colour flew into her cheeks.

The Macdonalds lived in the next door house. Five children there were. Looking through a hole in the vegetable garden fence the little girl saw them playing 'tag' in the evening — the Father with the 'baby Mac' on his shoulders, two little girls hanging on to his coat tails — ran round and round the flower beds, shaking with laughter. Once she saw the boys turn the hose on him — *turn the hose on him* — and he made a great grab at them, tickling them until they got hiccoughs.

Then it was she decided there were different sorts of Fathers.

Suddenly, one day, Mother became ill, and she and Grandmother drove into town in a closed carriage.

The little girl was left alone in the house with Alice, the 'general'. That was all right in the daytime, but while Alice was putting her to bed she grew suddenly afraid.

'What'll I do if I have nightmare?' she asked. 'I *often* have nightmare and then Grannie takes me into her bed — I can't stay in the dark — it all gets "whispery" ... What'll I do if I do?'

'You just go to sleep, child,' said Alice, pulling off her socks and whacking them against the bedrail, 'and don't holler out and wake your poor Pa.'

But the same old nightmare came — the butcher with a knife and a rope who grew nearer and nearer, smiling that dreadful smile, while she could not move — could only stand still, crying out, 'Grandma, Grand*ma*'. She woke shivering, to see Father beside her bed, a candle in his hand.

'What's the matter?' he said.

'Oh, a butcher — a knife — I want Grannie.' He blew out the candle, bent down and caught up the child in his arms, carrying her along the passage to the big bedroom. A newspaper was on the bed — a half-smoked cigar balanced against his reading lamp. He pitched the paper on to the floor — threw the cigar into the fireplace — then carefully tucked up the child. He lay down beside her. Half asleep still, still with the butcher's smile all about her, it seemed, she crept close to him, snuggled her head under his arm, held tightly to his pyjama jacket.

Then the dark did not matter; she lay still.

'Here, rub your feet against my legs and get them warm,' said Father.

Tired out, he slept before the little girl. A funny feeling came over her. Poor Father! Not so big after all — and with no one to look after him ... He was harder than the Grandmother, but it was a nice hardness ... And every day he had to work and was too tired to be a Mr Macdonald ... She had torn up all his beautiful writing ... She stirred suddenly, and sighed.

'What's the matter?' asked Father. 'Another dream?'

'Oh,' said the little girl, 'my head's on your heart; I can hear it going. What a big heart you've got, Father dear.'

Ole Underwood

Down the windy hill stalked Ole Underwood. He carried a black umbrella in one hand, in the other a red and white spotted hand-kerchief knotted into a lump. He wore a black peaked cap like a pilot; gold rings gleamed in his ears and his little eyes snapped like two sparks. Like two sparks they glowed in the smoulder of his bearded face. On one side of the hill grew a forest of pines from the road right down to the sea. On the other side short tufted grass and little bushes of white manuka flower. The pine-trees roared like waves in their topmost branches, their stems creaked like the timber of ships; in the windy air flew the white manuka flower. Ah–k! shouted Ole Underwood, shaking his umbrella at the wind bearing down upon him, beating him, half strangling him with his black cape. Ah–k! shouted the wind a hundred times as loud, and filled his mouth and nostrils with dust. Something inside Ole Underwood's breast beat like a ham-mer. One two — one two — never stopping, never changing. He couldn't do anything. It wasn't loud. No, it didn't make a noise — only a thud. One, two — one, two — like someone beating on an iron in a prison — someone in a secret place — bang — bang — bang — trying to get free. Do what he would, fumble at his coat, throw his arms about, spit, swear, he couldn't stop the noise. Stop! Stop! Stop! Stop! Ole Underwood began to shuffle and run.

Away below the sea heaving against the stone walls, and the little town just out of its reach close packed together, the better to face the grey water. And up on the other side of the hill the prison with high red walls. Over all bulged the grey sky with black web-like clouds streaming.

Ole Underwood slackened his pace as he neared the town, and when he came to the first house he flourished his umbrella like a herald's staff and threw out his chest, his head glancing quickly from right to left. They were ugly little houses leading into the town, built of wood — two windows and a door, a stumpy veranda and a green mat of grass before. Under one veranda yellow hens huddled out of the wind. Shoo! shouted Ole Underwood, and laughed to see them fly, and laughed again at the woman who came to the door and shook a red, soapy fist at him. A little girl stood in another yard untwisting some rags from a clothes line. When she saw Ole Underwood she let the clothes prop fall and rushed screaming to the door, beating it, screaming 'Mum-ma — Mum-ma!' That started the hammer in Ole Underwood's heart. Mum-ma — Mum-ma! He saw an old face with a trembling chin and grey hair nodding out of the window as they dragged him past. Mum-ma — Mum-ma! He looked up at the big red prison perched on the hill and he pulled a face as if he wanted to cry. At the corner in front of the pub some carts were pulled up, and some men sat in the porch of the pub drinking and talking. Ole Underwood wanted a drink. He slouched into the bar. It was half full of old and young men in big coats and top boots with stock whips in their hands. Behind the counter a big girl with red hair pulled the beer handles and cheeked the men. Ole Underwood sneaked to one side, like a cat. Nobody looked at him, only the men looked at each other, one or two of them nudged. The girl nodded and winked at the fellow she was serving. He took some money out of his knotted handkerchief and slipped it on to the counter. His hand shook. He didn't speak. The girl took no notice; she served everybody, went on with her talk, and then as if by accident shoved a mug towards him. A great big jar of red pinks stood on the bar counter. Ole Underwood stared at them as he drank and frowned at them. Red — red — red — red! beat the hammer. It was very warm in the bar and quiet as a pond, except for the talk and the girl. She kept on laughing. Ha! ha! That was what the men liked to see, for she threw back her head and her great breasts lifted and shook to her laughter. In one corner sat a stranger. He pointed at Ole Underwood. 'Cracked!' said one of the men. 'When he was a young fellow, thirty years ago, a man 'ere done in 'is woman, an' 'e foun' out an' killed 'er. Got twenty year in quod up on the 'ill. Came out cracked.' 'Oo done 'er in?' asked the man. 'Dunno. 'E don' no, nor nobody. 'E was a sailor till 'e marrid 'er. Cracked!' The man spat and smeared the spittle in the floor, shrugging his shoulders. ' 'E's 'armless enough.' Ole Underwood heard; he did not turn, but he shot out an old claw and crushed up the red pinks. 'Uh-Uh! You ole beast! Uh! You ole swine!' screamed the girl, leaning across the counter and banging him with a tin jug. 'Get art! Get art! Don' you never come 'ere no more!' Somebody kicked him: he scuttled like a rat.

He walked past the Chinamen's shops. The fruit and vegetables were all piled up against the windows. Bits of wooden cases, straw, and old newspapers were strewn over the pavement. A woman flounced out of a shop and slushed a pail of slops over his feet. He peered in at the windows, at the Chinamen sitting in little groups on old barrels playing cards. They made him smile. He looked and looked, pressing his face against the glass and sniggering. They sat still with their long pigtails bound round their heads and their faces yellow as lemons. Some of them had knives in their belts and one old man sat by himself on the floor plaiting his long crooked toes together. The Chinamen didn't mind Ole Underwood. When they saw him they nodded. He went to the door of a shop and cautiously opened it. In rushed the wind with him, scattering the cards. 'Ya-Ya! Ya-Ya!' screamed the Chinamen, and Ole Underwood rushed off, the hammer beating quick and hard. Ya-Ya! He turned a corner out of sight. He thought he heard one of the Chinks after him and he slipped into a timber-yard. There he lay panting ... Close by him, under another stack there was a heap of yellow shavings. As he watched them they moved and a little grey cat unfolded

herself and came out waving her tail. She trod delicately over to
Ole Underwood and rubbed against his sleeve. The hammer in
Ole Underwood's heart beat madly. It pounded up into his
throat, and then it seemed to half stop and beat very, very faintly. 'Kit! Kit! Kit!' That was what she used to call the little cat he
brought her off the ship. Kit! Kit! Kit! and stoop down with the
saucer in her hands. 'Ah! my God! — my Lord!' Ole
Underwood sat up and took the kitten in his arms and rocked to
and fro, crushing it against his face. It was warm and soft, and it
mewed faintly. He buried his eyes in its fur. My God! My Lord!
He tucked the little cat in his coat and stole out of the wood-
yard, and slouched down towards the wharves. As he came near
the sea, Ole Underwood's nostrils expanded. The mad wind
smelled of tar and ropes and slime and salt. He crossed the rail-
way line, he crept behind the wharf-sheds and along a little
cinder path that threaded through a patch of rank fennel to some
stone drain pipes carrying the sewage into the sea. And he stared
up at the wharves and at the ships with flags flying and suddenly
the old, old lust swept over Ole Underwood. 'I will! I will! I
will!' he muttered. He tore the little cat out of his coat and
swung it by its tail and flung it out to the sewer opening. The
hammer beat loud and strong. He tossed his head, he was young
again. He walked on to the wharves, past the wool-bales, past
the loungers and the loafers to the extreme end of the wharves.
The sea sucked against the wharf-poles as though it drank
something from the land. One ship was loading wool. He heard
a crane rattle and the shriek of a whistle. So he came to the little
ship lying by herself with a bit of plank for a gangway and no sign
of anybody, anybody at all. Ole Underwood looked once back at
the town, at the prison perched like a red bird, at the black,
webby clouds trailing. Then he went up the gangway and on to
the slippery deck. He grinned, and rolled in his walk, carrying
high in his hand the red and white handkerchief. His ship! Mine!

Mine! Mine! beat the hammer. There was a door latched open on the lee-side, labelled 'State-room'. He peered in. A man lay sleeping on a bunk — his bunk — a great big man in a seaman's coat with a long fair beard and hair on the red pillow. And looking down upon him from the wall there shone her picture — his woman's picture — smiling and smiling at the big sleeping man.

Millie

Millie stood leaning against the verandah until the men were out of sight. When they were far down the road Willie Cox turned round on his horse and waved. But she didn't wave back. She nodded her head a little and made a grimace. Not a bad young fellow, Willie Cox, but a bit too free and easy for her taste. Oh, my word! it was hot. Enough to fry your hair! Millie put her handkerchief over her head and shaded her eyes with her hand. In the distance along the dusty road she could see the horses — like brown spots dancing up and down, and when she looked away from them and over the burnt paddocks she could see them still — just before her eyes, jumping like mosquitoes. It was half-past two in the afternoon. The sun hung in the faded blue sky like a burning mirror, and away beyond the paddocks the blue mountains quivered and leapt like sea. Sid wouldn't be back until half-past ten. He had ridden over to the township with four of the boys to help hunt down the young fellow who'd murdered Mr Williamson. Such a dreadful thing! And Mrs Williamson left all alone with all those kids. Funny! she couldn't think of Mr Williamson being dead! He was such a one for a joke. Always having a lark. Willie Cox said they found him in the barn, shot bang through the head, and the young English 'johnny' who'd been on the station learning farming — disappeared. Funny! she wouldn't think of anyone shooting Mr Williamson, and him so popular and all. My word! when they caught that young man! Well — you couldn't be sorry for a young fellow like that. As Sid said, if he wasn't strung up where would they all be? A man like that doesn't stop at one go. There was blood all over the barn. And Willie Cox said he was that knocked out he picked a cigarette up out of the blood and smoked it. My word! he must have been half dotty.

Millie went back into the kitchen. She put some ashes on the stove and sprinkled them with water. Languidly, the sweat pouring down her face, and dropping off her nose and chin, she cleared away the dinner, and going into the bedroom, stared at herself in the fly-specked mirror, and wiped her face and neck with a towel. She didn't know what was the matter with herself that afternoon. She could have had a good cry — just for nothing — and then change her blouse and have a good cup of tea. Yes, she felt like that! She flopped down on the side of the bed and stared at the coloured print on the wall opposite, 'Garden Party at Windsor Castle'. In the foreground emerald lawns planted with immense oak trees, and in their grateful shade, a muddle of ladies and gentlemen and parasols and little tables. The background was filled with the towers of Windsor Castle, flying three Union Jacks, and in the middle of the picture the old Queen, like a tea cosy with a head on top of it. 'I wonder if it really looked like that.' Millie stared at the flowery ladies, who simpered back at her. 'I wouldn't care for that sort of thing. Too much side. What with the Queen an' one thing an' another.' Over the packing case dressing-table there was a large photograph of her and Sid, taken on their wedding day. Nice picture that — if you *do* like. She was sitting down in a basket chair, in her cream cashmere and satin ribbons, and Sid, standing with one hand on her shoulder, looking at her bouquet. And behind them there were some fern trees, and a waterfall, and Mount

Cook in the distance, covered with snow. She had almost forgotten her wedding day; time did pass so, and if you hadn't any one to talk things over with, they soon dropped out of your mind. 'I wunner why we never had no kids ... ' She shrugged her shoulders — gave it up. 'Well, *I've* never missed them. I wouldn't be surprised if Sid had, though. He's softer than me.'

And then she sat, quiet, thinking of nothing at all, her red swollen hands rolled in her apron, her feet stuck out in front of her, her little head with the thick screw of dark hair, drooped on her chest. 'Tick-tick' went the kitchen clock, the ashes clinked in the grate, and the venetian blind knocked against the kitchen window. Quite suddenly Millie felt frightened. A queer trembling started inside her — in her stomach — and then spread all over to her knees and hands. 'There's somebody about.' She tiptoed to the door and peered into the kitchen. Nobody there; the verandah doors were closed, and blinds were down, and in the dusky light the white face of the clock shone, and the furniture seemed to bulge and breathe ... and listen, too. The clock — the ashes — and the venetian — and then again — something else — like steps in the back hard. 'Go an' see what it is, Millie Evans.' She started to the back door, opened it, and at the same moment someone ducked behind the wood pile. 'Who's that,' she cried in a loud, bold voice. 'Come out o' that. I seen yer. I know where you are. I got my gun. Come out from behind of that wood stack.' She was not frightened any more. She was furiously angry. Her heart banged like a drum. 'I'll teach you to play tricks with a woman,' she yelled, and she took a gun from the kitchen corner, and dashed down the verandah steps, across the glaring yard to the other side of the wood stack. A young man lay there, on his stomach, one arm across his face. 'Get up! You're shamming!' Still holding the gun she kicked him in the shoulders. He gave no sign. 'Oh, my God, I believe he's dead.' She knelt down, seized hold of him, and turned him over on his back.

He rolled like a sack. She crouched back on her haunches, staring, her lips and nostrils fluttered with horror.

He was not much more than a boy, with fair hair, and a growth of fair down on his lips and chin. His eyes were open, rolled up, showing the whites, and his face was patched with dust caked with sweat. He wore a cotton shirt and trousers with sandshoes on his feet. One of the trousers stuck to his leg with a patch of dark blood. 'I *can't*,' said Millie, and then, 'You've got to.' She bent over and felt his heart. 'Wait a minute,' she stammered, 'wait a minute,' and she ran into the house for brandy and a pail of water. 'What are you going to do, Millie Evans? Oh, I don't know. I never seen anyone in a dead faint before.' She knelt down, put her arm under the boy's head and poured some brandy between his lips. It spilled down both sides of his mouth. She dipped a corner of her apron in the water and wiped his face, and his hair and his throat, with fingers that trembled. Under the dust and sweat his face gleamed, white as her apron, and thin, and puckered in little lines. A strange dreadful feeling gripped Millie Evans' bosom — some seed that had never flourished there, unfolded, and struck deep roots and burst into painful leaf. 'Are yer coming round? Feeling all right again?' The boy breathed sharply, half choked, his eyelids quivered, and he moved his head from side to side. 'You're better,' said Millie, smoothing his hair. 'Feeling fine now again, ain't you?' The pain in her bosom half suffocated her. 'It's no good you crying, Millie Evans. You got to keep your head.' Quite suddenly he sat up and leaned against the wood pile, away from her, staring on the ground. 'There now!' cried Millie Evans, in a strange, shaking voice. The boy turned and looked at her, still not speaking, but his eyes were so full of pain and terror that she had to shut her teeth and clench her hand to stop from crying. After a long pause he said in the little voice of a child talking in his sleep, 'I'm hungry.' His lips quivered. She scrambled to her feet and stood over him. 'You come right into the house and have a set down meal,' she said. 'Can you walk?' 'Yes,' he whispered, and swaying he followed her across the glaring yard to the verandah. At the bottom step he paused, looking at her again. 'I'm not coming in,' he said. He sat on the verandah step in the little pool of shade that lay round the house. Millie watched him. 'When did yer last 'ave anythink to eat?' He shook his head. She cut a chunk off the greasy corned beef and a round of bread plastered with butter; but when she brought it he was standing up, glancing round him, and paid no attention to the plate of food. 'When are they coming back?' he stammered.

At that moment she knew. She stood, holding the plate, staring. He was Harrison. He was the English johnny who'd killed Mr Williamson. 'I know who you are,' she said, very slowly, 'yer can't fox me. That's who you are. I must have been blind in me two eyes not to 'ave known from the first.' He made a movement with his hands as though that was all nothing. 'When are they coming back?' And she meant to say, 'Any minute. They're on their way now.' Instead she said to the dreadful, frightened face, 'Not till 'arf past ten.' He sat down, leaning against one of the verandah poles. His face broke up into little quivers. He shut his eyes and tears streamed down his cheeks. 'Nothing but a kid. An' all them fellows after 'im. 'E don't stand any more of a chance than a kid would.' 'Try a bit of beef,' said Millie. 'It's food you want. Something to steady your stomach.' She moved across the verandah and sat down beside him, the plate on her knees. ' 'Ere — try a bit.' She broke the bread and butter into little pieces, and she thought, 'They won't ketch 'im. Not if I can 'elp it. Men is all beasts. I don' care wot 'e's done, or wot 'e 'asn't done. See 'im through, Millie Evans. 'E's nothink but a sick kid.'

Millie lay on her back, her eyes wide open, listening. Sid turned over, hunched the quilt round his shoulders, muttered 'Good night, ole girl.' She heard Willie Cox and the other chap drop their clothes on to the kitchen floor, and then their voices, and Willie Cox saying, 'Lie down, Gumboil. Lie down, yer little devil,' to his dog. The house dropped quiet. She lay and listened. Little pulses tapped in her body, listening, too. It was hot. She was frightened to move because of Sid. ' 'E must get off. 'E must. I don' care anythink about justice an' all the rot they've been spouting to-night,' she thought, savagely. ' 'Ow are yer to know what anythink's like till yer *do* know. It's all rot.' She strained to the silence. He ought to be moving ... Before there was a sound from outside Willie Cox's Gumboil got up and padded sharply across the kitchen floor and sniffed at the back door. Terror started up in Millie. 'What's the dog doing? Uh! What a fool that young fellow is with a dog 'anging about. Why don't 'e lie down an' sleep.' The dog stopped, but she knew it was listening. Suddenly, with a sound that made her cry out in horror the dog started barking and rushing to and fro. 'What's that? What's up?' Sid flung out of bed. 'It ain't nothink. It's only Gumboil. Sid, Sid.' She clutched his arm, but he shook her off. 'My Christ, there's somethink up. My God.' Sid flung into his trousers. Willie Cox opened the back door. Gumboil in a fury darted out into the yard, round the corner of the house. 'Sid, there's someone in the paddock,' roared the other chap. 'What's it — what's that?' Sid dashed out on to the front verandah. 'Here, Millie, take the lantin. Willie, some skunk's got 'old of one of the 'orses.' The three men bolted out of the house and at the same moment Millie saw Harrison dash across the paddock on Sid's horse and down the road. 'Millie, bring that blasted lantin.' She ran in her bare feet, her nightdress flicking her legs. They were after him in a flash. And at the sight of Harrison in the distance, and the three men hot after, a strange mad joy smothered everything else. She rushed into the road — she laughed and shrieked and danced in the dust, jigging the lantern. 'A-ah! Arter 'im, Sid! A-a-a-ah! ketch 'im, Willie. Go it! Go it! A-ah, Sid! Shoot 'im down. Shoot 'im!'

Old Tar

Old Tar must have begun building his house when he was about five years old. Every Sunday morning after church his father and he, hand in hand, went for a bit of a stroll while Mother got dinner, up the new road, through a barbed-wire fence, and on to the great green shoulders of Makra Hill. There they sat down on the blowing grass and pink 'fairy trumpets' or on the white and yellow daisies and dandelions, and while his father had a chew of tobacco, old Tar (who was very young Tar indeed then) sat quiet and strained his little panting chest against his tight Sunday clothes. Far below, the sea ran with a crashing laugh up Makra beach and slipped back again, stealthy, quiet, and gathered together and came again, biting over the rocks and swallowing the sand. They could snuff it in their nostrils and taste it on their lips. There was nothing to be seen to left or right of them but other hill-tops bounded by dark, high masses of bush. Behind them there was the new road leading to Wadesville, and a further drop to the township, Karori; but all that was hidden, and might have been the length of days away. 'By gum!' the old man would mutter, lifting his worn head. 'It's a durn fine place ... it's a place to shake yer lungs out in — yer know, boy, my Pap bought this from the Maoris — he did. Ye-es! Got it off Ole Puhui for a "suit of clothes an' a lookin'-glass of yer Granmaw's." My stars! He had an eye! Larst thing the old man says to me was "James," 'e says, "don't you be muckin' about with that bit of land top of Makra Hill. Don't you sell it. 'And it on," 'e says, "to you an' yours." ' 'Wot d'you mean?' asked the little boy one day, sitting, his legs straight out, making finger gloves of the fairy trumpets. 'Why, wot I mean is — when I'm put away it'll be yours. See?' 'Wot — all this?' cried the little boy, frightened, clutching the hill, as though he expected it to jump away with him on its back, like a great green camel. 'All this!' echoed the father, solemn. 'All yours

— once you're through the fence.' Nothing more was said until dinner. He sat with his bib round his neck, drinking tinned soup with Worcester sauce. 'Pop,' he said, 'I'm goin' to build an 'ouse on my hill. Big as …' and he stretched his arms wide.

Tar was an only child. His father was fifty when he was born, and his mother forty-three. They were strict, upright people, owners of the Wadesville general store and post office. They did brisk business, and every Saturday night Tar helped his father fasten the wooden shutter on which was printed 'Closed in God's name. Those whom the Lord loveth He chasteneth.' He was brought up so severely that his animal spirits never bubbled at all, and he lived in a sober manner, behind his mother's skirts and his father's counter. The first thing that he remembered was that Sunday morning when his father told him Makra Hill would be his, and the telling took such strange hold of him that there was no room in his mind for anything else. All his plans and plots, all his games and dreams were of what he would do when he had it, and of the fine house he'd build. Sometimes it would be bigger than Government House in Wellington, with its hundred bedrooms and fine red carpets, with palm trees growing out of them, and other times it would be a little house, just room enough to hold him and 'something to set'. Then it would be a farm with all animals on it — even white pigs. At fourteen his father put him behind the counter — a little, pale, freckled boy, with a flop of black hair falling into his eyebrows. After the shop was shut he'd pull off his apron and get a hunk of bread and jam and be off at a run, not stopping to take breath or to look this side or that until he reached the windy hill with the brimming sea below. Every stone of the hill he thought he knew; every pocket and cranny he marched over, lord and master. Swelled up with pride he'd dig with his heel: 'I'll have me front door here, and the rain tanks here, under the balcony scuppers.' And on winter nights in the iron chapel when the rain beat with a million hammers on the roof and walls, and the preacher with a stuck-out beard boomed, 'An' the mountains shall skip like r-rams and the little hills like young sheep,' something jumped in Tar, like a flare in the dark. He saw himself running away from the place and through the fence on top of it. And the Day of Judgement was come and the hill leaping …

When Tar was twenty his mother died. She was chopping up a candle-box in the backyard, and suddenly the tomahawk fell from her hand and she dropped. Just like that. Not a word. He thought quick, 'If it'd been Pop I'd have had my hill — here,' and hid away the money she left him and began to save every penny for the house. He married at thirty a quiet girl who bossed him. And the business grew and grew, and by-and-by they were well off. They had to add a room now and again at the back of the shop for the children. 'Oh, why can't you build a nice place somewhere, Father?' the wife used to scold. 'You wait, my girl,' said Tar, his eyes suddenly fierce. At last, when he was fifty, and his father ninety-five, the old man stretched out, creaked his bones, and died. That was on a Sunday night. Monday morning, Old Tar hitched the buggy and drove off to Karori, like a man drunk or to his wedding-feast. He wore his best black suit, he cut at the trees as he passed, and greeted people with a grin and a chuckle, and stopped at the builder's. 'Look 'ere, Mr Stubbs. Will you come back with me? There's a piece of ground I want to show you. I've decided to build.' Not until they were half-way home he remembered to tell Stubbs the old man had gone.

All Wadesville and Karori watched the building of Tar's house. Parties drove up to see it, and picnicked on the piles of yellow, sweet-smelling wood. The store brimmed over with customers, and Mrs Tar, in black, with her troop of black alpaca children, turned into a fine lady, and talked of nothing but the hinconvenience she'd suffered living in the shop for the sake of her 'usband's father and his sentimentalness. Old Tar, after one

day's burst of excitement, kept his grim joy to himself. But he
was mad inside, so hot that he felt all the hard years in him melting away. He spent half the day with the workmen, and a great
big barn began to grow out of the scooped and jagged hole dug
in the side of the hill. It grew quickly. The stairs were up. The
flooring was done upstairs. He could creep up at evening to the
front room and look through the window-hole at the sea. He
would go up and take a lantern and walk from room to room,
silent as a cat, feeding his delight … And at last it was finished.
Old Tar's house, painted white with green 'pickings', reared up
ready at the top of the hill. 'We'll make a party an' all go up this
evening,' said his wife, 'an' have a fair look.' 'No you don't,' said
Old Tar. 'I got to be there. Business. Measuring. I got to have my
'ead quiet. You kin go tomorrow.' She shrugged and obeyed. Tar
left the shop early. The setting sun was drawing from the earth
the strong, sweet scents of day. There was no wind; just a breeze
rippled over the grass and shook the manuka flowers, like tiny
white stars down the yellow clay banks of the new road. He
walked slowly. No need to get through the fence — the fence
was down and carted away. Heavy ruts were carved in the side
of the hill, and there was a path to the front door strewn already
with a load of white shells. The big white house, with all its
hollow eyes, glared at Old Tar.

'It's big,' he thought, and he said as though he prayed, 'Oh,
Lord, it is big!' The builders had left the key under the verandah.
He felt and found it, and let himself in. At first the house was
very still, then it creaked a little, and he heard a tap drip. It smelt
strongly of paint and varnish and fine ripe wood. A pencil ray of
sun shone across the stairs. As he watched, it shifted and disappeared. The sun had set. Old Tar, tip-toe in his creaking boots,
walked through his dream, up and down, in and out, prying like
a woman, conscious as a lover, wondering and touching things,
and knocking them with his knuckles to hear how thick they

sounded. At last he felt a bit tired. He sat down on the stairs. It had begun to grow dusky. The shadows of the door lay across the front hall, sharp and long. He took off his hard hat and leaned his head with the boyish flop of hair against the stair-rail. In the quiet he heard the sea beat, beat up, and then he heard the wind, very slow, snuffling round the house like a lonely dog. 'Ooh Hee! Oooh Hee!' it sounded. 'A rare, sad noise,' thought Old Tar, shaking his head to it. 'Sounds as if it's lost something an' couldn't find it again.' 'Lost for evermore,' and the sad words fell into his quiet heart and started strange, uneasy ripples. Sitting by himself like that, he felt queer and frightened, somehow. 'Ooh Hee! Ooh Hee!' sounded the wind, rattling the window sashes. ' 'Tain't like it used to sound up here,' he thought. ' 'Tain't like it was in the old man's time.' 'Shake out yer lungs, me lad,' he heard old Pop say. Clear as a dream Old Tar saw his Pop and himself sitting where the house stood now, he with the pink, sticky flowers in his fingers, the hill shining and the sea shining below. And then, like a man in a dream, he took off his boots, and stole down into the hall, out of the house. It was getting darker every minute. Thin clouds flew over an ashen sky. The grass between his feet, Old Tar stepped back from the house and looked up at it. He saw in the dusky light the pits the workmen had dug in his hill. He saw the great trampled patches the timber piles had made, and he saw, between him and the sea, the white house perched, the big white nest for his wife and her brood on top of his hill. As though he saw it for the first time. Old Tar muttered in a strange voice, 'Wot's it doing there — wot's it for?' and 'Oh, Lord, wot 'ave I done — wot 'ave I done, Lord?' A long time Old Tar stood there, while the dark shifted over him and the house paled and stretched up to the sky. His feet seemed to freeze into the cold grass of the hill, and dark thoughts flew across his mind, like clouds, never quiet, never breaking.

The Wind Blows

Suddenly — dreadfully — she wakes up. What has happened? Something dreadful has happened. No — nothing has happened. It is only the wind shaking the house, rattling the windows, banging a piece of iron on the roof and making her bed tremble. Leaves flutter past the window, up and away; down in the avenue a whole newspaper wags in the air like a lost kite and falls, spiked on a pine tree. It is cold. Summer is over — it is autumn — everything is ugly. The carts rattle by, swinging from side to side; two Chinamen lollop along under their wooden yokes with the straining vegetable baskets — their pigtails and blue blouses fly out in the wind. A white dog on three legs yelps past the gate. It is all over! What is? Oh, everything! And she begins to plait her hair with shaking fingers, not daring to look in the glass. Mother is talking to grandmother in the hall.

'A perfect idiot! Imagine leaving anything out on the line in weather like this ... Now my best little Teneriffe-work teacloth is simply in ribbons. *What* is that extraordinary smell? It's the porridge burning. Oh, heavens — this wind!'

She has a music lesson at ten o'clock. At the thought the minor movement of the Beethoven begins to play in her head, the trills long and terrible like little rolling drums ... Marie Swainson runs into the garden next door to pick the 'chrysanths' before they are ruined. Her skirt flies up above her waist; she tries to beat it down, to tuck it between her legs while she stoops, but it is no use — up it flies. All the trees and bushes beat about her. She picks as quickly as she can, but she is quite distracted. She doesn't mind what she does — she pulls the plants up by the roots and bends and twists them, stamping her foot and swearing.

'For heaven's sake keep the front door shut! Go round to the back,' shouts someone. And then she hears Bogey:

'Mother, you're wanted on the telephone. Telephone, Mother. It's the butcher.'

How hideous life is — revolting, simply revolting ... And now her hat-elastic's snapped. Of course it would. She'll wear her old tam and slip out the back way. But Mother has seen.

'Matilda. Matilda. Come back im-me-diately! What on earth have you got on your head? It looks like a tea cosy. And why have you got that mane of hair on your forehead.'

'I can't come back, Mother. I'll be late for my lesson.'

'Come back immediately!'

She won't. She won't. She hates Mother. 'Go to hell,' she shouts, running down the road.

In waves, in clouds, in big round whirls the dust comes stinging, and with it little bits of straw and chaff and manure. There is a loud roaring sound from the trees in the gardens, and standing at the bottom of the road outside Mr Bullen's gate she can hear the sea sob: 'Ah! ... Ah! ... Ah-h!' But Mr Bullen's drawing-room is as quiet as a cave. The windows are closed, the blinds half pulled, and she is not late. The-girl-before-her has just started playing Macdowell's 'To an Iceberg'. Mr Bullen looks over at her and half smiles.

'Sit down,' he says. 'Sit over in the sofa corner, little lady.'

How funny he is. He doesn't exactly laugh at you ... but there is just something ... Oh, how peaceful it is here. She likes this room. It smells of art serge and stale smoke and chrysanthemums ... there is a big vase of them on the mantelpiece behind the pale photograph of Rubinstein ... *à mon ami Robert Bullen* ... Over the black glittering piano hangs 'Solitude' — a dark tragic woman draped in white, sitting on a rock, her knees crossed, her chin on her hands.

'No, no!' says Mr Bullen, and he leans over the other girl, puts his arms over her shoulders and plays the passage for her. The stupid — she's blushing! How ridiculous!

Now the-girl-before-her has gone; the front door slams. Mr Bullen comes back and walks up and down, very softly, waiting for her. What an extraordinary thing. Her fingers tremble so that she can't undo the knot in the music satchel. It's the wind ... And her heart beats so hard she feels it must lift her blouse up and down. Mr Bullen does not say a word. The shabby red piano seat is long enough for two people to sit side by side. Mr Bullen sits down by her.

'Shall I begin with scales,' she asks, squeezing her hands together. 'I had some arpeggios, too.'

But he does not answer. She doesn't believe he even hears ... and then suddenly his fresh hand with the ring on it reaches over and opens Beethoven.

'Let's have a little of the old master,' he says.

But why does he speak so kindly — so awfully kindly — and as though they had known each other for years and years and knew everything about each other.

He turns the page slowly. She watches his hand — it is a very nice hand and always looks as though it had just been washed.

'Here we are,' says Mr Bullen.

Oh, that kind voice — Oh, that minor movement. Here come the little drums ...

'Shall I take the repeat?'

'Yes, dear child.'

His voice is far, far too kind. The crotchets and quavers are dancing up and down the stave like little black boys on a fence. Why is he so ... She will not cry — she has nothing to cry about ...

'What is it, dear child?'

Mr Bullen takes her hands. His shoulder is there — just by her head. She leans on it ever so little, her cheek against the springy tweed.

'Life is so dreadful,' she murmurs, but she does not feel it's dreadful at all. He says something about 'waiting' and 'marking time' and 'that rare thing, a woman', but she does not hear. It is so comfortable … for ever …

Suddenly the door opens and in pops Marie Swainson, hours before her time.

'Take the allegretto a little faster,' says Mr Bullen, and gets up and begins to walk up and down again.

'Sit in the sofa corner, little lady,' he says to Marie.

The wind, the wind. It's frightening to be here in her room by herself. The bed, the mirror, the white jug and basin gleam like the sky outside. It's the bed that is frightening. There it lies, sound asleep … Does Mother imagine for one moment that she is going to darn all those stockings knotted up on the quilt like a coil of snakes? She's not. No, Mother. I do not see why I should … The wind — the wind! There's a funny smell of soot blowing down the chimney. Hasn't anyone written poems to the wind? … 'I bring fresh flowers to the leaves and showers.' … What nonsense.

'Is that you, Bogey?'

'Come for a walk round the esplanade, Matilda. I can't stand this any longer.'

'Right-o. I'll put on my ulster. Isn't it an awful day!' Bogey's ulster is just like hers. Hooking the collar she looks at herself in the glass. Her face is white, they have the same excited eyes and hot lips. Ah, they know those two in the glass. Good-bye, dears; we shall be back soon.

'This is better, isn't it?'

'Hook on,' says Bogey.

They cannot walk fast enough. Their heads bent, their legs just touching, they stride like one eager person through the town, down the asphalt zigzag where the fennel grows wild and on to the esplanade. It is dusky — just getting dusky. The wind is so strong that they have to fight their way through it, rocking like two old drunkards. All the poor little pahutukawas on the esplanade are bent to the ground.

'Come on! Come on! Let's get near.'

Over by the breakwater the sea is very high. They pull off their hats and her hair blows across her mouth, tasting of salt. The sea is so high that the waves do not break at all; they thump against the rough stone wall and suck up the weedy, dripping steps. A fine spray skims from the water right across the esplanade. They are covered with drops; the inside of her mouth tastes wet and cold.

Bogey's voice is breaking. When he speaks he rushes up and down the scale. It's funny — it makes you laugh — and yet it just suits the day. The wind carries their voices — away fly the sentences like the narrow ribbons.

'Quicker! Quicker!'

It is getting very dark. In the harbour the coal hulks show two lights — one high on a mast, and one from the stern.

'Look, Bogey. Look over there.'

A big black steamer with a long loop of smoke streaming, with the portholes lighted, with lights everywhere, is putting out to sea. The wind does not stop her; she cuts through the waves, making for the open gate between the pointed rocks that leads to … It's the light that makes her look so awfully beautiful and mysterious … *They* are on board leaning over the rail arm in arm.

' … Who are they?'

'Brother and sister.'

'Look, Bogey, there's the town. Doesn't it look small? There's the post office clock chiming for the last time. There's the esplanade where we walked that windy day. Do you remember? I cried at my music lesson that day — how many years ago! Good-bye, little island, good-bye … '

Now the dark stretches a wing over the tumbling water. They can't see those two any more. Good-bye, good-bye. Don't forget … But the ship is gone, now.

The wind — the wind.

Kezia and Tui

All that day school seemed unreal and silly to Kezia. Round and round, like a musical box with only one tune, went her mind on what had happened the evening before. Her head ached with trying to remember every little detail and every word. She did not want to remember — but somehow, she could not stop trying. She answered questions and made mistakes in her sums and recited 'How Horatious kept the Bridge' like a little girl in a dream. The day crawled by. 'That was the first time I've ever stood up to him,' she thought. 'I wonder if everything will be different now. We can't even pretend to like each other again.' Bottlenose! Bottlenose! She smiled again remembering the word, but at the same time she felt frightened. She had not seen her father that morning. The Grandmother told her that he had promised not to mention the subject again. 'But I didn't believe that,' though Kezia. 'I wish it hadn't happened. No, I'm glad it has ... I wish that he was dead — Oh, what Heaven that would be for us!' But she could not imagine that sort of person dying. She remembered suddenly the way he sucked in his moustache when he drank and the long hairs he had on his hands, and the noises he made when he had indigestion — No, that sort of person seemed too real to die. She worried the thought of him until she was furious with rage. 'How I detest him — detest him!' The class stood up to sing. Kezia shared a book with Tui.

> 'O forest, green and fair,
> O pine-trees waving high,
> How sweet their cool retreat,
> How full of rest!'

sang the little girls. Kezia looked out through the big bare windows to the wattle trees, their gold tassels nodding in the sunny air, and suddenly the sad tune and the tree moving so gently made her feel quite calm. She looked down at the withered sweet-pea that drooped from her blouse. She saw herself sitting on the Grandmother's lap and leaning against the Grandmother's bodice. That was what she wanted. To sit there and hear Grannie's watch ticking against her ear and bury her face in the soft warm place smelling of lavender and put up her hand and feel the five owls sitting on the moon.

Mrs Fairfield was in the garden when she came home — stooping over the pansies. She had a little straw basket on her arm, half filled with flowers. Kezia went up to her and leant against her and played with her spectacle case.

'Sweetheart, listen,' she said. 'It's no good saying I'm sorry because I'm not. And I'm not ashamed either. It's no good trying to make me.' Her face grew hard. 'I *hate* that man and I won't pretend. But because you're more — ' she hesitated, groping for the word, 'more *valuable* than he is, I won't behave like that again — not unless I absolutely feel I can't help it, Grannie.' She looked up and smiled. 'See?'

'I can't make you do what you don't want to, Kezia,' said Mrs Fairfield.

'No,' said she. 'Nobody can, can they? Otherwise it wouldn't be any good wanting anything for your own self — would it? Aren't the pansies pretties, Grannie? I'd like to make pets of them.'

'I think they're rather like my little scaramouch in the face,' said Mrs Fairfield, smiling and pulling Kezia's pink ear.

'Oh, thank goodness!' sighed Kezia. 'You're yourself again. We've made it up, haven't we? I can't bear being serious for a long time together. Oh my Grannie, I've got to be happy with you. When I go thinking of serious things, I could poke out my tongue at myself.' She took Mrs Fairfield's hand and stroked it. 'You do love me, don't you?'

'Of course, you silly billy.'

'We-ll,' laughed Kezia. 'That's the only real thing, isn't it?'

'There are two bits of cold pudding inside for you and Tui,' said Mrs Fairfield. 'Run along and take it to her while I finish the ironing. I only came out while the iron was getting hot.'

'You won't be wretched if I leave you alone?' asked Kezia. She danced into the house, found the pudding and danced over to the Beads'.

'Mrs Bead! Tui! where are you?' she called, stepping over a saucepan, two big cabbages and Tui's hat and coat inside the kitchen door.

'We're upstairs. I'm washing my hair in the bathroom. Come up, darling,' cooed Tui. Kezia bounded up the stairs. Mrs Bead in a pink flannel dressing-gown sat on the edge of the bath, and Tui stood in torn calico drawers, a towel round her shoulders and her head in a basin.

'Hallo, Mrs Bead,' said Kezia. She buried her head in the Maori woman's neck and put her teeth in a roll of soft fat. Mrs Bead pulled Kezia between her knees and had a good look at her.

'Well, Tui,' she said, 'you are a little fibber. Tui told me you'd had a fight with your father and he'd given you two black eyes.'

'I didn't — I didn't,' cried Tui, stamping. 'No one is looking after me. Pour a jug of water on my head, Mummy. Oh, Kezia don't listen to her.'

'Pooh! it's nothing new,' said Kezia. 'You're always lying. I'll pour the water over your head.' She rolled up her sleeves and deluged Tui, who gave little moaning cries.

'I'm drowned, drowned, drowned,' she said, wringing out her long black hair.

'You have a lot of it,' said Kezia.

'Yes.' Tui twisted it round her head. 'But I shan't be content till it is down to my knees. Don't you think it would be nice to be able to wrap yourself up in your hair?'

'What funny ideas you have,' said Kezia, considering Tui. 'Mrs Bead, don't you think Tui's getting awfully conceited?'

'Oh, not more than she ought to,' said Mrs Bead, stretching herself and yawning. 'I believe in girls thinking about their appearance. Tui could do a lot with herself if she liked.'

'Well, she doesn't think about anything else, do you, Tui?'

'No, darling,' Tui smiled.

'Well, why should she?' remarked Mrs Bead easily. 'She's not like you, Kezia. She hasn't got any brain for books, but she's real smart in making up complexion mixtures and she keeps her feet as neat as her hands.'

'When I grow up,' said Tui, 'I mean to be a terri-fic beauty. Mother's going to take me to Sydney when I'm sixteen — but I mean to be the rage if I die for it. And then I'm going to marry a rich Englishman and have five little boys with beautiful blue eyes.'

'Well, you never know,' said Mrs Bead. 'And if you turn out into a raging beauty, Tui, I'll take you to Sydney, sure. What a pity you couldn't come too, Kezia.'

'We'd make such an uncommon pair,' suggested Tui. Kezia shook her head.

'No, Grannie and I are going to live by ourselves when I grow up, and I'm going to make money out of flowers and veg-etables and bees.'

'But don't you want to be rich?' cried Tui, 'and travel all over the world and have perfect clothes? Oh, dear, if I thought I was going to live all my life with Mummy in this piggy little house I believe I'd die of grief.'

'Yes, that's a good thing about you, Tui,' said Mrs Bead. 'Though you're lazy like me, you want a lot to be lazy on; and you're quite right, dearie, quite right. I made a great mistake coming to a little town like this. But then I'd got sick of things and I had enough money to keep us, and once I got the furniture in here I seemed to lose heart, somehow. You ought to have ambition, Kezia, but I think you'll come on slower than Tui. You do keep skinny, don't you,' said Mrs Bead. 'Why, Tui's got quite a figure beside you.'

'She hasn't got any front at all, Mummy,' gurgled Tui. 'Have you, chérie? Mummy, go downstairs and make us some cocoa, and I'll get dressed and come down to finish my hair at the fire.'

Mrs Bead left the two little girls. They went into Tui's bedroom.

'Look!' said Tui. 'Doesn't it surprise you? Mummy and I fixed it yesterday.' The shabby untidy little room had changed to suit Tui's romantic mood. White muslin curtains made out of an old skirt of her mother's adorned the bed, and everywhere Kezia looked there were pink sateen bows. Over the looking-glass, on the back of the chair, on the gas bracket and the four black iron bed-poles.

'Why don't you put a bow on each of the knobs of the chest of drawers,' said Kezia, sarcastically, 'and round the washstand jug, too!'

'Oh!' Tui's face fell. 'Don't you like it, darling? We thought it was lovely. Mummy thought you'd think it fearfully artistic.'

'I think it looks awful,' said Kezia, 'and just like you. You're off your head lately, Tui Bead.'

'Really and truly you think so?' said Tui, making tragic eyes at herself in the looking-glass.

'Yes. Besides, if I were you, I would mend my drawers first,' she answered, scorning Tui's eyes.

'I wonder what makes you so hard, hard, hard. You're never nice to me now, Kezia.'

'Yes, I am. But you're so dotty. You seem to be getting all different.'

'Darling,' Tui put her arm round Kezia's waist, 'in my heart I'm just the same. Feel my hair. Do you think I've washed it successfully? Feel this bit. Is it silky?' Kezia gave it a pull.

'It's nearly as soft as you.'

'Come along downstairs, you kids,' called Mrs Bead. 'And, Kezia, you can take a piece of my coconut cake to your Grandma. It hasn't riz at all and it's a little damp in the middle, but the ingredients are all the best quality.'

It was dark when she left the Beads'. She went home by the front way through their weedy garden and out of the gate into their own. Hawk Street was quiet. All over the sky there were little stars and the garden with its white flowers looked as though it were steeped in milk. The blinds were pulled down in their house but lamplight shone from the sitting-room and she knew her Father was there. But she did not care.

'What a lovely thing night is,' thought Kezia. 'I wish I could stay out here and watch it.' She bent her face over the spicy arum lilies and could not have enough of their scent. 'I shall *remember* just this moment,' decided the little girl. 'I shall always remember what I like and forget what I don't like.' How still and quiet it was! She could hear the dew dripping off the leaves. 'I wonder,' she thought, dreamy and grave, looking up at the stars, 'I wonder if there really *is* a God!'

A Pic-nic

(The Evening Before)
(Miranda Richmond, laden with parcels, is fighting her way out of the tram.)

MIRANDA: Oh, dear, it's simply impossible. People won't move. They seem to be hypnotised. Let me pass, please. Excuse me. I want to get out. Now, I dropped one; I knew I should.

(A young man picks it up. It is Andrew Gold, the artist.)

MIRANDA *(to herself)*: What a surprise! I never noticed him.

(Smiles sweetly.) Thank you so much.

GOLD: I'm getting out, too. Don't worry. I'll give it to you when we're safe ashore.

(In the streets. The lamps are just lighted. A fine evening.)

MIRANDA: Now give me that wretched parcel. What a relief to be out of that car. I didn't notice you until you came to my rescue.

GOLD: No? I got in when you did. I knew you didn't see me. You were awfully deep in thought.

MIRANDA *(who had been wondering whether it was safe to fry that fish, or if it had better be boiled)*: Was I? Heaven knows what I was thinking about. My horror of crowds, I expect … I've just two fingers for the parcel.

GOLD: Please let me carry it. I am going your way. Give me some more. Give me this, and this and this.

MIRANDA: Yes, I will, then. I hate parcels. I am always on the point of simply throwing them away. *(Sees herself, a charming naughty child, throwing them away, and stamping an adorable little foot.)*

GOLD: Ha! I know what this one is. It's a pineapple.

MIRANDA: Yes, I love pineapples — don't you? Not only the taste, but the colour and shape of them — their solidity. They are so really barbaric — don't you think? *(A pause.)* The first painting I ever saw of yours was a dish of nectarines and black grapes. *(Smiles.)* I never forgot it.

GOLD: Oh, yes. I think I know the one you mean. *(Doesn't he, just!)* Awfully glad you liked it. It was one of my favourites. I had rather a feeling that I brought it off.

MIRANDA: Well, this is my gate. *(They stop.)* Isn't it a divine evening!

(Little Dickie in the garden gathering snails in a tin pail.)

DICKIE: Mummy! Mummy!

MIRANDA *(charmingly tender)*: Well, my little sweet.

DICKIE: Jennie is awfully cross. She been waitin' an' waitin' for that fish.

MIRANDA *(hands him a wettish paper bag)*: Run with it into the kitchen, my precious. *(To Gold)*: I'm not going to ask you to come in. Houses are so absurd on a night like this — aren't they. Stifling! One only wants to walk about and breathe the lovely air.

GOLD *(ardently)*: I only wish you would.

MIRANDA *(shakes her head, smiling into his eyes)*: Alas! *(Has a happy thought)*: We're all going for a pic-nic to Days Bay, to-morrow. Won't you come?

GOLD: But I'd love to.

MIRANDA: Do, then. Good-bye *(shyly)* until to-morrow.

GOLD *(fervently)*: Until to-morrow. *(Stands bareheaded until she disappears.)* My God! She's a gorgeous woman. She's wonderful. And to think she's wasted on that ass of a Richmond. She's such an amazing type to find in a place like this. Awfully primitive. Extraordinarily barbaric. *(He sees himself in a strange country, dressed as a hunter, striding back to the camp fire at evening. A woman crouches over the fireglow.)*

WOMAN: Andrew!

HUNTER: Miranda!

(On the wharf by the ferry boat. The women look quite charming in their summer dresses, with wide hats and coloured parasols; the men, very disreputable in old flannel trousers and sweaters. Dear little Dickie rushes up and down the gangway, tumbles over coils of rope, balances himself on one leg on the edge of the wharf, piping: 'Look at me. Look! Look what I'm doing now!')

MRS HILL: Who are we waiting for? Aren't we all here? Oh, your husband's not come yet, has he?

MIRANDA: No, he had to go to the office first. But he promised to be here in good time.

MRS HILL: Oh, he does have to work hard — doesn't he! What a shame it is! My dear, why on earth has Mrs Barker brought her mother? She's such an old bore; she always wants to do what everybody else does. She actually bathed last year, my dear, in an immense chemise. And do you see what she's carrying over her arm? An air-cushion. Isn't she too disgusting!

MIRANDA: Dreadful. I wish Frank would come.

MRS HILL: Good gracious! Look who's coming. Andrew Gold. My dear, who ever can have invited him? I'm sure I didn't.

MIRANDA: I haven't the least idea.

MRS HILL: But how mysterious. He's evidently come for the picnic. I wonder who invited him. I must ask. (*She rushes away and asks each separate lady.*) It really is too mysterious for words.

(*Gold comes up to Miranda. Raises his hat, and is just about to speak, when the siren blows a terrific blast.*)

MRS HILL (*taking command*): Now, then — all aboard! We can't wait any longer. Come on, everybody. Stow the lunch-baskets on the upper deck.

MRS HILL: But poor Mr Richmond, Harry!

(*Cries of: 'Here he is! Here he comes! Don't pull up the gangway!' Frank Richmond dashes down the wharf, and leaps on board, panting and perspiring.*)

RICHMOND: By jove, that was a narrow shave. I couldn't manage to get away a moment before. Morning, everybody! Grand day! (*Shouts to Captain.*) Let her go, Captain! (*He feels triumphant; he feels like a King's Messenger arriving.*) Had to answer an important letter by this morning's mail. Just managed to get it off in time.

OLD MRS BARKER (*with great relish*): He'll catch his death of cold out on the water in that state of perspir-ation.

RICHMOND *(very hearty)*: Oh, don't you mind me, Mrs Barker. I can afford to take a risk or two at my age.

HILL *(to Richmond)*: Just a word, ole man. *(Leads him away mysteriously)*: Have a nip of whisky. I've got a drop of the very best. How's that — eh?

RICHMOND: OK, ole man. I say, who invited that chap, Gold?

HILL: Deuce knows. Bit of a wet blanket — isn't he?

RICHMOND: I can't stick the fellow. He's one of those lop-eared artist chaps. Slippery as an eel. Never know when you've got him.

GOLD: How lovely she looks under that yellow umbrella. The Yellow Umbrella — portrait by Andrew Gold. One thousand guineas. And sold the day the exhibition opened … What on earth have I been doing ever since I came to this rotten little town? I never seemed to see her until last night when she made that remark about the pineapple. She's utterly unlike all the women here. I must get her to myself for a bit. I must talk to her. Why can't we give these people the slip when we get off the boat … Would she?

MIRANDA: Isn't it a divine morning?

GOLD *(looks a trifle dashed)*: Er — yes.

MIRANDA *(perceiving it)*: I don't know if you are like me. I really feel that climate is almost the only thing that matters. If the sun comes out one expands and becomes a human being, and — anything seems possible. And when the sun goes in I want to creep into a hollow tree and die …

GOLD *(enthusiastically)*: I understand absolutely what you mean. Yes, I am just like that myself. I feel more and more strongly …

DICKIE: Mummy, kin I have a be-nana?

MIRANDA: Not now, darling; run away. *(To Gold)*: Yes, so do I. Everything else seems to be such a false complexity. People seem to take a huge delight in denying the simple richness of life — don't you feel?

GOLD: But of course I do. It's so extraordinary that you should say that. It's my creed, absolutely.

DICKIE: Mummy, why can't I have a be-nana now?

MIRANDA (*hands him one as if it were a lily*): Run and play with Bobbie Hill, sweetheart. (*To Gold*): And, after all, one's life is lived in such strange places, that one is simply forced to cling to what is really ultimate ... The sun, the sea — the earth (*laughs*) they're the only Gods I pray to.

(They lean over the side.)

GOLD: You must be very lonely here.

MIRANDA (*looks at him, smiling bravely*): Yes, I am. Very lonely.

GOLD: Couldn't we escape from these people after we arrive, and have a real talk — (*very low*) — you and I?

MIRANDA (*simply*): I should like to.

(They arrive.)

MR HILL (*still in command*): Come along, now, everybody. Bathing is the first item on the programme. You ladies can undress behind the rocks, and we'll go among the sand hills.

MIRANDA: I don't think I'll bathe, Frank.

RICHMOND: Why, of course you will, my dear girl. What the hell's the good of a pic-nic if you're afraid of getting your feet wet.

MRS HILL: Oh, Mrs Richmond! We won't bathe if you don't.

YOUNG MRS BARKER: No, indeed, we won't.

MR HILL: Now, then, Mrs Richmond, don't spoil the party.

MIRANDA (*to Gold*): Later, then ...

GOLD (*bows and makes for the sand hills*).

(In the water.)

MIRANDA (*swims away from the others; Gold follows*): Isn't it divine! (*To herself*): Why on earth do I keep on saying 'divine'? That's the third time since I met him last night.

GOLD: Try and escape from the others when this is over. Will you?

MIRANDA *(to herself)*: I feel as light as a feather. How lovely it is to be lifted, lifted by these lovely waves. *(She cries to him: like a mermaid, she thinks)*: Yes, I will escape. I will! *(To herself)*: What a good thing it is that I can swim so well. For I do swim very well. So smoothly and gracefully. We are like creatures of another world, he and I. For surely, I am in my way an artist, too. He makes me feel one. It is strange how when I am with him, everything I see seems to turn into a picture. What is going to happen? What does it matter ... I will escape — I will!

(A cold hand clasps her ankle and drags her under.)

RICHMOND: Ha! Ha! Ha! That gave you a good surprise, didn't it. Ha! Ha! Ha! Did you see that, Hill?

(After the bathe.)

HILL: Now, then, ladies, look sharp. Don't mind your back hair. We're all married men, except Gold, and he's an artist, and don't count. Get a move on with those sandwiches.

MIRANDA: Oh, what am I doing among these vulgar people? I never realised until to-day how far, far away I was from them. Why can't we simply disappear? I, too, feel that we've something to say to each other. He makes me feel so myself in the truest sense ...

MRS HILL: Will you butter, Mrs Richmond, while I mustard, or will you mustard, while I butter?

MIRANDA: Certainly, Mrs Hill.

(They have lunch.)

MR HILL *(opening bottles)*: Now, then, ladies. We'll soon have you twinkling.

RICHMOND: Pass your glass along, Gold. I suppose you're

accustomed to this kind of thing. Pic-nic every day of the year, if you want one — what. By Jove, you can't think what it means to a chap like me, who spends his life sweating in an office — eh, Hill?

OLD MRS BARKER *(tartly)*: I'll have an-other glass of wine.

YOUNG MRS B. *(warningly)*: Mother!

GOLD: Will you have an almond-biscuit, Mrs Richmond? Try and escape after this — will you?

MIRANDA *(meaningly)*: Yes, I will!

(After lunch.)

MIRANDA: What a wonderful view there must be from the top of that hill. *(Very skittish.)* I'm going up there.

GOLD *(very gay)*: May I come, too, Mrs Richmond?

MIRANDA: Yes, if you promise not to faint by the way.

(They go.)

MRS HILL *(to young Mrs B.)*: Now I know who asked young Mr Gold.

(They climb.)

MIRANDA *(standing on the top of the hill, facing the wind)*: Oh, it's perfectly div — wonderful!

GOLD: I should like to paint you, just like that.

MIRANDA *(archly)*: Well, why don't you?

GOLD: Seriously?

MIRANDA *(gravely)*: I'd be only too proud.

GOLD: Let us sit down here. Thank God we've escaped. Mrs Richmond — Miranda!

(Old Mrs Barker crashes through the bushes.)

OLD MRS B. *(trumpeting)*: Well, I wasn't so far behind you, after all. I always was one for pre-cip-i-tous hills!

(At tea.)

DICKIE: Daddie, there's a sailor coming at us.

RICHMOND: Great Scott! So there is. What the dickens can he want!

SAILOR: Captain says we'll have to start at once. There's a big storm blowing up.

GOLD: Let us escape from the others on the boat. We must talk.

MIRANDA: Yes, I will. I will.

Mr Hill: Now, then, ladies and gentlemen *(etc., etc.)*.

(On the boat.)

GOLD: They won't follow us here. My God if they do, I'll kill the first person who comes along. Miranda!

MIRANDA *(turning pale)*: I can't stay here; one feels the motion so.

(The boat rocks, quivers, dives. It gets very cold.)

GOLD: Let us stand behind a funnel. Miranda!

MIRANDA *(paler)*: I can't stay here. There is such a smell of oil.
    (The boat gives a tremendous roll. Miranda is hurled across the deck against the railings. Gold disappears.)

MIRANDA *(sobbing)*: Why doesn't somebody look after me. Why am I always utterly alone!

(Two minutes later.)

MIRANDA: Oh, Frank, why didn't you come before? I'm all alone. I feel horribly ill. I'm so cold.

RICHMOND: Great Scott! I thought Gold was looking after you. My poor little pole cat, you are a sight! Here, take my coat. I don't want the damned thing. Come over here. Sit down. You won't feel the motion so much. Lean on me. That's right. Your poor little hat's all crooked. That's the ticket.

MIRANDA *(feeling death is near)*: Where is our Dickie?

RICHMOND: Old mother Barker's got him. He's all right.

MIRANDA *(a trifle warmer)*: Isn't it dreadful!

RICHMOND: Oh, nothing much. Bit of a swell on.

MIRANDA *(to herself)*: He really is brave. And he holds me so beautifully. I don't feel the motion half so much. I like leaning against him. And he gave me his coat — without a thought — so simply — beautifully even. Yes, beautifully. *(A trifle warmer)*: Frank.

RICHMOND: Yes?

MIRANDA: Do you remember I used to call you Big Bear?

RICHMOND: No. Clean forgotten.

MIRANDA: I love him even for that — for forgetting. *(To Richmond)*: Is there any danger?

RICHMOND: Good Lord, no, little woman. Can I get you anything? A nip of whisky?

MIRANDA: No, no, don't move. Stay there. Hold me. Don't let me go. Don't leave me. *(Feels his shoulder shake)*: Are you — laughing?

RICHMOND: I'm wondering what you'll feel like when this is all over, old girl.

MIRANDA *(fervently: the past a dream)*: Just as I do now!

Richmond *(sees Hill appear. Tips him a wink and leans over Miranda)*: There — there — little woman. Nearly there, now!

Prelude

I

There was not an inch of room for Lottie and Kezia in the buggy. When Pat swung them on top of the luggage they wobbled; the grandmother's lap was full and Linda Burnell could not possibly have held a lump of a child on hers for any distance. Isabel, very superior, was perched beside the new handy-man on the driver's seat. Hold-alls, bags and boxes were piled upon the floor. 'These are absolute necessities that I will not let out of my sight for one instant,' said Linda Burnell, her voice trembling with fatigue and excitement.

Lottie and Kezia stood on the patch of lawn just inside the gate all ready for the fray in their coats with brass anchor buttons and little round caps with battleship ribbons. Hand in hand, they stared with round solemn eyes first at the absolute necessities and then at their mother.

'We shall simply have to leave them. That is all. We shall simply have to cast them off,' said Linda Burnell. A strange little laugh flew from her lips; she leaned back against the buttoned leather cushions and shut her eyes, her lips trembling with laughter. Happily at that moment Mrs Samuel Josephs, who had been watching the scene from behind her drawing-room blind, waddled down the garden path.

'Why nod leave the chudren with be for the afterdoon, Brs Burnell? They could go on the dray with the storeban when he comes in the eveding. Those thigs on the path have to go, dod't they?'

'Yes, everything outside the house is supposed to go,' said Linda Burnell, and she waved a white hand at the tables and chairs standing on their heads on the front lawn. How absurd they looked! Either they ought to be the other way up, or Lottie and Kezia ought to stand on their heads, too. And she longed to say: 'Stand on your heads, children, and wait for the storeman.' It seemed to her that would be so exquisitely funny that she could not attend to Mrs Samuel Josephs.

The fat creaking body leaned across the gate, and the big jelly of a face smiled. 'Dod't you worry, Brs Burnell. Loddie and Kezia can have tea with by chudren in the dursery, and I'll see theb on the dray afterwards.'

The grandmother considered. 'Yes, it really is quite the best plan. We are very obliged to you, Mrs Samuel Josephs. Children, say "Thank you" to Mrs Samuel Josephs.'

Two subdued chirrups: 'Thank you, Mrs Samuel Josephs.'

'And be good little girls, and — come closer — ' they advanced, 'don't forget to tell Mrs Samuel Josephs when you want to … '

'No, granma.'

'Dod't worry, Brs Burnell.'

At the last moment Kezia let go Lottie's hand and darted towards the buggy.

'I want to kiss my granma good-bye again.'

But she was too late. The buggy rolled off up the road, Isabel bursting with pride, her nose turned up at all the world, Linda Burnell prostrated, and the grandmother rummaging among the very curious oddments she had put in her black silk reticule at the last moment, for something to give her daughter. The buggy twinkled away in the sunlight and fine golden dust up the hill and over. Kezia bit her lip, but Lottie, carefully finding her handkerchief first, set up a wail.

'Mother! Granma!'

Mrs Samuel Josephs, like a huge warm black silk tea cosy, enveloped her.

'It's all right, by dear. Be a brave child. You come and blay in the dursery!'

She put her arm around weeping Lottie and led her away. Kezia followed, making a face at Mrs Samuel Josephs' placket, which was undone as usual, with two long pink corset laces hanging out of it …

Lottie's weeping died down as she mounted the stairs, but the sight of her at the nursery door with swollen eyes and a blob of a nose gave great satisfaction to the S. J.'s, who sat on two benches before a long table covered with American cloth and set out with immense plates of bread and dripping and two brown jugs that faintly steamed.

'Hullo! You've been crying!'

'Ooh! Your eyes have gone right in.'

'Doesn't her nose look funny.'

'You're all red-and-patchy.'

Lottie was quite a success. She felt it and swelled, smiling timidly.

'Go and sit by Zaidee, ducky,' said Mrs Samuel Josephs, 'and Kezia, you sid ad the end by Boses.'

Moses grinned and gave her a nip as she sat down; but she pretended not to notice. She did hate boys.

'Which will you have?' asked Stanley, leaning across the table very politely, and smiling at her. 'Which will you have to begin with — strawberries and cream or bread and dripping?'

'Strawberries and cream, please,' said she.

'Ah-h-h-h.' How they all laughed and beat the table with their tea-spoons. Wasn't that a take in! Wasn't it now! Didn't he fox her! Good old Stan!

'Ma! She thought it was real.'

Even Mrs Samuel Josephs, pouring out the milk and water, could not help smiling. 'You bustn't tease theb on their last day,' she wheezed.

But Kezia bit a big piece out of her bread and dripping, and then stood the piece up on her plate. With the bite out it made a dear little sort of a gate. Pooh! She didn't care! A tear rolled down her cheek, but she wasn't crying. She couldn't have cried in front of those awful Samuel Josephs. She sat with her head bent, and as the tear dripped slowly down, she caught it with a neat little whisk of her tongue and ate it before any of them had seen.

II

After tea Kezia wandered back to their own house. Slowly she walked up the back steps, and through the scullery into the kitchen. Nothing was left in it but a lump of gritty yellow soap in one corner of the kitchen window sill and a piece of flannel stained with a blue bag in another. The fireplace was choked up with rubbish. She poked among it but found nothing except a hair-tidy with a heart painted on it that had belonged to the servant girl. Even that she left lying, and she trailed through the narrow passage into the drawing-room. The Venetian blind was pulled down but not drawn close. Long pencil rays of sunlight shone through and the wavy shadow of a bush outside danced on the gold lines. Now it was still, now it began to flutter again, and now it came almost as far as her feet. Zoom! Zoom! a bluebottle knocked against the ceiling; the carpet-tacks had little bits of red fluff sticking to them.

The dining-room window had a square of coloured glass at each corner. One was blue and one was yellow. Kezia bent down to have one more look at the blue lawn with blue arum lilies growing at the gate, and then at a yellow lawn with yellow lilies and a yellow fence. As she looked a little Chinese Lottie came out on to the lawn and began to dust the tables and chairs with a corner of her pinafore. Was that really Lottie? Kezia was not quite sure until she had looked through the ordinary window.

Upstairs in her father's and mother's room she found a pill box black and shiny outside and red in, holding a blob of cotton wool.

'I could keep a bird's egg in that,' she decided.

In the servant girl's room there was a stay-button stuck in a crack of the floor, and in another crack some beads and a long needle. She knew there was nothing in her grandmother's room; she had watched her pack. She went over to the window and leaned against it, pressing her hands against the pane.

Kezia liked to stand so before the window. She liked the feeling of the cold shining glass against her hot palms, and she liked to watch the funny white tops that came on her fingers when she pressed them hard against the pane. As she stood there, the day flickered out and dark came. With the dark crept the wind snuffling and howling. The windows of the empty house shook, a creaking came from the walls and floors, a piece of loose iron on the roof banged forlornly. Kezia was suddenly quite, quite still, with wide open eyes and knees pressed together. She was frightened. She wanted to call Lottie and to go on calling all the while she ran downstairs and out of the house. But IT was just behind her, waiting at the door, at the head of the stairs, at the bottom of the stairs, hiding in the passage, ready to dart out at the back door. But Lottie was at the back door, too.

'Kezia!' she called cheerfully. 'The storeman's here. Everything is on the dray and three horses, Kezia. Mrs Samuel Josephs has given us a big shawl to wear round us, and she says to button up your coat. She won't come out because of asthma.'

Lottie was very important.

'Now then, you kids,' called the storeman. He hooked his big thumbs under their arms and up they swung. Lottie arranged the shawl 'most beautifully' and the storeman tucked up their feet in a piece of old blanket.

'Lift up. Easy does it.'

They might have been a couple of young ponies. The storeman felt over the cords holding his load, unhooked the brakechain from the wheel, and whistling, he swung up beside them.

'Keep close to me,' said Lottie, 'because otherwise you pull the shawl away from my side, Kezia.'

But Kezia edged up to the storeman. He towered beside her big as a giant and he smelled of nuts and new wooden boxes.

III

It was the first time that Lottie and Kezia had ever been out so late. Everything looked different — the painted wooden houses far smaller than they did by day, the gardens far bigger and wilder. Bright stars speckled the sky and the moon hung over the harbour dabbling the waves with gold. They could see the lighthouse shining on Quarantine Island, and the green lights on the old coal hulks.

'There comes the Picton boat,' said the storeman, pointing to a little steamer all hung with bright beads.

But when they reached the top of the hill and began to go down the other side the harbour disappeared, and although they were still in the town they were quite lost. Other carts rattled past. Everybody knew the storeman.

'Night, Fred.'

'Night O,' he shouted.

Kezia liked very much to hear him. Whenever a cart appeared in the distance she looked up and waited for his voice. He was an old friend; and she and her grandmother had often been to his place to buy grapes. The storeman lived alone in a cottage that had a glasshouse against one wall built by himself. All the glasshouse was spanned and arched over with one beautiful vine. He took her brown basket from her, lined it with three large leaves, and then he felt in his belt for a little horn knife, reached up and snapped off a big blue cluster and laid it on the leaves so tenderly that Kezia held her breath to watch. He was a very big man. He wore brown velvet trousers, and he had a long brown beard. But he never wore a collar, not even on Sunday. The back of his neck was burnt bright red.

'Where are we now?' Every few minutes one of the children asked him the question.

'Why, this is Hawk Street, or Charlotte Crescent.'

'Of course it is.' Lottie pricked up her ears at the last name; she always felt that Charlotte Crescent belonged specially to her. Very few people had streets with the same name as theirs.

'Look, Kezia, there is Charlotte Crescent. Doesn't it look different?' Now everything familiar was left behind. Now the big dray rattled into unknown country, along new roads with high clay banks on either side, up steep, steep hills, down into bushy valleys, through wide shallow rivers. Further and further. Lottie's head wagged; she drooped, she slipped half into Kezia's lap and lay there. But Kezia could not open her eyes wide enough. The wind blew and she shivered; but her cheeks and ears burned.

'Do stars ever blow about?' she asked.

'Not to notice,' said the storeman.

'We've got a nuncle and a naunt living near our new house,' said Kezia. 'They have got two children, Pip, the eldest is called, and the youngest's name is Rags. He's got a ram. He has to feed it with a nenamal teapot and a glove top over the spout. He's going to show us. What is the difference between a ram and a sheep?'

'Well, a ram has horns and runs for you.'

Kezia considered. 'I don't want to see it frightfully,' she said. 'I hate rushing animals like dogs and parrots. I often dream that animals rush at me — even camels — and while they are rushing, their heads swell e-enormous.'

The storeman said nothing. Kezia peered up at him, screwing up her eyes. Then she put her finger out and stroked his sleeve; it felt hairy. 'Are we near?' she asked.

'Not far off, now,' answered the storeman. 'Getting tired?'

'Well, I'm not an atom bit sleepy,' said Kezia. 'But my eyes keep curling up in such a funny sort of way.' She gave a long sigh, and to stop her eyes from curling she shut them ... When she opened them again they were clanking through a drive that cut through the garden like a whip lash, looping suddenly an island of green, and behind the island, but out of sight until you came upon it, was the house. It was long and low built, with a pillared verandah and balcony all the way round. The soft white bulk of it lay stretched upon the green garden like a sleeping beast. And now one and now another of the windows leaped into light. Someone was walking through the empty rooms carrying a lamp. From a window downstairs the light of a fire flickered.

A strange beautiful excitement seemed to stream from the house in quivering ripples.

'Where are we?' said Lottie, sitting up. Her reefer cap was all on one side and on her cheek there was the print of an anchor button she had pressed against while sleeping. Tenderly the storeman lifted her, set her cap straight, and pulled down her crumpled clothes. She stood blinking on the lowest verandah step watching Kezia who seemed to come flying through the air to her feet.

'Ooh!' cried Kezia, flinging up her arms. The grandmother came out of the dark hall carrying a little lamp. She was smiling.

'You found your way in the dark?' said she.

'Perfectly well.'

But Lottie staggered on the lowest verandah step like a bird fallen out of the nest. If she stood still for a moment she fell asleep, if she leaned against anything her eyes closed. She could not walk another step.

'Kezia,' said the grandmother, 'can I trust you to carry the lamp?'

'Yes, my granma.'

The old woman bent down and gave the bright breathing thing into her hands and then she caught up drunken Lottie. 'This way.'

Through a square hall filled with bales and hundreds of parrots (but the parrots were only on the wall-paper) down a narrow passage where the parrots persisted in flying past Kezia with her lamp.

'Be very quiet,' warned the grandmother, putting down Lottie and opening the dining-room door. 'Poor little mother has got such a headache.'

Linda Burnell, in a long cane chair, with her feet on a hassock, and a plaid over her knees, lay before a crackling fire. Burnell and Beryl sat at the table in the middle of the room eating a dish of fried chops and drinking tea out of a brown china teapot. Over the back of her mother's chair leaned Isabel.

She had a comb in her fingers and in a gentle absorbed fashion she was combing the curls from her mother's forehead. Outside the pool of lamp and firelight the room stretched dark and bare to the hollow windows.

'Are those the children?' But Linda did not really care; she did not even open her eyes to see.

'Put down the lamp, Kezia,' said Aunt Beryl, 'or we shall have the house on fire before we are out of the packing cases. More tea, Stanley?'

'Well, you might just give me five-eighths of a cup,' said Burnell, leaning across the table. 'Have another chop, Beryl. Tip-top meat, isn't it? Not too lean and not too fat.' He turned to his wife. 'You're sure you won't change your mind, Linda darling?'

'The very thought of it is enough.' She raised one eyebrow in the way she had. The grandmother brought the children bread and milk and they sat up to the table, flushed and sleepy behind the wavy steam.

'I had meat for my supper,' said Isabel, still combing gently.

'I had a whole chop for my supper, the bone and all and Worcester Sauce. Didn't I, father?'

'Oh, don't boast, Isabel,' said Aunt Beryl.

Isabel looked astounded. 'I wasn't boasting, was I, Mummy? I never thought of boasting. I thought they would like to know. I only meant to tell them.'

'Very well. That's enough,' said Burnell. He pushed back his plate, took a tooth-pick out of his pocket and began picking his strong white teeth.

'You might see that Fred has a bit of something in the kitchen before he goes, will you, mother?'

'Yes, Stanley.' The old woman turned to go.

'Oh, hold on half a jiffy. I suppose nobody knows where my slippers were put? I suppose I shall not be able to get at them for a month or two — what?'

'Yes,' came from Linda. 'In the top of the canvas hold-all marked "urgent necessities".'

'Well you might get them for me will you, mother?'

'Yes, Stanley.'

Burnell got up, stretched himself, and going over to the fire he turned his back to it and lifted up his coat tails.

'By jove, this is a pretty pickle. Eh, Beryl?'

Beryl, sipping tea, her elbows on the table, smiled over the cup at him. She wore an unfamiliar pink pinafore; the sleeves of her blouse were rolled up to her shoulders showing her lovely freckled arms, and she had let her hair fall down her back in a long pig-tail.

'How long do you think it will take to get straight — couple of weeks — eh?' he chaffed.

'Good heavens, no,' said Beryl airily. 'The worst is over already. The servant girl and I have simply slaved all day, and ever since mother came she has worked like a horse, too. We have never sat down for a moment. We have had a day.'

Stanley scented a rebuke.

'Well, I suppose you did not expect me to rush away from the office and nail carpets — did you?'

'Certainly not,' laughed Beryl. She put down her cup and ran out of the dining-room.

'What the hell does she expect us to do?' asked Stanley. 'Sit down and fan herself with a palm leaf while I have a gang of professionals to do the job? By Jove, if she can't do a hand's turn occasionally without shouting about it in return for ... '

And he gloomed as the chops began to fight the tea in his sensitive stomach. But Linda put up a hand and dragged him down to the side of her long chair.

'This is a wretched time for you, old boy,' she said. Her cheeks were very white but she smiled and curled her fingers into the big red hand she held. Burnell became quiet. Suddenly he began to whistle 'Pure as a lily, joyous and free' — a good sign.

'Think you're going to like it?' he asked.

'I don't want to tell you, but I think I ought to, mother,' said Isabel. 'Kezia is drinking tea out of Aunt Beryl's cup.'

I V

They were taken off to bed by the grandmother. She went first with a candle; the stairs rang to their climbing feet. Isabel and Lottie lay in a room to themselves, Kezia curled in her grandmother's soft bed.

'Aren't there going to be any sheets, my granma?'

'No, not to-night.'

'It's tickly,' said Kezia, 'but it's like Indians.' She dragged her grandmother down to her and kissed her under the chin. 'Come to bed soon and be my Indian brave.'

'What a silly you are,' said the old woman, tucking her in as she loved to be tucked.

'Aren't you going to leave me a candle?'

'No. Sh-h. Go to sleep.'

'Well, can I have the door left open?'

She rolled herself up into a round but she did not go to sleep. From all over the house came the sound of steps. The house itself creaked and popped. Loud whispering voices came from downstairs. Once she heard Aunt Beryl's rush of high laughter, and once she heard a loud trumpeting from Burnell blowing his nose. Outside the window hundreds of black cats with yellow eyes sat in the sky watching her — but she was not frightened. Lottie was saying to Isabel:

'I'm going to say my prayers in bed to-night.'

'No you can't, Lottie.' Isabel was very firm. 'God only excuses you saying your prayers in bed if you've got a temperature.' So Lottie yielded:

> Gentle Jesus meek anmile,
>> Look pon a little chile,
>> Pity me, simple Lizzie
> Suffer me to come to thee.

And then they lay down back to back, their little behinds just touching, and fell asleep.

Standing in a pool of moonlight Beryl Fairfield undressed herself. She was tired, but she pretended to be more tired that she really was — letting her clothes fall, pushing back with a languid gesture her warm, heavy hair.

'Oh, how tired I am — very tired.'

She shut her eyes a moment, but her lips smiled. Her breath rose and fell in her breast like two fanning wings. The window was wide open; it was warm, and somewhere out there in the garden a young man, dark and slender, with mocking eyes, tiptoed among the bushes, and gathered the flowers into a big bouquet, and slipped under her window and held it up to her. She saw herself bending forward. He thrust his head among the bright waxy flowers, sly and laughing. 'No, no,' said Beryl. She turned from the window and dropped her nightgown over her head.

'How frightfully unreasonable Stanley is sometimes,' she thought, buttoning. And then, as she lay down, there came the old thought, the cruel thought — ah, if only she had money of her own.

A young man, immensely rich, has just arrived from England. He meets her quite by chance ... The new governor is unmarried ... There is a ball at Government house ... Who is that exquisite creature in *eau de nil* satin? Beryl Fairfield ...

'The thing that pleases me,' said Stanley, leaning against the side of the bed and giving himself a good scratch on his shoulders and back before turning in, 'is that I've got the place dirt cheap, Linda. I was talking about it to little Wally Bell to-day and he said he simply could not understand why they had accepted my figure. You see land about here is bound to become more and more valuable ... in about ten years' time ... of course we shall have to go very slow and cut down expenses as fine as possible. Not asleep — are you?'

'No, dear, I've heard every word,' said Linda. He sprang into bed, leaned over her and blew out the candle.

'Good night, Mr Business Man,' said she, and she took hold of his head by the ears and gave him a quick kiss. Her faint far-away voice seemed to come from a deep well.

'Good night, darling.' He slipped his arm under her neck and drew her to him.

'Yes, clasp me,' said the faint voice from the deep well.

Pat the handy man sprawled in his little room behind the kitchen. His sponge-bag, coat and trousers hung from the door-peg like a hanged man. From the edge of the blanket his twisted toes protruded, and on the floor beside him there was an empty cane bird-cage. He looked like a comic picture.

'Honk, honk,' came from the servant girl. She had adenoids.

Last to go to bed was the grandmother.

'What. Not asleep yet?'

'No, I'm waiting for you,' said Kezia. The old woman sighed and lay down beside her. Kezia thrust her head under the grandmother's arm and gave a little squeak. But the old woman only pressed her faintly, and sighed again, took out her teeth, and put them in a glass of water beside her on the floor.

In the garden some tiny owls, perched on the branches of a lace-bark tree, called: 'More pork; more pork.' And far away in the bush there sounded a harsh rapid chatter: 'Ha-ha-ha ... Ha-ha-ha.'

V

Dawn came sharp and chill with red clouds on a faint green sky and drops of water on every leaf and blade. A breeze blew over the garden, dropping dew and dropping petals, shivered over the drenched paddocks, and was lost in the sombre bush. In the sky some tiny stars floated for a moment and then they were gone — they were dissolved like bubbles. And plain to be heard in the early quiet was the sound of the creek in the paddock running over the brown stones, running in and out of the sandy hollows, hiding under clumps of dark berry bushes, spilling into a swamp of yellow water flowers and cresses.

And then at the first beam of sun the birds began. Big cheeky birds, starlings and mynahs, whistled on the lawns, the little birds, the goldfinches and linnets and fantails flicked from bough to bough. A lovely kingfisher perched on the paddock fence preening his rich beauty, and a *tui* sang his three notes and laughed and sang them again.

'How loud the birds are,' said Linda in her dream. She was walking with her father through a green paddock sprinkled with daisies. Suddenly he bent down and parted the grasses and showed her a tiny ball of fluff just at her feet. 'Oh, Papa, the darling.' She made a cup of her hands and caught the tiny bird and stroked its head with her finger. It was quite tame. But a funny thing happened. As she stroked it began to swell, it ruffled and pouched, it grew bigger and bigger and its round eyes seemed to smile knowingly at her. Now her arms were hardly wide enough to hold it and she dropped it into her apron. It had become a baby with a big naked head and gaping bird-mouth, opening and shutting. Her father broke into a loud clattering laugh and she woke to see Burnell standing by the windows rattling the Venetian blind up to the very top.

'Hullo,' he said. 'Didn't wake you, did I? Nothing much wrong with the weather this morning.'

He was enormously pleased. Weather like this set a final seal on his bargain. He felt, somehow, that he had bought the lovely day, too — got it chucked in dirt cheap with the house and ground. He dashed off to his bath and Linda turned over and raised herself on one elbow to see the room by daylight. All the furniture had found a place — all the old paraphernalia — as she expressed it. Even the photographs were on the mantelpiece and the medicine bottles on the shelf above the wash-stand. Her clothes lay across a chair — her outdoor things, a purple cape and a round hat with a plume in it. Looking at them she wished that she was going away from this house, too. And she saw herself driving away from them all in a little buggy, driving away from everybody and not even waving.

Back came Stanley girt with a towel, glowing and slapping his thighs. He pitched the wet towel on top of her hat and cape, and standing firm in the exact centre of a square of sunlight he began to do his exercises. Deep breathing, bending and squatting like a frog and shooting out his legs. He was so delighted with his firm, obedient body that he hit himself on the chest and gave a loud 'Ah'. But this amazing vigour seemed to set him worlds away from Linda. She lay on the white tumbled bed and watched him as if from the clouds.

'Oh, damn! Oh, blast!' said Stanley, who had butted into a crisp white shirt only to find that some idiot had fastened the neck-band and he was caught. He stalked over to Linda waving his arms.

'You look like a big fat turkey,' said she.

'Fat. I like that,' said Stanley. 'I haven't a square inch of fat on me. Feel that.'

'It's rock — it's iron,' mocked she.

'You'd be surprised,' said Stanley, as though this were intensely interesting, 'at the number of chaps at the club who have got a corporation. Young chaps, you know — men of my

age.' He began parting his bushy ginger hair, his blue eyes fixed
and round in the glass, his knees bent, because the dressing table
was always — confound it — a bit too low for him. 'Little Wally
Bell, for instance,' and he straightened, describing upon himself
an enormous curve with the hairbrush. 'I must say I've a perfect
horror … '

'My dear, don't worry. You'll never be fat. You are far too
energetic.'

'Yes, yes, I suppose that's true,' said he, comforted for the
hundredth time, and taking a pearl pen-knife out of his pocket he
began to pare his nails.

'Breakfast, Stanley.' Beryl was at the door. 'Oh, Linda,
mother says you are not to get up yet.' She popped her head in
at the door. She had a big piece of syringa stuck through her hair.

'Everything we left on the verandah last night is simply sopping this morning. You should see poor dear mother wringing
out the tables and the chairs. However, there is no harm done
— ' this with the faintest glance at Stanley.

'Have you told Pat to have the buggy round in time? It's a
good six and a half miles to the office.'

'I can imagine what this early start for the office will be like,'
thought Linda. 'It will be very high pressure indeed.'

'Pat, Pat.' She heard the servant girl calling. But Pat was evidently hard to find; the silly voice went baa-aaing through the
garden.

Linda did not rest again until the final slam of the front door
told her that Stanley was really gone.

Later she heard her children playing in the garden. Lottie's
stolid, compact little voice cried: 'Ke — zia. Isa — bel.' She was
always getting lost or losing people only to find them again, to
her great surprise, round the next tree or the next corner. 'Oh,
there you are after all.' They had been turned out after breakfast
and told not to come back to the house until they were called.

Isabel wheeled a neat pramload of prim dolls and Lottie was allowed for a great treat to walk beside her holding the doll's parasol over the face of the wax one.

'Where are you going to, Kezia?' asked Isabel, who longed to find some light and menial duty that Kezia might perform and so be roped in under her government.

'Oh, just away,' said Kezia ...

Then she did not hear them any more. What a glare there was in the room. She hated blinds pulled up to the top at any time, but in the morning it was intolerable. She turned over to the wall and idly, with one finger, she traced a poppy on the wall-paper with a leaf and a stem and a fat bursting bud. In the quiet, and under her tracing finger, the poppy seemed to come alive. She could feel the sticky, silky petals, the stem, hairy like a goose-berry skin, the rough leaf and the tight glazed bud. Things had a habit of coming alive like that. Not only large substantial things like furniture but curtains and the patterns of stuffs and the fringes of quilts and cushions. How often she had seen the tassel fringe of her quilt change into a funny procession of dancers with priests attending ... For there were some tassels that did not dance at all but walked stately, bent forward as if praying or chanting. How often the medicine bottles had turned into a row of little men with brown top-hats on; and the washstand jug had a way of sitting in the basin like a fat bird in a round nest.

'I dreamed about birds last night,' thought Linda. What was it? She had forgotten. But the strangest part of this coming alive of things was what they did. They listened, they seemed to swell out with some mysterious important content, and when they were full she felt that they smiled. But it was not for her, only, their sly secret smile; they were members of a secret society and they smiled among themselves. Sometimes, when she had fallen asleep in the daytime, she woke and could not lift a finger, could not even turn her eyes to left or right because THEY were there; sometimes when she went out of a room and left it empty, she knew as she clicked the door to that THEY were filling it. And there were times in the evenings when she was upstairs, perhaps, and everybody else was down, when she could hardly escape from them. Then she could not hurry, she could not hum a tune; if she tried to say ever so carelessly — 'Bother that old thimble' — THEY were not deceived. THEY knew how frightened she was; THEY saw how she turned her head away as she passed the mirror. What Linda always felt was that THEY wanted something of her, and she knew that if she gave herself up and was quiet, more than quiet, silent, motionless, something would really happen.

'It's very quiet now,' she thought. She opened her eyes wide, and she heard the silence spinning its soft endless web. How lightly she breathed; she scarcely had to breathe at all.

Yes, everything had come alive down to the minutest, tiniest particle, and she did not feel her bed, she floated, held up in the air. Only she seemed to be listening with her wide open watchful eyes, waiting for someone to come who just did not come, watching for something to happen that just did not happen.

V I

In the kitchen at the long deal table under two windows old Mrs Fairfield was washing the breakfast dishes. The kitchen window looked out on to a big grass patch that led down to the vegetable garden and the rhubarb beds. On one side the grass patch was bordered by the scullery and wash-house and over this white-washed lean-to there grew a knotted vine. She had noticed yesterday that a few tiny corkscrew tendrils had come right through some cracks in the scullery ceiling and all the windows of the lean-to had a thick frill of ruffled green.

'I am very fond of a grape vine,' declared Mrs Fairfield, 'but I do not think that the grapes will ripen here. It takes Australian sun.' And she remembered how Beryl when she was a baby had been picking some white grapes from the wine on the back verandah of their Tasmanian house and had been stung on the leg by a huge red ant. She saw Beryl in a little plaid dress with red ribbon tie-ups on the shoulders screaming so dreadfully that half the street rushed in. And how the child's leg had swelled! 'T-t-t-t!' Mrs Fairfield caught her breath remembering. 'Poor child, how terrifying it was.' And she set her lips tight and went over to the stove for some more hot water. The water frothed up in the big soapy bowl with pink and blue bubbles on top of the foam. Old Mrs Fairfield's arms were bare to the elbow and stained a bright pink. She wore a grey foulard dress patterned with large purple pansies, a white linen apron and a high cap shaped like a jelly mould of white muslin. At her throat there was a silver crescent moon with five little owls seated on it, and round her neck she wore a watch-guard made of black beads.

It was hard to believe that she had not been in that kitchen for years; she was so much a part of it. She put the crocks away with a sure, precise touch, moving leisurely and ample from the stove to the dresser, looking into the pantry and the larder as though there were not an unfamiliar corner. When she had finished, everything in the kitchen had become part of a series of patterns. She stood in the middle of the room wiping her hands on a check cloth; a smile beamed on her lips; she thought it looked very nice, very satisfactory.

'Mother! Mother! Are you there?' called Beryl.

'Yes, dear. Do you want me?'

'No. I'm coming,' and Beryl rushed in, very flushed, dragging with her two big pictures.

'Mother, whatever can I do with these awful hideous Chinese paintings that Chung Wah gave Stanley when he went bankrupt? It's absurd to say that they are valuable, because they were hanging in Chung Wah's fruit shop for months before. I can't make out why Stanley wants them kept. I'm sure he thinks them just as hideous as we do, but it's because of the frames,' she said spitefully. 'I suppose he thinks the frames might fetch something some day or other.'

'Why don't you hang them in the passage?' suggested Mrs Fairfield; 'they would not be much seen there.'

'I can't. There is no room. I've hung all the photographs of his office there before and after building, and the signed photos of his business friends, and that awful enlargement of Isabel lying on the mat in her singlet.' Her angry glance swept the placid kitchen. 'I know what I'll do. I'll hang them here. I will tell Stanley they got a little damp in the moving so I have put them in here for the time being.'

She dragged a chair forward, jumped on it, took a hammer and a big nail out of her pinafore pocket and banged away.

'There! That is enough! Hand me the picture, mother.'

'One moment, child.' Her mother was wiping over the carved ebony frame.

'Oh, mother, really you need not dust them. It would take years to dust all those little holes.' And she frowned at the top of her mother's head and bit her lip with impatience. Mother's deliberate way of doing things was simply maddening. It was old age, she supposed, loftily.

At last the two pictures were hung side by side. She jumped off the chair, stowing away the little hammer.

'They don't look so bad there, do they?' said she. 'And at any rate nobody need gaze on them except Pat and the servant girl — have I got a spider's web on my face, mother? I've been poking into that cupboard under the stairs and now something keeps tickling my nose.'

But before Mrs Fairfield had time to look Beryl had turned away. Someone tapped on the window: Linda was there, nodding and smiling. They heard the latch of the scullery door lift and she came in. She had no hat on; her hair stood up on her head in curling rings and she was wrapped up in an old cashmere shawl.

'I'm so hungry,' said Linda: 'where can I get something to eat, mother? This is the first time I've been in the kitchen. It says "mother" all over; everything is in pairs.'

'I will make you some tea,' said Mrs Fairfield, spreading a clean napkin over a corner of the table, 'and Beryl can have a cup with you.'

'Beryl, do you want half my gingerbread?' Linda waved the knife at her. 'Beryl, do you like the house now that we are here?'

'Oh yes, I like the house immensely and the garden is beautiful, but it feels very far from everything to me. I can't imagine people coming out from town to see us in that dreadful jolting bus, and I am sure there is not anyone here to come and call. Of course it does not matter to you because — '

'But there's the buggy,' said Linda. 'Pat can drive you into town whenever you like.'

That was a consolation, certainly, but there was something at the back of Beryl's mind, something she did not even put into words for herself.

'Oh, well, at any rate it won't kill us,' she said dryly, putting down her empty cup and standing up and stretching. 'I am going to hang curtains.' And she ran away singing:

> How many thousand birds I see
> That sing aloud from every tree …

' … birds I see/That sing aloud from every tree … ' But when she reached the dining-room she stopped singing, her face changed; it became gloomy and sullen.

'One may as well rot here as anywhere else,' she muttered savagely, digging the stiff brass safety-pins into the red serge curtains.

The two left in the kitchen were quiet for a little. Linda leaned her cheek on her fingers and watched her mother. She thought her mother looked wonderfully beautiful with her back to the leafy window. There was something comforting in the sight of her that Linda felt she could never do without. She needed the sweet smell of her flesh, and the soft feel of her cheeks and her arms and shoulders still softer. She loved the way her hair curled, silver at her forehead, lighter at her neck, and bright brown still in the big coil under the muslin cap. Exquisite were her mother's hands, and the two rings she wore seemed to melt into her creamy skin. And she was always so fresh, so delicious. The old woman could bear nothing but linen next to her body and she bathed in cold water winter and summer.

'Isn't there anything for me to do?' asked Linda.

'No, darling. I wish you would go into the garden and give an eye to your children; but that I know you will not do.'

'Of course I will, but you know Isabel is much more grown up than any of us.'

'Yes, but Kezia is not,' said Mrs Fairfield.

'Oh, Kezia has been tossed by a bull hours ago,' said Linda, winding herself up in her shawl again.

But no, Kezia had seen a bull through a hole in a knot of wood in the paling that separated the tennis lawn from the paddock. But she had not liked the bull frightfully, so she had walked away back through the orchard, up the grassy slope, along the path by the lace bark tree and so into the spread tangled garden. She did not believe that she would ever not get lost in this garden. Twice she had found her way back to the big iron gates they had driven through the night before, and then had turned to walk up the drive that led to the house, but there were so many little paths on either side. On one side they all led into a tangle of tall dark trees and strange bushes with flat velvet leaves and feathery cream flowers that buzzed with flies when you shook them — this was the frightening side, and no garden at all. The little paths here were wet and clayey with tree roots spanned across them like the marks of big fowls' feet.

But on the other side of the drive there was a high box border and the paths had box edges and all of them led into a deeper and deeper tangle of flowers. The camellias were in bloom, white and crimson and pink and white striped with flashing leaves. You could not see a leaf on the syringa bushes for the white clusters. The roses were in flower — gentlemen's buttonhole roses, little white ones, but far too full of insects to hold under anyone's nose, pink monthly roses with a ring of fallen petals round the bushes, cabbage roses on thick stalks, moss roses, always in bud, pink smooth beauties opening curl on curl, red ones so dark they seemed to turn black as they fell, and a certain exquisite cream kind with a slender red stem and bright scarlet leaves.

There were clumps of fairy bells, and all kinds of geraniums, and there were little trees of verbena and bluish lavender bushes and a bed of pelargoniums with velvet eyes and leaves like moths' wings. There was a bed of nothing but mignonette and another of nothing but pansies — borders of double and single daisies and all kinds of little tufty plants she had never seen before.

The red-hot pokers were taller than she; the Japanese sunflowers grew in a tiny jungle. She sat down on one of the box borders. By pressing hard at first it made a nice seat. But how dusty it was inside! Kezia bent down to look and sneezed and rubbed her nose.

And then she found herself at the top of the rolling grassy slope that led down to the orchard ... She looked down at the slope a moment; then she lay down on her back, gave a squeak and rolled over and over into the thick flowery orchard grass. As she lay waiting for things to stop spinning, she decided to go up to the house and ask the servant girl for an empty match-box. She wanted to make a surprise for the grandmother ... First she would put a leaf inside with a big violet lying on it, then she would put a very small white picotee, perhaps, on each side of the violet, and then she would sprinkle some lavender on the top, but not to cover their heads.

She often made these surprises for the grandmother, and they were always most successful.

'Do you want a match, my granny?'

'Why, yes, child, I believe a match is just what I'm looking for.'

The grandmother slowly opened the box and came upon the picture inside.

'Good gracious, child! How you astonished me!'

'I can make her one every day here,' she thought, scrambling up the grass on her slippery shoes.

But on her way back to the house she came to that island that lay in the middle of the drive, dividing the drive into two arms that met in front of the house. The island was made of grass banked up high. Nothing grew on the top except one huge plant with thick, grey-green, thorny leaves, and out of the middle there sprang up a tall stout stem. Some of the leaves of the plant were so old that they curled up in the air no longer; they turned back, they were split and broken; some of them lay flat and withered on the ground.

Whatever could it be? She had never seen anything like it before. She stood and stared. And then she saw her mother coming down the path.

'Mother, what is it?' asked Kezia.

Linda looked up at the fat swelling plant with its cruel leaves and fleshy stem. High above them, as though becalmed in the air, and yet holding so fast to the earth it grew from, it might have had claws instead of roots. The curving leaves seemed to be hiding something; the blind stem cut into the air as if no wind could ever shake it.

'That is an aloe, Kezia,' said her mother.

'Does it ever have any flowers?'

'Yes, Kezia,' and Linda smiled down at her, and half shut her eyes. 'Once every hundred years.'

VII

On his way home from the office Stanley Burnell stopped the buggy at the Bodega, got out and bought a large bottle of oysters. At the Chinaman's shop next door he bought a pineapple in the pink of condition, and noticing a basket of fresh black cherries he told John to put him a pound of those as well. The oysters and the pine he stowed away in the box under the front seat, but the cherries he kept in his hand.

Pat, the handy-man, leapt off the box and tucked him up again in the brown rug.

'Life yer feet, Mr Burnell, while I give yer a fold under,' said he.

'Right! Right! First-rate!' said Stanley. 'You can make straight for home now.'

Pat gave the grey mare a touch and the buggy sprang forward.

'I believe this man is a first-rate chap,' thought Stanley. He liked the look of him sitting up there in his neat brown coat and brown bowler. He liked the way Pat had tucked him in, and he liked his eyes. There was nothing servile about him — and if there was one thing he hated more than another it was servility. And he looked as if he was pleased with his job happy and contented already.

The grey mare went very well; Burnell was impatient to be out of the town. He wanted to be home. Ah, it was splendid to live in the country — to get right out of that hole of a town once the office was closed; and this drive in the fresh warm air, knowing all the while that his own house was at the other end, with its garden and paddocks, its three tip-top cows and enough fowls and ducks to keep them in poultry, was splendid too.

As they left the town finally and bowled away up the deserted road his heart beat for joy. He rooted in the bag and began to eat the cherries, three or four at a time, chucking the stones over the side of the buggy. They were delicious, so plump and cold, without a spot or a bruise on them.

Look at those two, now — black one side and white the other — perfect! A perfect little pair of Siamese twins. And he stuck them in his button-hole ... by Jove, he wouldn't mind giving that chap up there a handful — but no, better not. Better wait until he had been with him a bit longer.

He began to plan what he would do with his Saturday afternoons and his Sundays. He wouldn't go to the club for lunch on Saturday. No, cut away from the office as soon as possible and get them to give him a couple of slices of cold meat and half a lettuce when he got home. And then he'd get a few chaps out from town to play tennis in the afternoon. Not too many — three at most. Beryl was a good player, too ... He stretched out his right arm and slowly bent it, feeling the muscle ... a bath, a good rubdown, a cigar on the verandah after dinner ...

On Sunday morning they would go to church — children and all. Which reminded him that he must hire a pew, in the sun if possible and well forward so as to be out of the draught from the door. In fancy he heard himself intoning extremely well: 'When thou did overcome the *Sharp*ness of Death Thou didst open the *King*dom of Heaven to *all* Believers.' And he saw the neat brass-edged card on the corner of the pew — Mr Stanley Burnell and family ... The rest of the day he'd loaf about with Linda ... Now they were walking about the garden; she was on his arm, and he was explaining to her at length what he intended doing at the office the week following. He heard her saying: 'My dear, I think that is most wise.' ... Talking things over with Linda was a wonderful help even though they were apt to drift away from the point.

Hang it all! They weren't getting along very fast. Pat had put the brake on again. Ugh! What a brute of a thing it was. He could feel it in the pit of his stomach.

A sort of panic overtook Burnell whenever he approached near home. Before he was well inside the gate he would shout to anyone within sight: 'Is everything all right?' And then he did not believe it was until he heard Linda say: 'Hullo! Are you home again?' That was the worst of living in the country — it took the deuce of a long time to get back ... But now they weren't far off. They were on the top of the last hill; it was a gentle slope all the way now and not more than half a mile.

Pat trailed the whip over the mare's back and he coaxed her: 'Goop now. Goop now.'

It wanted a few minutes to sunset. Everything stood motionless bathed in bright, metallic light and from the paddocks on either side there streamed the milky scent of ripe grass. The iron gates were open. They dashed through and up the drive and round the island, stopping at the exact middle of the verandah.

'Did she satisfy yer, Sir?' said Pat, getting off the box and grinning at his master.

'Very well indeed, Pat,' said Stanley.

Linda came out of the glass door; her voice rang in the shadowy quiet. 'Hullo! Are you home again?'

At the sound of her his heart beat so hard that he could hardly stop himself dashing up the steps and catching her in his arms.

'Yes, I'm home again. Is everything all right?'

Pat began to lead the buggy round to the side gate that opened into the courtyard.

'Here, half a moment,' said Burnell. 'Hand me those two parcels.' And he said to Linda, 'I've brought you back a bottle of oysters and a pineapple,' as though he had brought her back all the harvest of the earth.

They went into the hall; Linda carried the oysters in one hand and the pineapple in the other. Burnell shut the glass door, threw his hat down, put his arms around her and strained her to him, kissing the top of her head, her ears, her lips, her eyes.

'Oh, dear! Oh, dear!' said she. 'Wait a moment. Let me put down these silly things,' and she put the bottle of oysters and the pine on a little carved chair. 'What have you got in your button-hole — cherries?' She took them out and hung them over his ear.

'Don't do that, darling. They are for you.'

So she took them off his ear again. 'You don't mind if I save them. They'd spoil my appetite for dinner. Come and see your children. They are having tea.'

The lamp was lighted on the nursery table. Mrs Fairfield was cutting and spreading bread and butter. The three little girls sat up to table wearing large bibs embroidered with their names. They wiped their mouths as their father came in ready to be kissed. The windows were open; a jar of wild flowers stood on the mantelpiece, and the lamp made a big soft bubble of light on the ceiling.

'You seem pretty snug, mother,' said Burnell, blinking at the light. Isabel and Lottie sat one on either side of the table, Kezia at the bottom — the place at the top was empty.

'That's where my boy ought to sit,' thought Stanley. He tightened his arm round Linda's shoulder. By God, he was a perfect fool to feel as happy as this!

'We are, Stanley. We are very snug,' said Mrs Fairfield, cutting Kezia's bread into fingers.

'Like it better than town — eh, children?' asked Burnell.

'Oh, yes,' said the three little girls, and Isabel added as an after-thought: 'Thank you very much indeed, father dear.'

'Come upstairs,' said Linda. 'I'll bring your slippers.'

But the stairs were too narrow for them to go up arm in arm. It was quite dark in the room. He heard her ring tapping the marble mantelpiece as she felt for the matches.

'I've got some, darling. I'll light the candles.'

But instead he came up behind her and again he put his arms round her and pressed her head into his shoulder.

'I'm so confoundedly happy,' he said.

'Are you?' She turned and put her hands on his breast and looked up at him.

'I don't know what has come over me,' he protested.

It was quite dark outside now and heavy dew was falling. When Linda shut the window the cold dew touched her finger tips. Far away a dog barked. 'I believe there is going to be a moon,' she said.

At the words, and with the cold wet dew on her fingers, she felt as though the moon had risen — that she was being strangely discovered in a flood of cold light. She shivered; she came away from the window and sat down upon the box ottoman beside Stanley.

In the dining-room, by the flicker of a wood fire, Beryl sat on a hassock playing the guitar. She had bathed and changed all her clothes. Now she wore a white muslin dress with black spots on it and in her hair she had pinned a black silk rose.

> Nature has gone to her rest, love,
>   See, we are alone.
> Give me your hand to press, love,
>   Lightly within my own.

She played and sang half to herself, for she was watching herself playing and singing. The firelight gleamed on her shoes, on the ruddy belly of the guitar, and on her white fingers …

'If I were outside the window and looked in and saw myself I really would be rather struck,' thought she. Still more softly she played the accompaniment — not singing now but listening.

… 'The first time that I ever saw you, little girl — oh, you had no idea that you were not alone — you were sitting with your little feet upon a hassock, playing the guitar. God, I can never forget … ' Beryl flung up her head and began to sing again:

> Even the moon is aweary …

But there came a loud bang at the door. The servant girl's crimson face popped through.

'Please, Miss Beryl, I've got to come and lay.'

'Certainly, Alice,' said Beryl, in a voice of ice. She put the guitar in a corner. Alice lunged in with a heavy black iron tray.

'Well, I have had a job with that oving,' said she. 'I can't get nothing to brown.'

'Really!' said Beryl.

But no, she could not stand that fool of a girl. She ran into the dark drawing-room and began walking up and down … Oh, she was restless, restless. There was a mirror over the mantel. She leaned her arms along and looked at her pale shadow in it. How beautiful she looked, but there was nobody to see, nobody.

'Why must you suffer so?' said the face in the mirror. 'You were not made for suffering … Smile!'

Beryl smiled, and really her smile *was* so adorable that she smiled again — but this time because she could not help it.

VIII

'Good morning, Mrs Jones.'

'Oh, good morning, Mrs Smith. I'm so glad to see you. Have you brought your children?'

'Yes, I've brought both my twins. I have had another baby since I saw you last, but she came so suddenly that I haven't had time to make her any clothes, yet. So I left her … How is your husband?'

'Oh, he is very well, thank you. At least he had a nawful cold but Queen Victoria — she's my godmother, you know — sent him a case of pineapples and that cured it im-mediately. Is that your new servant?'

'Yes, her name's Gwen. I've only had her two days. Oh, Gwen, this is my friend, Mrs Smith.'

'Good morning, Mrs Smith. Dinner won't be ready for about ten minutes.'

'I don't think you ought to introduce me to the servant. I think I ought to just begin talking to her.'

'Well, she's more of a lady-help than a servant and you do introduce lady-helps, I know, because Mrs Samuel Josephs had one.'

'Oh, well, it doesn't matter,' said the servant, carelessly, beating up a chocolate custard with half a broken clothes peg. The dinner was baking beautifully on a concrete step. She began to lay the cloth on a pink garden seat. In front of each person she put two geranium leaf plates, a pine needle fork and a twig knife. There were three daisy heads on a laurel leaf for poached eggs, some slices of fuchsia petal cold beef, some lovely little rissoles made of earth and water and dandelion seeds, and the chocolate custard which she had decided to serve in the pawa shell she had cooked it in.

'You needn't trouble about my children,' said Mrs Smith graciously. 'If you'll just take this bottle and fill it at the tap — I mean at the dairy.'

'Oh, all right,' said Gwen, and she whispered to Mrs Jones: 'Shall I go and ask Alice for a little bit of real milk?'

But someone called from the front of the house and the luncheon party melted away, leaving the charming table, leaving the rissoles and the poached eggs to the ants and to an old snail who pushed his quivering horns over the edge of the garden seat and began to nibble a geranium plate.

'Come round to the front, children. Pip and Rags have come.'

The Trout boys were the cousins Kezia had mentioned to the storeman. They lived about a mile away in a house called Monkey Tree Cottage. Pip was tall for his age, with lank black hair and a white face, but Rags was very small and so thin that when he was undressed his shoulder blades stuck out like two little wings. They had a mongrel dog with pale blue eyes and a long tail turned up at the end who followed them everywhere; he was called Snooker. They spent half their time combing and brushing Snooker and dosing him with various awful mixtures concocted by Pip, and kept secretly by him in a broken jug covered with an old kettle lid. Even faithful little Rags was not allowed to know the full secret of these mixtures ... Take some carbolic tooth powder and a pinch of sulphur powdered up fine, and perhaps a bit of starch to stiffen up Snooker's coat ... But that was not all; Rags privately thought that the rest was gun-powder ... And he never was allowed to help with the mixing because of the danger ... 'Why, if a spot of this flew in your eye, you would be blinded for life,' Pip would say, stirring the mixture with an iron spoon. 'And there's always the chance — just the chance, mind you — of it exploding if you whack it hard enough ... Two spoons of this in a kerosene tin will be enough to kill thousands of fleas.' But Snooker spent all his spare time biting and snuffling, and he stank abominably.

'It's because he is such a grand fighting dog,' Pip would say, 'All fighting dogs smell.'

The Trout boys had often spent the day with the Burnells in town, but now that they lived in this fine house and boncer garden they were inclined to be very friendly. Besides, both of them liked playing with girls — Pip, because he could fox them so, and because Lottie was so easily frightened, and Rags for a shameful reason. He adored dolls. How he would look at a doll as it lay asleep, speaking in a whisper and smiling timidly, and what a treat it was to him to be allowed to hold one ...

'Curve your arms round her. Don't keep them stiff like that. You'll drop her,' Isabel would say sternly.

Now they were standing on the verandah and holding back Snooker who wanted to go into the house but wasn't allowed to because Aunt Linda hated decent dogs.

'We came over in the bus with Mum,' they said, 'and we're going to spend the afternoon with you. We brought over a batch of our gingerbread for Aunt Linda. Our Minnie made it. It's all over nuts.'

'I skinned the almonds,' said Pip. 'I just stuck my hand into a saucepan of boiling water and grabbed them out and gave them a kind of pinch and the nuts flew out of the skins, some of them as high as the ceiling. Didn't they, Rags?'

Rags nodded. 'When they make cakes at our place,' said Pip, 'we always stay in the kitchen, Rags and me, and I get the bowl and he gets the spoon and the egg beater. Sponge cake's best. It's all frothy stuff, then.'

He ran down the verandah steps to the lawn, planted his hands on the grass, bent forward, and just did not stand on his head.

'That lawn's all bumpy,' he said. 'You have to have a flat place for standing on your head. I can walk round the monkey tree on my head at our place. Can't I, Rags?'

'Nearly,' said Rags faintly.

'Stand on your head on the verandah. That's quite flat,' said Kezia.

'No, smarty,' said Pip. 'You have to do it on something soft. Because if you give a jerk and fall over, something in your neck goes click, and it breaks off. Dad told me.'

'Oh, do let's play something,' said Kezia.

'Very well,' said Isabel quickly, 'we'll play hospitals. I will be the nurse and Pip can be the doctor and you and Lottie and Rags can be the sick people.'

Lottie didn't want to play that, because last time Pip had squeezed something down her throat and it hurt awfully.

'Pooh,' scoffed Pip. 'It was only the juice out of a bit of mandarin peel.'

'Well, let's play ladies,' said Isabel. 'Pip can be the father and you can be all our dear little children.'

'I hate playing ladies,' said Kezia. 'You always make us go to church hand in hand and come home and go to bed.'

Suddenly Pip took a filthy handkerchief out of his pocket. 'Snooker! Here, sir,' he called. But Snooker, as usual, tried to sneak away, his tail between his legs. Pip leapt on top of him, and pressed him between his knees.

'Keep his head firm, Rags,' he said, and he tied the handkerchief round Snooker's head with a funny knot sticking up at the top.

'Whatever is that for?' asked Lottie.

'It's to train his ears to grow more close to his head — see?' said Pip. 'All fighting dogs have ears that lie back. But Snooker's ears are a bit too soft.'

'I know,' said Kezia. 'They are always turning inside out. I hate that.'

Snooker lay down, made one feeble effort with his paw to get the handkerchief off, but finding he could not, trailed after the children, shivering with misery.

I X

Pat came swinging along; in his hand he held a little tomahawk that winked in the sun.

'Come with me,' he said to the children, 'and I'll show you how the kings of Ireland chop the head off a duck.'

They drew back — they didn't believe him, and besides, the Trout boys had never seen Pat before.

'Come on now,' he coaxed, smiling and holding out his hand to Kezia.

'Is it a real duck's head? One from the paddock?'

'It is,' said Pat. She put her hand in his hard dry one, and he stuck the tomahawk in his belt and held out the other to Rags. He loved little children.

'I'd better keep hold of Snooker's head if there's going to be any blood about,' said Pip, 'because the sight of blood makes him awfully wild.' He ran ahead dragging Snooker by the handkerchief.

'Do you think we ought to go?' whispered Isabel. 'We haven't asked or anything. Have we?'

At the bottom of the orchard a gate was set in the paling fence. On the other side a steep bank led down to a bridge that spanned the creek, and once up the bank on the other side you were on the fringe of the paddocks. A little old stable in the first paddock had been turned into a fowl house. The fowls had strayed far away across the paddock down to a dumping ground, in a hollow, but the ducks kept close to that part of the creek that flowed under the bridge.

Tall bushes overhung the stream with red leaves and yellow flowers and clusters of blackberries. At some place the stream was wide and shallow, but at others it tumbled into deep little pools with foam at the edges and quivering bubbles. It was in these pools that the big white ducks had made themselves at home, swimming and guzzling along the weedy banks.

Up and down they swam, preening their dazzling breasts, and other ducks with the same dazzling breasts and yellow bills swam upside down with them.

'There is the little Irish navy,' said Pat, 'and look at the old admiral there with the green neck and the grand little flagstaff on his tail.'

He pulled a handful of grain from his pocket and began to walk towards the fowl house, lazy, his straw hat with the broken crown pulled over his eyes.

'Lid. Lid-lid-lid-lid — ' he called.

'Qua. Qua-qua-qua-qua — ' answered the ducks, making for land, and flapping and scrambling up the bank they streamed after him in a long waddling line. He coaxed them, pretending to throw the grain, shaking it in his hands and calling to them until they swept round him in a white ring.

From far away the fowls heard the clamour and they too came running across the paddock, their heads thrust forward, their wings spread, turning in their feet in the silly way fowls run and scolding as they came.

Then Pat scattered the grain and the greedy ducks began to gobble. Quickly he stooped, seized two, one under each arm, and strode across to the children. Their darting heads and round eyes frightened the children — all except Pip.

'Come on, sillies,' he cried, 'they can't bite. They haven't any teeth. They've only got those two little holes in their beaks for breathing through.'

'Will you hold one while I finish with the other?' asked Pat. Pip let go of Snooker. 'Won't I? Won't I? Give us one. I don't mind how much he kicks.'

He nearly sobbed with delight when Pat gave the white lump into his arms.

There was an old stump beside the door of the fowl house. Pat grabbed the duck by the legs, laid it flat across the stump, and almost at the same moment down came the little tomahawk and the duck's head flew off the stump. Up the blood spurted over the white feathers and over his hand.

When the children saw the blood they were frightened no longer. They crowded round him and began to scream. Even Isabel leaped about crying: 'The blood! The blood!' Pip forgot all about his duck. He simply threw it away from him and shouted, 'I saw it. I saw it,' and jumped round the wood block.

Rags, with cheeks as white as paper, ran up to the little head, put out a finger as if he wanted to touch it, shrank back again and then again put out a finger. He was shivering all over.

Even Lottie, frightened little Lottie, began to laugh and pointed at the duck and shrieked: 'Look, Kezia, look.'

'Watch it!' shouted Pat. He put down the body and it began to waddle — with only a long spurt of blood where the head had been; it began to pad away without a sound towards the steep bank that led to the stream … That was the crowning wonder.

'Do you see that? Do you see that?' yelled Pip. He ran among the little girls tugging at their pinafores.

'It's like a little engine. It's like a funny little railway engine,' squealed Isabel.

But Kezia suddenly rushed at Pat and flung her arms round his legs and butted her head as hard as she could against his knees.

'Put head back! Put head back!' she screamed.

When he stooped to move her she would not let go or take her head away. She held on as hard as she could and sobbed: 'Head back! Head back!' until it sounded like a loud strange hiccup.

'It's stopped. It's tumbled over. It's dead,' said Pip.

Pat dragged Kezia up into his arms. Her sun-bonnet had fallen back, but she would not let him look at her face. No, she pressed her face into a bone in his shoulder and clasped her arms round his neck.

The children stopped screaming as suddenly as they had begun. They stood round the dead duck. Rags was not frightened of the head any more. He knelt down and stroked it, now.

'I don't think the head is quite dead yet,' he said. 'Do you think it would keep alive if I gave it something to drink?'

But Pip got very cross: 'Bah! You baby.' He whistled to Snooker and went off.

When Isabel went up to Lottie, Lottie snatched away.

'What are you always touching me for, Isabel?'

'There now,' said Pat to Kezia. 'There's a grand little girl.'

She put up her hands and touched his ears. She felt something. Slowly she raised her quivering face and looked. Pat wore little round gold ear-rings. She never knew that men wore ear-rings. She was very much surprised.

'Do they come on and off?' she asked huskily.

X

Up in the house, in the warm tidy kitchen, Alice, the servant girl, was getting the afternoon tea. She was 'dressed'. She had on a black stuff dress that smelt under the arms, a white apron like a large sheet of paper, and a lace bow pinned on to her hair with two jetty pins. Also her comfortable carpet slippers were changed for a pair of black leather ones that pinched her corn on her little toe something dreadful ...

It was warm in the kitchen. A blow-fly buzzed, a fan of whity steam came out of the kettle, and the lid kept up a rattling jig as the water bubbled. The clock ticked in the warm air, slow and deliberate, like the click of an old woman's knitting needle, and sometimes — for no reason at all, for there wasn't any breeze — the blind swung out and back, tapping the window.

Alice was making water-cress sandwiches. She had a lump of butter on the table, a barracouta loaf, and the cresses tumbled in a white cloth.

But propped against the butter dish there was a dirty, greasy little book, half unstitched, with curled edges, and while she mashed the butter she read:

'To dream of black-beetles drawing a hearse is bad. Signifies death of one you hold near or dear, either father, husband, brother, son, or intended. If beetles crawl backwards as you watch them it means death from fire or from great height such as flight of stairs, scaffolding, etc.

'Spiders. To dream of spiders creeping over you is good. Signifies large sum of money in near future. Should party be in family way an easy confinement may be expected. But care should be taken in sixth month to avoid eating of probable present of shellfish ... '

'How many thousand birds I see.'

Oh, life. There was Miss Beryl. Alice dropped the knife and slipped the *Dream Book* under the butter dish. But she hadn't time to hide it quite, for Beryl ran into the kitchen and up to the table, and the first thing her eye lighted on were those greasy edges. Alice saw Miss Beryl's meaning little smile and the way she raised her eyebrows and screwed up her eyes as though she were not quite sure what that could be. She decided to answer if Miss Beryl should ask her: 'Nothing as belongs to you, Miss.' But she knew Miss Beryl would not ask her.

Alice was a mild creature in reality, but she had the most marvellous retorts ready for questions that she knew would never be put to her. The composing of them and the turning of them over and over in her mind comforted her just as much as if they'd been expressed. Really, they kept her alive in places where she'd been that chivvied she'd been afraid to go to bed at night with a box of matches on the chair in case she bit the tops off in her sleep, as you might say.

'Oh, Alice,' said Miss Beryl. 'There's one extra to tea, so heat a plate of yesterday's scones, please. And put on the Victoria sandwich as well as the coffee cake. And don't forget to put little doyleys under the plates — will you? You did yesterday, you know, and the tea looked so ugly and common. And, Alice, don't put that dreadful old pink and green cosy on the afternoon teapot again. That is only for the mornings. Really, I think it ought to be kept for the kitchen — it's so shabby, and quite smelly. Put on the Japanese one. You quite understand, don't you?'

Miss Beryl had finished.

'That sing aloud from every tree ... '

she sang as she left the kitchen, very pleased with her firm handling of Alice.

Oh, Alice was wild. She wasn't one to mind being told, but there was something in the way Miss Beryl had of speaking to her that she couldn't stand. Oh, that she couldn't. It made her curl up inside, as you might say, and she fair trembled. But what Alice really hated Miss Beryl for was that she made her feel low. She talked to Alice in a special voice as though she wasn't quite all there; and she never lost her temper with her — never. Even when Alice dropped anything or forgot anything important Miss Beryl seemed to have expected it to happen.

'If you please, Mrs Burnell,' said an imaginary Alice, as she buttered the scones, 'I'd rather not take my orders from Miss Beryl. I may be only a common servant girl as doesn't know how to play the guitar, but … '

This last thrust pleased her so much that she quite recovered her temper.

'The only thing to do,' she heard, as she opened the dining-room door, 'is to cut the sleeves out entirely and just have a broad band of black velvet over the shoulders instead … '

X I

The white duck did not look as if it had ever had a head when Alice placed it in front of Stanley Burnell that night. It lay, in beautifully basted resignation, on a blue dish — its legs tied together with a piece of string and a wreath of little balls of stuffing round it.

It was hard to say which of the two, Alice or the duck, looked the better basted; they were both such a rich colour and they both had the same air of gloss and strain. But Alice was fiery red and the duck a Spanish mahogany.

Burnell ran his eye along the edge of the carving knife. He prided himself very much upon his carving, upon making a first-class job of it. He hated seeing a woman carve; they were always too slow and they never seemed to care what the meat looked like afterwards. Now he did; he took a real pride in cutting delicate shaves of cold beef; little wads of mutton, just the right thickness, and in dividing a chicken or a duck with nice precision …

'Is this the first of the home products?' he asked, knowing perfectly well that it was.

'Yes, the butcher did not come. We have found out that he only calls twice a week.'

But there was no need to apologise. It was a superb bird. It wasn't meat at all, but a kind of very superior jelly. 'My father would say,' said Burnell, 'this must have been one of those birds whose mother played to it in infancy upon the German flute. And the sweet strains of the dulcet instrument acted with such effect upon the infant mind … have some more, Beryl? You and I are the only ones in this house with a real feeling for food. I'm perfectly willing to state, in a court of law, if necessary, that I love good food.'

Tea was served in the drawing-room, and Beryl, who for some reason had been very charming to Stanley ever since he came home, suggested a game of crib. They sat at a little table near one of the open windows. Mrs Fairfield disappeared, and Linda lay in a rocking-chair, her arms above her head, rocking to and fro.

'You don't want the light — do you, Linda?' said Beryl. She moved the tall lamp so that she sat under its soft light.

How remote they looked, those two, from where Linda sat and rocked. The green table, the polished cards, Stanley's big hands and Beryl's tiny ones, all seemed to be part of one mysterious movement. Stanley himself, big and solid, in his dark suit, took his ease, and Beryl tossed her bright head and pouted. Round her throat she wore an unfamiliar velvet ribbon. It changed her, somehow — altered the shape of her face — but it was charming, Linda decided. The room smelled of lilies; there were two big jars of arums in the fire-place.

'Fifteen two — fifteen four — and a pair is six and a run of three is nine,' said Stanley, so deliberately, he might have been counting sheep.

'I've nothing but two pairs,' said Beryl, exaggerating her woe because she knew how he loved winning.

The cribbage pegs were like two little people going up the road together, turning round the sharp corner, and coming down the road again. They were pursuing each other. They did not so much want to get ahead as to keep near enough to talk — to keep near, perhaps that was all.

But no, there was always one who was impatient and hopped away as the other came up, and would not listen. Perhaps the white peg was frightened of the red one, or perhaps he was cruel and would not give the red one a chance to speak ...

In the front of her dress Beryl wore a bunch of pansies, and once when the little pegs were side by side, she bent over and the pansies dropped out and covered them.

'What a shame,' said she, picking up the pansies. 'Just as they had a chance to fly into each other's arms.'

'Farewell, my girl,' laughed Stanley, and away the red peg hopped.

The drawing-room was long and narrow with glass doors that gave on to the verandah. It had a cream paper with a pattern of gilt roses, and the furniture, which had belonged to old Mrs Fairfield, was dark and plain. A little piano stood against the wall with yellow pleated silk let into the carved front. Above it hung an oil painting by Beryl of a large cluster of surprised looking clematis. Each flower was the size of a small saucer, with a centre like an astonished eye fringed in black. But the room was not finished yet. Stanley had set his heart on a Chesterfield and two decent chairs. Linda liked it best as it was ...

Two big moths flew in through the window and round and round the circle of lamplight.

'Fly away before it is too late. Fly out again.'

Round and round they flew; they seemed to bring the silence and the moonlight in with them on their silent wings ...

'I've two kings,' said Stanley. 'Any good?'

'Quite good,' said Beryl.

Linda stopped rocking and got up. Stanley looked across. 'Anything the matter, darling?'

'No, nothing. I'm going to find mother.'

She went out of the room and standing at the foot of the stairs she called, but her mother's voice answered her from the verandah.

The moon that Lottie and Kezia had seen from the storeman's wagon was full, and the house, the garden, the old woman and Linda — all were bathed in dazzling light.

'I have been looking at the aloe,' said Mrs Fairfield. 'I believe it is going to flower this year. Look at the top there. Are those buds, or is it only an effect of light?'

As they stood on the steps, the high grassy bank on which the aloe rested rose up like a wave, and the aloe seemed to ride upon it like a ship with the oars lifted. Bright moonlight hung upon the lifted oars like water, and on the green wave glittered the dew.

'Do you feel it, too,' said Linda, and she spoke to her mother with the special voice that women use at night to each other as though they spoke in their sleep or from some hollow cave — 'Don't you feel that it is coming towards us?'

She dreamed that she was caught up out of the cold water into the ship with the lifted oars and the budding mast. Now the oars fell striking quickly, quickly. They rowed far away over the top of the garden trees, the paddocks and the dark bush beyond. Ah, she heard herself cry: 'Faster! Faster!' to those who were rowing.

How much more real this dream was than that they should go back to the house where the sleeping children lay and where Stanley and Beryl played cribbage.

'I believe those are buds,' said she. 'Let us go down into the garden, mother. I like that aloe. I like it more than anything here. And I am sure I shall remember it long after I've forgotten all the other things.'

She put her hand on her mother's arm and they walked down the steps, round the island and on to the main drive that led to the front gates.

Looking at it from below she could see the long sharp thorns that edged the aloe leaves, and at the sight of them her heart grew hard … She particularly liked the long sharp thorns … Nobody would dare to come near the ship or to follow after.

'Not even my Newfoundland dog,' thought she, 'that I'm so fond of in the daytime.'

For she really was fond of him; she loved and admired and respected him tremendously. Oh, better than anyone else in the world. She knew him through and through. He was the soul of truth and decency, and for all his practical experience he was awfully simple, easily pleased and easily hurt …

If only he wouldn't jump at her so, and bark so loudly, and watch her with such eager, loving eyes. He was too strong for her; she had always hated things that rush at her, from a child. There were times when he was frightening — really frightening. When she just had not screamed at the top of her voice: 'You are killing me.' And at those times she had longed to say the most coarse, hateful things …

'You know I'm very delicate. You know as well as I do that my heart is affected, and the doctor has told you I may die any moment. I have had three great lumps of children already … '

Yes, yes, it was true. Linda snatched her hand from mother's arm. For all her love and respect and admiration she hated him. And how tender he always was after times like those, how submissive, how thoughtful. He would do anything for her; he longed to serve her … Linda heard herself saying in a weak voice:

'Stanley, would you light a candle?'

And she heard his joyful voice answer: 'Of course I will, my darling,' and he leapt out of bed as though he were going to leap at the moon for her.

It had never been so plain to her as it was at this moment. There were all her feelings for him, sharp and defined, one as true as the other. And there was this other, this hatred, just as real as the rest. She could have done her feelings up in little packets and given them to Stanley. She longed to hand him that last one, for a surprise. She could see his eyes as he opened that …

She hugged her folded arms and began to laugh silently. How absurd life was — it was laughable, simply laughable. And why this mania of hers to keep alive at all? For it really was a mania, she thought, mocking and laughing.

'What am I guarding myself for so preciously? I shall go on having children and Stanley will go on making money and the children and the gardens will grow bigger and bigger, with whole fleets of aloes in them for me to choose from.'

She had been walking with her head bent, looking at nothing. Now she looked up and about her. They were standing by the red and white camellia trees. Beautiful were the rich dark leaves spangled with light and the round flowers that perch among them like red and white birds. Linda pulled a piece of verbena and crumpled it, and held her hands to her mother.

'Delicious,' said the old woman. 'Are you cold, child? Are you trembling? Yes, your hands are cold. We had better go back to the house.'

'What have you been thinking about?' said Linda. 'Tell me.'

'I haven't really been thinking of anything. I wondered as we passed the orchard what the fruit trees were like and whether we should be able to make much jam this autumn. There are splendid healthy currant bushes in the vegetable garden. I noticed them today. I should like to see those pantry shelves thoroughly well stocked with our own jam … '

XII

'My Darling Nan,

Don't think me a piggy wig because I haven't written before. I haven't had a moment, dear, and even now I feel so exhausted that I can hardly hold a pen.

Well, the dreadful deed is done. We have actually left the

giddy whirl of town, and I can't see how we shall ever go back again, for my brother-in-law has bought this house "lock, stock and barrel", to use his own words.

In a way, of course, it is an awful relief, for he has been threatening to take a place in the country ever since I've lived with them — and I must say the house and garden are awfully nice — a million times better than that awful cubby-hole in town.

But buried, my dear. Buried isn't the word.

We have got neighbours, but they are only farmers — big louts of boys who seem to be milking all day, and two dreadful females with rabbit teeth who brought us some scones when we were moving and said they would be pleased to help. But my sister who lives a mile away doesn't know a soul here, so I am sure we never shall. It's pretty certain nobody will ever come out from town to see us, because though there is a bus it's an awful old rattling thing with black leather sides that any decent person would rather die than ride in for six miles.

Such is life. It's a sad ending for poor little B. I'll get to be a most awful frump in a year or two and come and see you in a mackintosh and a sailor hat tied on with a white china silk motor veil. So pretty.

Stanley says that now we are settled — for after the most awful week of my life we really are settled — he is going to bring out a couple of men from the club on Saturday afternoons for tennis. In fact, two are promised as a great treat to-day. But, my dear, if you could see Stanley's men from the club ... rather fattish, the type who look frightfully indecent without waistcoats — always with toes that turn in rather — so conspicuous when you are walking about a court in white shoes. And they are pulling up their trousers every minute — don't you know — and whacking at imaginary things with their rackets.

I used to play with them at the club last summer, and I am sure you will know the type when I tell you that after I'd been there about three times they all called me Miss Beryl. It's a weary world. Of course mother simply loves the place, but then I suppose when I am mother's age I shall be content to sit in the sun and shell peas into a basin. But I'm not — not — not.

What Linda thinks about the whole affair, per usual, I haven't the slightest idea. Mysterious as ever ...

My dear, you know that white satin dress of mine. I have taken the sleeves out entirely, put bands of black velvet across the shoulders and two big red poppies off my dear sister's *chapeau*. It is a great success, though when I shall wear it I do not know.'

Beryl sat writing this letter at a little table in her room. In a way, of course, it was all perfectly true, but in another way it was all the greatest rubbish and she didn't believe a word of it. No, that wasn't true. She felt all those things, but she didn't really feel them like that.

It was her other self who had written that letter. It not only bored, it rather disgusted her real self.

'Flippant and silly,' said her real self. Yet she knew that she'd send it and she'd always write that kind of twaddle to Nan Pym. In fact, it was a very mild example of the kind of letter she generally wrote.

Beryl leaned her elbows on the table and read it through again. The voice of the letter seemed to come up to her from the page. It was faint already, like a voice heard over the telephone, high, gushing, with something bitter in the sound. Oh, she detested it to-day.

'You've always got so much animation,' said Nan Pym. 'That's why men are so keen on you.' And she had added, rather mournfully, for men were not at all keen on Nan, who was a solid kind of girl, with fat hips and a high colour — 'I can't understand how you can keep it up. But it is your nature, I suppose.'

What rot. What nonsense, it wasn't her nature at all. Good heavens, if she had ever been her real self with Nan Pym, Nannie would have jumped out of the window with surprise. My dear, you know that white satin of mine ... Beryl slammed the letter-case to.

She jumped up and half unconsciously, half consciously she drifted over to the looking-glass.

There stood a slim girl in white — a white serge skirt, a white silk blouse, and a leather belt drawn in very tightly at her tiny waist.

Her face was heart-shaped, wide at the brows and with a pointed chin — but not too pointed. Her eyes, her eyes were perhaps her best feature; they were such a strange uncommon colour — greeny blue with little gold points in them.

She had fine black eyebrows and long lashes — so long that when they lay on her cheeks they positively caught the light in them, someone or other had told her.

Her mouth was rather large. Too large? No, not really. Her underlip protruded a little; she had a way of sucking it in that somebody else had told her was awfully fascinating.

Her nose was her least satisfactory feature. Not that it was really ugly. But it was not half as fine as Linda's. Linda really had a perfect little nose. Hers spread rather — not badly. And in all probability she exaggerated the spreadiness of it just because it was her nose, and she was so awfully critical of herself. She pinched it with a thumb and first finger and made a little face ...

Lovely, lovely hair. And such a mass of it. It had the colour of fresh fallen leaves, brown and red with a glint of yellow. When she did it in a long plait she felt it on her backbone like a long snake. She loved to feel the weight of it dragging her head back, and she loved to feel it loose, covering her bare arms. 'Yes, my dear, there is no doubt about it, you really are a lovely little thing.'

At the words her bosom lifted; she took a long breath of delight, half closing her eyes.

But even as she looked the smile faded from her lips and eyes.

Oh God, there she was, back again, playing the same old game. False — false as ever. False as when she'd written to Nan Pym. False even when she was alone with herself, now.

What had that creature in the glass to do with her, and why was she staring? She dropped down to one side of her bed and buried her face in her arms.

'Oh,' she cried, 'I am so miserable — so frightfully miserable. I know that I'm silly and spiteful and vain; I'm always acting a part. I'm never my real self for a moment.' And plainly, plainly, she saw her false self running up and down the stairs, laughing a special trilling laugh if they had visitors, standing under the lamp if a man came to dinner, so that he should see the light on her hair, pouting and pretending to be a little girl when she was asked to play the guitar. Why? She even kept it up for Stanley's benefit. Only last night when he was reading the paper her false self had stood beside him and leaned against his shoulder on purpose. Hadn't she put her hand over his, pointing out something so that he should see how white her hand was beside his brown one.

How despicable! Despicable! Her heart was cold with rage. 'It's marvellous how you keep it up,' said she to the false self. But then it was only because she was so miserable — so miserable. If she had been happy and leading her own life, her false life would cease to be. She saw the real Beryl — a shadow ... a shadow. Faint and unsubstantial she shone. What was there of her except the radiance? And for what tiny moments she was really she. Beryl could almost remember every one of them. At those times she had felt: 'Life is rich and mysterious and good, and I am rich and mysterious and good, too.' Shall I ever be that Beryl for ever? Shall I? How can I? And was there ever a time when I did not have a false self? ... But just as she had got that far she heard the sound of little steps running along the passage; the door handle rattled. Kezia came in.

'Aunt Beryl, mother says will you please come down? Father is home with a man and lunch is ready.'

Botheration! How she had crumpled her skirt, kneeling in that idiotic way.

'Very well, Kezia.' She went over to the dressing table and powdered her nose.

Kezia crossed too, and unscrewed a little pot of cream and sniffed it. Under her arm she carried a very dirty calico cat.

When Aunt Beryl ran out of the room she sat the cat up on the dressing table and stuck the top of the cream jar over its ear.

'Now look at yourself,' said she sternly.

The calico cat was so overcome by the sight that it toppled over backwards and bumped and bumped on to the floor. And the top of the cream jar flew through the air and rolled like a penny in a round on the linoleum — and did not break.

But for Kezia it had broken the moment it flew through the air, and she picked it up, hot all over, and put it back on the dressing table.

Then she tip-toed away, far too quickly and airily …

The Stranger

It seemed to the little crowd on the wharf that she was never going to move again. There she lay, immense, motionless on the grey crinkled water, a loop of smoke over her, an immense flock of gulls screaming and diving after the galley droppings at the stern. You could just see little couples parading — little flies walking up and down the dish on the grey crinkled tablecloth. Other flies clustered and swarmed at the edge. Now there was a gleam of white on the lower deck — the cook's apron or the stewardess perhaps. Now a tiny black spider raced up the ladder on to the bridge.

In the front of the crowd a strong-looking, middle-aged man, dressed very well, very snugly in a grey overcoat, grey silk scarf, thick gloves and dark felt hat, marched up and down, twirling his folded umbrella. He seemed to be the leader of the little crowd on the wharf and at the same time to keep them together. He was something between the sheep-dog and the shepherd.

But what a fool — what a fool he had been not to bring any glasses! There wasn't a pair of glasses between the whole lot of them.

'Curious thing, Mr Scott, that none of us thought of glasses. We might have been able to stir 'em up a bit. We might have managed a little signalling. *Don't hesitate to land. Natives harmless.* Or: *A welcome awaits you. All is forgiven.* What? Eh?'

Mr Hammond's quick eager glance, so nervous and yet so friendly and confiding, took in everybody on the wharf, roped in even those old chaps lounging against the gangways. They knew, every man-jack of them, that Mrs Hammond was on that boat, and he was so tremendously excited it never entered his head not to believe that this marvellous fact meant something to them too. It warmed his heart towards them. They were, he decided, as decent a crowd of people — those old chaps over by the gangways, too — fine, solid old chaps. What chests — by Jove! And he squared his own, plunged his thick-gloved hands into his pockets, rocked from heel to toe.

'Yes, my wife's been in Europe for the last ten months. On a visit to our eldest girl, who was married last year. I brought her up here, as far as Auckland, myself. So I thought I'd better come and fetch her back. Yes, yes, yes.' The shrewd grey eyes narrowed again and searched anxiously, quickly, the motionless liner. Again his overcoat was unbuttoned. Out came the thin, butter-yellow watch again, and for the twentieth — fiftieth — hundredth time he made the calculation.

'Let me see, now. It was two fifteen when the doctor's launch went off. Two fifteen. It is now exactly twenty-eight minutes past four. That is to say, the doctor's been gone two hours and thir-teen minutes. Two hours and thirteen minutes! Whee-ooh!' He gave a queer little half-whistle and snapped his watch to again. 'But I think we should have been told if there was anything up — don't you, Mr Gaven?'

'Oh, yes, Mr Hammond! I don't think there's anything to — anything to worry about,' said Mr Gaven, knocking out his pipe against the heel of his shoe. 'At the same time — '

'Quite so! Quite so!' cried Mr Hammond. 'Dashed annoy-ing!' He paced quickly up and down and came back again to his stand between Mr and Mrs Scott and Mr Gaven. 'It's getting quite dark, too,' and he waved his folding umbrella as though the dusk at least might have had the decency to keep off for a bit. But the dusk came slowly, spreading like a slow stain over the water. Little Jean Scott dragged at her mother's hand.

'I wan' my tea, mammy!' she wailed.

'I expect you do,' said Mr Hammond. 'I expect all these ladies want their tea.' And his kind, flushed, almost pitiful glance roped them all in again. He wondered whether Janey was having a final cup of tea in the saloon out there. He hoped so; he thought not. It would be just like her not to leave the deck. In that case perhaps the deck steward would bring her up a cup. If he'd been there he'd have got it for her — somehow. And for a moment he was on deck, standing over her, watching her little hand fold round the cup in the way she had, while she drank the only cup of tea to be got on board ... But now he was back here, and the Lord only knew when that cursed Captain would stop hanging about in the stream. He took another turn, up and down, up and down. He walked as far as the cab-stand to make sure his driver hadn't disappeared; back he swerved again to the little flock hud-dled in the shelter of the banana crates. Little Jean Scott was still wanting her tea. Poor little beggar! He wished he had a bit of chocolate on him.

'Here, Jean!' he said. 'Like a lift up?' And easily, gently, he swung the little girl on to a higher barrel. The movement of holding her, steadying her, relieved him wonderfully, lightened his heart.

'Hold on,' he said, keeping an arm round her.

'Oh, don't worry about *Jean*, Mr Hammond!' said Mrs Scott.

'That's all right, Mrs Scott. No trouble. It's a pleasure. Jean's a little pal of mine, aren't you, Jean?'

'Yes, Mr Hammond,' said Jean, and she ran her finger down the dent on his felt hat.

But suddenly she caught him by the ear and gave a loud scream. 'Lo-ok, Mr Hammond! She's moving! Look, she's coming in!'

By Jove! So she was. At last! She was slowly, slowly turning round. A bell sounded far over the water and a great spout of steam gushed into the air. The gulls rose; they fluttered away like bits of white paper. And whether that deep throbbing was her engines or his heart Mr Hammond couldn't say. He had to nerve himself to bear it, whatever it was. At that moment old Captain Johnson, the harbour-master, came striding down the wharf, a leather portfolio under his arm.

'Jean'll be all right,' said Mr Scott. 'I'll hold her.' He was just in time. Mr Hammond had forgotten about Jean. He sprang away to greet old Captain Johnson.

'Well, Captain,' the eager, nervous voice rang out again, 'you've taken pity on us at last.'

'It's no good blaming me, Mr Hammond,' wheezed old Captain Johnson, staring at the liner. 'You got Mrs Hammond on board, ain't yer?'

'Yes, yes!' said Hammond, and he kept by the harbour-master's side. 'Mrs Hammond's there. Hul-lo! We shan't be long now!'

With her telephone ring-ringing, the thrum of her screw filling the air, the big liner bore down on them, cutting sharp through the dark water so that big white shavings curled to either side. Hammond and the harbour-master kept in front of the rest. Hammond took off his hat; he raked the decks — they were crammed with passengers; he waved his hat and bawled a loud, strange 'Hul-lo!' across the water, and then turned round and burst out laughing and said something — nothing — to old Captain Johnson.

'Seen her?' asked the harbour-master.

'No, not yet. Steady — wait a bit!' And suddenly, between two great clumsy idiots — 'Get out of the way there!' he signed with his umbrella — he saw a hand raised — a white glove shaking a handkerchief. Another moment, and — thank God, thank God! — there she was. There was Janey. There was Mrs Hammond, yes, yes, yes — standing by the rail and smiling and nodding and waving her handkerchief.

'Well, that's first class — first class! Well, well, well!' He positively stamped. Like lightning he drew out his cigar-case and offered it to old Captain Johnson. 'Have a cigar, Captain! They're pretty good. Have a couple! Here' — and he pressed all the cigars in the case on the harbour-master — 'I've a couple of boxes up at the hotel.'

'Thanks, Mr Hammond!' wheezed old Captain Johnson.

Hammond stuffed the cigar-case back. His hands were shaking, but he'd got hold of himself again. He was able to face Janey. There she was, leaning on the rail, talking to some woman and at the same time watching him, ready for him. It struck him, as the gulf of water closed, how small she looked on that huge ship. His heart was wrung with such a spasm that he could have cried out. How little she looked to have come all that long way and back by herself! Just like her, though. Just like Janey. She had the courage of a — And now the crew had come forward and parted the passengers; they had lowered the rails for the gangways.

The voices on shore and the voices on board flew to greet each other.

'All well?'

'All well.'

'How's mother?'

'Much better.'

'Hello, Jean!'

'Hillo, Aun' Emily!'

'Had a good voyage?'

'Splendid!'

'Shan't be long now!'

'Not long now.'

The engines stopped. Slowly she edged to the wharf-side.

'Make way there — make way — make way!' And the wharf hands brought the heavy gangways along at a sweeping run. Hammond signed to Janey to stay where she was. The old harbour-master stepped forward; he followed. As to 'ladies first', or any rot like that, it never entered his head.

'After you, Captain!' he cried genially. And, treading on the old man's heels, he strode up the gangway on to the deck in a bee-line to Janey, and Janey was clasped in his arms.

'Well, well, well! Yes, yes! Here we are at last!' he stammered. It was all he could say. And Janey emerged, and her cool little voice — the only voice in the world for him — said,

'Well, darling! Have you been waiting long?'

No; not long. Or, at any rate, it didn't matter. It was over now. But the point was, he had a cab waiting at the end of the wharf. Was she ready to go off? Was her luggage ready? In that case they could cut off sharp with her cabin luggage and let the rest go hang until to-morrow. He bent over her and she looked up with her familiar half-smile. She was just the same. Not a day changed. Just as he'd always known her. She laid her small hand on his sleeve.

'How are the children, John?' she asked.

(Hang the children!) 'Perfectly well. Never better in their lives.'

'Haven't they sent me letters?'

'Yes, yes — of course! I've left them at the hotel for you to digest later on.'

'We can't go quite so fast,' said she. 'I've got people to say good-bye to — and then there's the Captain.' As his face fell she gave his arm a small understanding squeeze. 'If the Captain comes off the bridge I want you to thank him for having looked after your wife so beautifully.' Well, he'd got her. If she wanted another ten minutes — As he gave way she was surrounded. The whole first-class seemed to want to say good-bye to Janey.

'Good-bye, *dear* Mrs Hammond! And next time you're in Sydney I'll *expect* you.'

'Darling Mrs Hammond! You won't forget to write to me, will you?'

'Well, Mrs Hammond, what this boat would have been without you!'

It was as plain as a pikestaff that she was by far the most popular woman on board. And she took it all — just as usual. Absolutely composed. Just her little self — just Janey all over; standing there with her veil thrown back. Hammond never noticed what his wife had on. It was all the same to him whatever she wore. But to-day he did notice that she wore a black 'costume' — didn't they call it? — with white frills, trimmings he supposed they were, at the neck and sleeves. All this while Janey handed him round.

'John, dear!' And then: 'I want to introduce you to — '

Finally they did escape, and she led the way to her state-room. To follow Janey down the passage that she knew so well — that was so strange to him; to part the green curtains after her and to step into the cabin that had been hers gave him exquisite happiness. But — confound it! — the stewardess was there on the floor, strapping up the rugs.

'That's the last, Mrs Hammond,' said the stewardess, rising and pulling down her cuffs.

He was introduced again, and then Janey and the stewardess disappeared into the passage. He heard whisperings. She was getting the tipping business over, he supposed. He sat down on the striped sofa and took his hat off. There were the rugs she had taken with her; they looked good as new. All her luggage looked fresh, perfect. The labels were written in her beautiful little clear hand — 'Mrs John Hammond'.

'Mrs John Hammond!' He gave a long sigh of content and leaned back, crossing his arms. The strain was over. He felt he could have sat there for ever sighing his relief — the relief at being rid of that horrible tug, pull, grip on his heart. The danger was over. That was the feeling. They were on dry land again.

But at that moment Janey's head came round the corner.

'Darling — do you mind? I just want to go and say good-bye to the doctor.'

Hammond started up. 'I'll come with you.'

'No, no!' she said. 'Don't bother. I'd rather not. I'll not be a minute.'

And before he could answer she was gone. He had half a mind to run after her; but instead he sat down again.

Would she really not be long? What was the time now? Out came the watch; he stared at nothing. That was rather queer of Janey, wasn't it? Why couldn't she have told the stewardess to say good-bye for her? Why did she have to go chasing after the ship's doctor? She could have sent a note from the hotel even if the affair had been urgent. Urgent? Did it — could it mean that she had been ill on the voyage — she was keeping something from him? That was it! He seized his hat. He was going off to find that fellow and to wring the truth out of him at all costs. He thought he'd noticed just something. She was just a touch too calm — too steady. From the very first moment —

The curtains rang. Janey was back. He jumped to his feet.

'Janey, have you been ill on this voyage? You have!'

'Ill?' Her airy little voice mocked him. She stepped over the rugs, came up close, touched his breast, and looked up at him.

'Darling,' she said, 'don't frighten me. Of course I haven't! Whatever makes you think I have? Do I look ill?'

But Hammond didn't see her. He only felt that she was looking at him and that there was no need to worry about anything. She was here to look after things. It was all right. Everything was.

The gentle pressure of her hand was so calming that he put his over hers to hold it there. And she said:

'Stand still. I want to look at you. I haven't seen you yet. You've had your beard beautifully trimmed, and you look — younger, I think, and decidedly thinner! Bachelor life agrees with you.'

'Agrees with me!' He groaned for love and caught her close again. And again, as always, he had the feeling he was holding something that never was quite his — his. Something too delicate, too precious, that would fly away once he let go.

'For God's sake let's get off to the hotel so that we can be by ourselves!' And he rang the bell hard for someone to look sharp with the luggage.

Walking down the wharf together she took his arm. He had her on his arm again. And the difference it made to get into the cab after Janey — to throw the red-and-yellow striped blanket round them both — to tell the driver to hurry because neither of them had had any tea. No more going without his tea or pouring out his own. She was back. He turned to her, squeezed her hand, and said gently, teasingly, in the 'special' voice he had for her: 'Glad to be home again, dearie?' She smiled; she didn't even bother to answer, but gently she drew his hand away as they came to the lighted streets.

'We've got the best room in the hotel,' he said. 'I wouldn't be put off with another. And I asked the chambermaid to put in a bit of a fire in case you felt chilly. She's a nice, attentive girl. And I thought now we were here we wouldn't bother to go home to-morrow, but spend the day looking round and leave the morning after. Does that suit you? There's no hurry, is there? The children will have you soon enough … I thought a day's sight-seeing might make a nice break in your journey — eh, Janey?'

'Have you taken the tickets for the day after?' she asked.

'I should think I have!' He unbuttoned his overcoat and took out his bulging pocket-book. 'Here we are! I reserved a first-class carriage to Napier. There it is — "Mr *and* Mrs John Hammond". I thought we might as well do ourselves comfort-ably, and we don't want other people butting in, do we? But if you'd like to stop here a bit longer — ?'

'Oh, no!' said Janey quickly. 'Not for the world! The day after to-morrow, then. And the children — '

But they had reached the hotel. The manager was standing in the broad, brilliantly lighted porch. He came down to greet them. A porter ran from the hall for their boxes.

'Well, Mr Arnold, here's Mrs Hammond at last!'

The manager led them through the hall himself and pressed the elevator-bell. Hammond knew there were business pals of his sitting at the little hall tables having a drink before dinner. But he wasn't going to risk interruption; he looked neither to the right nor the left. They could think what they pleased. If they didn't understand, the more fools they — and he stepped out of the lift, unlocked the door of their room, and shepherded Janey in. The door shut. Now, at last, they were alone together. He turned up the light. The curtains were drawn; the fire blazed. He flung his hat on to the huge bed and went towards her.

But — would you believe it! — again they were interrupted. This time it was the porter with the luggage. He made two journeys of it, leaving the door open in between, taking his time, whistling through his teeth in the corridor. Hammond paced up and down the room, tearing off his gloves, tearing off his scarf. Finally he flung his overcoat on to the bedside.

At last the fool was gone. The door clicked. Now they *were* alone. Said Hammond: 'I feel I'll never have you to myself again. These cursed people! Janey' — and he bent his flushed, eager gaze upon her — 'let's have dinner up here. If we go down to the restaurant we'll be interrupted, and then there's the confounded music' (the music he'd praised so highly, applauded so loudly last night!). 'We shan't be able to hear each other speak. Let's have something up here in front of the fire. It's too late for tea. I'll order a little supper, shall I? How does the idea strike you?'

'Do, darling!' said Janey. 'And while you're away — the children's letters — '

'Oh, later on will do!' said Hammond.

'But then we'd get it over,' said Janey. 'And I'd first have time to — '

'Oh, I needn't go down!' explained Hammond. 'I'll just ring and give the order ... you don't want to send me away, do you?'

Janey shook her head and smiled.

'But you're thinking of something else. You're worrying about something,' said Hammond. 'What is it? Come and sit here — come and sit on my knee before the fire.'

'I'll just unpin my hat,' said Janey, and she went over to the dressing-table. 'A-ah!' She gave a little cry.

'What is it?'

'Nothing, darling. I've just found the children's letters. That's all right! They will keep. No hurry now!' She turned to him, clasping them. She tucked them into her frilled blouse. She cried quickly, gaily: 'Oh, how typical this dressing-table is of you!'

'Why? What's the matter with it?' said Hammond.

'If it were floating in eternity I should say "John!" ' laughed Janey, staring at the big bottle of hair tonic, the wicker bottle of eau-de-Cologne, the two hair-brushes, and a dozen new collars tied with pink tape. 'Is this all your luggage?'

'Hang my luggage!' said Hammond; but all the same he liked being laughed at by Janey. 'Let's talk. Let's get down to things. Tell me' — and as Janey perched on his knees he leaned back and drew her into the deep, ugly chair — 'tell me you're really glad to be back, Janey.'

'Yes, darling, I am glad,' she said.

But just as when he embraced her he felt she would fly away, so Hammond never knew — never knew for dead certain that she was as glad as he was. How could he know? Would he ever know? Would he always have this craving — this pang like hunger, some-how, to make Janey so much part of him that there wasn't any of her to escape? He wanted to blot out everybody, everything. He wished now he'd turned off the light. That might have brought her nearer. And now those letters from the children rustled in her blouse. He could have chucked them into the fire.

'Janey,' he whispered.

'Yes, dear?' She lay on his breast, but so lightly, so remotely. Their breathing rose and fell together.

'Janey!'

'What is it?'

'Turn to me,' he whispered. A slow, deep flush flowed into his forehead. 'Kiss me, Janey! You kiss me!'

It seemed to him there was a tiny pause — but long enough for him to suffer torture — before her lips touched his, firmly, lightly — kissing them as she always kissed him, as though the kiss — how could he describe it? — confirmed what they were saying, signed the contract. But that wasn't what he wanted; that wasn't at all what he thirsted for. He felt suddenly, horribly tired.

'If you knew,' he said, opening his eyes, 'what it's been like — waiting to-day. I thought the boat never would come in. There we were, hanging about. What kept you so long?'

She made no answer. She was looking away from him at the fire. The flames hurried — hurried over the coals, flickered, fell.

'Not asleep, are you?' said Hammond, and he jumped her up and down.

'No,' she said. And then: 'Don't do that, dear. No, I was thinking. As a matter of fact,' she said, 'one of the passengers died last night — a man. That's what held us up. We brought him in — I mean, he wasn't buried at sea. So, of course, the ship's doctor and the shore doctor — '

'What was it?' asked Hammond uneasily. He hated to hear of death. He hated this to have happened. It was, in some queer way, as though he and Janey had met a funeral on their way to the hotel.

'Oh, it wasn't anything in the least infectious!' said Janey. She was speaking scarcely above her breath. 'It was *heart*.' A pause. 'Poor fellow!' she said. 'Quite young.' And she watched the fire flicker and fall. 'He died in my arms,' said Janey.

The blow was so sudden that Hammond thought he would faint. He couldn't move; he couldn't breathe. He felt all his strength flowing — flowing into the big dark chair, and the big dark chair held him fast, gripped him, forced him to bear it.

'What?' he said dully. 'What's that you say?'

'The end was quite peaceful,' said the small voice. 'He just' — and Hammond saw her lift her gentle hand — 'breathed his life away at the end.' And her hand fell.

'Who — else was there?' Hammond managed to ask.

'Nobody. I was alone with him.'

Ah, my God, what was she saying! What was she doing to him! This would kill him! And all the while she spoke:

'I saw the change coming and I sent the steward for the

doctor, but the doctor was too late. He couldn't have done anything, anyway.'

'But — why *you*, why *you*?' moaned Hammond.

At that Janey turned quickly, quickly searched his face.

'You don't *mind*, John, do you?' she asked. 'You don't — It's nothing to do with you and me.'

Somehow or other he managed to shake some sort of smile at her. Somehow or other he stammered: 'No — go — on, go on! I want you to tell me.'

'But, John darling — '

'Tell me, Janey!'

'There's nothing to tell,' she said, wondering. 'He was one of the first-class passengers. I saw he was very ill when he came on board … But he seemed to be so much better until yesterday. He had a severe attack in the afternoon — excitement — nervousness, I think about arriving. And after that he never recovered.'

'But why didn't the stewardess — '

'Oh, my dear — the stewardess!' said Janey. 'What would he have felt? And besides … he might have wanted to leave a message … to — '

'Didn't he?' muttered Hammond. 'Didn't he say anything?'

'No, darling, not a word!' She shook her head softly. 'All the time I was with him he was too weak … he was too weak even to move a finger … '

Janey was silent. But her words, so light, so soft, so chill, seemed to hover in the air, to rain into his breast like snow.

The fire had gone red. Now it fell in with a sharp sound and the room was colder. Cold crept up his arms. The room was huge, immense, glittering. It filled his whole world. There was the great blind bed, with his coat flung across it like some headless man saying his prayers. There was the luggage, ready to be carried away again, anywhere, tossed into trains, carted on to boats.

… 'He was too weak. He was too weak to move a finger.' And

yet he died in Janey's arms. She — who'd never — never once in all these years — never on one single solitary occasion —

No; he mustn't think of it. Madness lay in thinking of it. No, he wouldn't face it. He couldn't stand it. It was too much to bear!

And now Janey touched his tie with her fingers. She pinched the edges of the tie together.

'You're not — sorry I told you, John darling? It hasn't made you sad? It hasn't spoilt our evening — our being alone together?'

But at that he had to hide his face. He put his face into her bosom and his arms enfolded her.

Spoilt their evening! Spoilt their being alone together! They would never be alone together again.

An Ideal Family

That evening for the first time in his life, as he pressed through the swing door and descended the three broad steps to the pavement, old Mr Neave felt he was too old for the spring. Spring — warm, eager, restless — was there, waiting for him in the golden light, ready in front of everybody to run up, to blow in his white beard, to drag sweetly on his arm. And he couldn't meet her, no; he couldn't square up once more and stride off, jaunty as a young man. He was tired and, although the late sun was still shining, curiously cold, with a numbed feeling all over. Quite suddenly he hadn't the energy, he hadn't the heart to stand this gaiety and bright movement any longer; it confused him. He wanted to stand still, to wave it away with his stick, to say, 'Be off with you!' Suddenly it was a terrible effort to greet as usual — tipping his wide-awake with his stick — all the people whom he knew, the friends, acquaintances, shop-keepers, postmen, drivers. But the gay glance that went with the gesture, the kindly twinkle that seemed to say, 'I'm a match and more for any of you' — that old Mr Neave could not manage at all. He stumped along, lifting his knees high as if he were walking through air that had somehow grown heavy and solid like water. And the homeward-going crowd hurried by, the trams clanked, the light carts clattered, the big swinging cabs bowled along with that reckless, defiant indifference that one knows only in dreams …

It had been a day like other days at the office. Nothing special had happened. Harold hadn't come back from lunch until close on four. Where had he been? What had he been up to? He wasn't going to let his father know. Old Mr Neave had happened to be in the vestibule, saying good-bye to a caller, when Harold sauntered in, perfectly turned out as usual, cool, suave, smiling that peculiar little half-smile that women found so fascinating.

Ah, Harold was too handsome, too handsome by far; that had been the trouble all along. No man had a right to such eyes, such lashes and such lips; it was uncanny. As for his mother, his sisters, and the servants, it was not too much to say they made a young god of him; they worshipped Harold, they forgave him everything; and he had needed some forgiving ever since the time when he was thirteen and he had stolen his mother's purse, taken the money, and hidden the purse in the cook's bedroom. Old Mr Neave struck sharply with his stick upon the pavement edge. But it wasn't his family who spoiled Harold, he reflected, it was everybody; he had only to look and to smile, and down they went before him. So perhaps it wasn't to be wondered at that he expected the office to carry on the tradition. H'm, h'm! But it couldn't be done. No business — not even a successful, established, big paying concern — could be played with. A man had either to put his whole heart and soul into it, or it went all to pieces before his eyes …

And then Charlotte and the girls were always at him to make the whole thing over to Harold, to retire, and to spend his time enjoying himself. Enjoying himself! Old Mr Neave stopped dead under a group of ancient cabbage palms outside the Government buildings! Enjoying himself! The wind of evening shook the dark leaves to a thin airy cackle. Sitting at home, twiddling his thumbs, conscious all the while that his life's work was slipping away, dissolving, disappearing through Harold's fine fingers, while Harold smiled …

'Why will you be so unreasonable, father? There's absolutely no need for you to go to the office. It only makes it very awkward for us when people persist in saying how tired you're looking. Here's this huge house and garden. Surely you could be happy in — in — appreciating it for a change. Or you could take up some hobby.'

And Lola the baby had chimed in loftily, 'All men ought to have hobbies. It makes life impossible if they haven't.'

Well, well! He couldn't help a grim smile as painfully he began to climb the hill that led into Harcourt Avenue. Where would Lola and her sisters and Charlotte be if he'd gone in for hobbies, he'd like to know? Hobbies couldn't pay for the town house and the seaside bungalow, and their horses, and their golf, and the sixty-guinea gramophone in the music-room for them to dance to. Not that he grudged them these things. No, they were smart, good-looking girls, and Charlotte was a remarkable woman; it was natural for them to be in the swim. As a matter of fact, no other house in the town was as popular as theirs; no other family entertained so much. And how many times old Mr Neave, pushing the cigar box across the smoking-room table, had listened to praises of his wife, his girls, of himself even.

'You're an ideal family, sir, an ideal family. It's like something one reads about or sees on the stage.'

'That's all right, my boy,' old Mr Neave would reply. 'Try one of those; I think you'll like them. And if you care to smoke in the garden, you'll find the girls on the lawn, I dare say.'

That was why the girls had never married, so people said. They could have married anybody. But they had too good a time at home. They were too happy together, the girls and Charlotte. H'm, h'm! Well, well! Perhaps so …

By this time he had walked the length of fashionable Harcourt Avenue; he had reached the corner house, their house. The carriage gates were pushed back; there were fresh marks of wheels on the drive. And then he faced the big white-painted house, with its wide-open windows, its tulle curtains floating outwards, its blue jars of hyacinths on the broad sills. On either side of the carriage porch their hydrangeas — famous in the town — were coming into flower; the pinkish, bluish masses of flower lay like light among the spreading leaves. And somehow, it seemed to old Mr Neave that the house and the flowers, and even the fresh marks on the drive, were saying, 'There is young life here. There are girls — '

The hall, as always, was dusky with wraps, parasols, gloves, piled on the oak chests. From the music-room sounded the piano, quick, loud and impatient. Through the drawing-room door that was ajar voices floated.

'And were there ices?' came from Charlotte. Then the creak, creak of her rocker.

'Ices!' cried Ethel. 'My dear mother you never saw such ices. Only two kinds. And one a common little strawberry shop ice, in a sopping wet frill.'

'The food altogether was too appalling,' came from Marion.

'Still, it's rather early for ices,' said Charlotte easily.

'But why, if one has them at all ... ' began Ethel.

'Oh, quite so, darling,' crooned Charlotte.

Suddenly the music-room door opened and Lola dashed out. She started, she nearly screamed, at the sight of old Mr Neave.

'Gracious, father! What a fright you gave me! Have you just come home? Why isn't Charles here to help you off with your coat?'

Her cheeks were crimson from playing, her eyes glittered, the hair fell over her forehead. And she breathed as though she had come running through the dark and was frightened. Old Mr Neave stared at his youngest daughter; he felt he had never seen her before. So that was Lola, was it? But she seemed to have forgotten her father; it was not for him that she was waiting there. Now she put the tip of her crumpled handkerchief between her teeth and tugged at it angrily. The telephone rang. A-ah! Lola gave a cry like a sob and dashed past him. The door of the telephone-room slammed, and at the same moment Charlotte called, 'Is that you, father?'

'You're tired again,' said Charlotte reproachfully, and she stopped the rocker and offered him her warm plum-like cheek. Bright-haired Ethel pecked his beard; Marion's lips brushed his ear.

'Did you walk back, father?' asked Charlotte.

'Yes, I walked home,' said old Mr Neave, and he sank into one of the immense drawing-room chairs.

'But why didn't you take a cab?' said Ethel. 'There are hundreds of cabs about at that time.'

'My dear Ethel,' cried Marion, 'if father prefers to tire himself out, I really don't see what business of ours it is to interfere.'

'Children, children!' coaxed Charlotte.

But Marion wouldn't be stopped. 'No, mother, you spoil father, and it's not right. You ought to be stricter with him. He's very naughty.' She laughed her hard, bright laugh and patted her hair in a mirror. Strange! When she was a little girl she had such a soft, hesitating voice; she had even stuttered, and now, whatever she said — even if it was only 'Jam, please, father' — it rang out as though she were on the stage.

'Did Harold leave the office before you, dear?' asked Charlotte, beginning to rock again.

'I'm not sure,' said old Mr Neave.

'I'm not sure. I didn't see him after four o'clock.'

'He said — ' began Charlotte.

But at that moment Ethel, who was twitching over the leaves of some paper or other, ran to her mother and sank down beside her chair.

'There, you see,' she cried. 'That's what I mean, mummy. Yellow, with touches of silver. Don't you agree?'

'Give it to me, love,' said Charlotte. She fumbled for her tortoise-shell spectacles and put them on, gave the page a little dab with her plump small fingers, and pursed up her lips. 'Very sweet!' she crooned vaguely; she looked at Ethel over her spectacles. 'But I shouldn't have the train.'

'Not the train!' wailed Ethel tragically. 'But the train's the whole point.'

'Here, mother, let me decide.' Marion snatched the paper playfully from Charlotte. 'I agree with mother,' she cried triumphantly. 'The train overweights it.'

Old Mr Neave, forgotten, sank into the broad lap of his chair, and, dozing, heard them as though he dreamed. There was no doubt about it, he was tired out; he had lost his hold. Even Charlotte and the girls were too much for him to-night. They were too ... too ... But all his drowsing brain could think of was — too *rich* for him. And somewhere at the back of everything he was watching a little withered ancient man climbing up endless flights of stairs. Who was he?

'I shan't dress to-night,' he muttered.

'What do you say, father?'

'Eh, what, what?' Old Mr Neave woke with a start and stared across at them. 'I shan't dress to-night,' he repeated.

'But, father, we've got Lucile coming, and Henry Davenport, and Mrs Teddie Walker.'

'It will look so *very* out of the picture.'

'Don't you feel well, dear?'

'You needn't make any effort. What is Charles *for*?'

'But if you're really not up to it,' Charlotte wavered.

'Very well! Very well!' Old Mr Neave got up and went to join that little old climbing fellow just as far as his dressing-room ...

There young Charles was waiting for him. Carefully, as though everything depended on it, he was tucking a towel round the hot-water can. Young Charles had been a favourite of his ever since as a little red-faced boy he had come into the house to look after the fires. Old Mr Neave lowered himself into the cane lounge by the window, stretched out his legs, and made his little evening joke, 'Dress him up, Charles!' And Charles, breathing intensely and frowning, bent forward to take the pin out of his tie.

H'm, h'm! Well, well! It was pleasant by the open window, very pleasant — a fine mild evening. They were cutting the grass on the tennis court below; he heard the soft churr of the mower. Soon the girls would begin their tennis parties again. And at the thought he seemed to hear Marion's voice ring out, 'Good for you, partner ... Oh, *played*, partner ... Oh, *very* nice indeed.' Then Charlotte call-ing from the veranda, 'Where is Harold?' And Ethel, 'He's certain-ly not here, mother.' And Charlotte's vague, 'He said — '

Old Mr Neave sighed, got up, and putting one hand under his beard, he took the comb from young Charles, and carefully combed the white beard over.

Charles gave him a folded handkerchief, his watch and seals, and spectacle case.

'That will do, my lad.' The door shut, he sank back, he was alone ...

And now that little ancient fellow was climbing down end-less flights that led to a glittering, gay dining-room. What legs he had! They were like a spider's — thin, withered.

'You're an ideal family, sir, an ideal family.'

But if that were true, why didn't Charlotte or the girls stop him? Why was he all alone, climbing up and down? Where was Harold? Ah, it was no good expecting anything from Harold. Down, down went the little old spider, and then, to his horror, old Mr Neave saw him slip past the dining-room and make for the porch, the dark drive, the carriage gates, the office. Stop him, stop him somebody!

Old Mr Neave started up. It was dark in his dressing-room; the window shone pale. How long had he been asleep? He listened, and through the big, airy, darkened house there floated far-away voices, far-away sounds. Perhaps, he thought vaguely, he had been asleep for a long time. He'd been forgotten. What had all this to do with him — this house and Charlotte, the girls and Harold — what did he know about them? They were strangers to him. Life had passed him by. Charlotte was not his wife. His wife!

... A dark porch, half hidden by a passion-vine, that drooped sorrowful, mournful, as though it understood. Small, warm arms were round his neck. A face, little and pale, lifted to his, and a voice breathed, 'Good-bye, my treasure.'

My treasure! 'Good-bye, my treasure!' Which of them had spoken? Why had they said good-bye? There had been some terrible mistake. *She* was his wife, that little pale girl, and all the rest of his life had been a dream.

Then the door opened, and young Charles, standing in the light, put his hands by his side and shouted like a young soldier, 'Dinner is on the table, sir!'

'I'm coming, I'm coming,' said old Mr Neave.

Her First Ball

Exactly when the ball began Leila would have found it hard to say. Perhaps her first real partner was the cab. It did not matter that she shared the cab with the Sheridan girls and their brother. She sat back in her own little corner of it, and the bolster on which her hand rested felt like the sleeve of an unknown young man's dress suit; and away they bowled, past waltzing lamp-posts and houses and fences and trees.

'Have you really never been to a ball before, Leila? But, my child, how too weird' — cried the Sheridan girls.

'Our nearest neighbour was fifteen miles,' said Leila softly, gently opening and shutting her fan.

Oh, dear, how hard it was to be indifferent like the others! She tried not to smile too much; she tried not to care. But every single thing was so new and exciting ... Meg's tuberoses, Jose's long loop of amber, Laura's little dark head, pushing above her white fur like a flower through snow. She would remember for ever. It even gave her a pang to see her cousin Laurie throw away the wisps of tissue paper he pulled from the fastenings of his new gloves. She would like to have kept those wisps as a keepsake, as a remembrance. Laurie leaned forward and put his hand on Laura's knee.

'Look here, darling,' he said. 'The third and the ninth as usual. Twig?'

Oh, how marvellous to have a brother! In her excitement Leila felt that if there had been time, if it hadn't been impossible, she couldn't have helped crying because she was an only child, and no brother had ever said 'Twig?' to her; no sister would ever say, as Meg said to Jose that moment, 'I've never known your hair go up more successfully than it has to-night!'

But, of course, there was no time. They were at the drill hall already; there were cabs in front of them and cabs behind. The road was bright on either side with moving fan-like lights, and on the pavement gay couples seemed to float through the air; little satin shoes chased each other like birds.

'Hold on to me, Leila; you'll get lost,' said Laura.

'Come on, girls, let's make a dash for it,' said Laurie.

Leila put two fingers on Laura's pink velvet cloak, and they were somehow lifted past the big golden lantern, carried along the passage, and pushed into the little room marked 'Ladies'. Here the crowd was so great there was hardly space to take off their things; the noise was deafening. Two benches on either side were stacked high with wraps. Two old women in white aprons ran up and down tossing fresh armfuls. And everybody was pressing forward trying to get at the little dressing-table and mirror at the far end.

A great quivering jet of gas lighted the ladies' room. It couldn't wait; it was dancing already. When the door opened again and there came a burst of tuning from the drill hall, it leaped almost to the ceiling.

Dark girls, fair girls were patting their hair, tying ribbons again, tucking handkerchiefs down the fronts of their bodices, smoothing marble-white gloves. And because they were all laughing it seemed to Leila that they were all lovely.

'Aren't there any invisible hair-pins?' cried a voice. 'How most extraordinary! I can't see a single invisible hair-pin.'

'Powder my back, there's a darling,' cried some one else.

'But I must have a needle and cotton. I've torn simply miles and miles of the frill,' wailed a third.

Then, 'Pass them along, pass them along!' The straw basket of programmes was tossed from arm to arm. Darling little pink-and-silver programmes, with pink pencils and fluffy tassels. Leila's fingers shook as she took one out of the basket. She wanted to ask some one, 'Am I meant to have one too?' but she had just time to read: 'Waltz 3. *Two, Two in a Canoe*. Polka 4. *Making the Feathers Fly*,' when Meg cried, 'Ready, Leila?' and they pressed their way through the crush in the passage towards the big double doors of the drill hall.

Dancing had not begun yet, but the band had stopped tuning, and the noise was so great it seemed that when it did begin to play it would never be heard. Leila, pressing close to Meg, looking over Meg's shoulder, felt that even the little quivering coloured flags strung across the ceiling were talking. She quite forgot to be shy; she forgot how in the middle of dressing she had sat down on the bed with one shoe off and one shoe on and begged her mother to ring up her cousins and say she couldn't go after all. And the rush of longing she had had to be sitting on the verandah of their forsaken up-country home, listening to the baby owls crying 'More pork' in the moonlight, was changed to a rush of joy so sweet that it was hard to bear alone. She clutched her fan, and, gazing at the gleaming, golden floor, the azaleas, the lanterns, the stage at one end with its red carpet and gilt chairs and the band in a corner, she thought breathlessly, 'How heavenly; how simply heavenly!'

All the girls stood grouped together at one side of the doors, the men at the other, and the chaperones in dark dresses, smiling rather foolishly, walked with little careful steps over the polished floor towards the stage.

'This is my little country cousin Leila. Be nice to her. Find her partners; she's under my wing,' said Meg, going up to one girl after another.

Strange faces smiled at Leila — sweetly, vaguely. Strange voices answered, 'Of course, my dear.' But Leila felt the girls didn't really see her. They were looking towards the men. Why didn't the men begin? What were they waiting for? There they stood, smoothing their gloves, patting their glossy hair and smiling among themselves. Then, quite suddenly, as if they had only just made up their minds that that was what they had to do, the men came gliding over the parquet. There was a joyful flutter among the girls. A tall, fair man flew up to Meg, seized her programme, scribbled something; Meg passed him on to Leila. 'May I have the pleasure?' He ducked and smiled. There came a dark man wearing an eyeglass, then cousin Laurie with a friend, and Laura with a little freckled fellow whose tie was crooked. Then quite an old man — fat, with a big bald patch on his head — took her programme and murmured, 'Let me see, let me see!' And he was a long time comparing his programme, which looked black with names, with hers. It seemed to give him so much trouble that Leila was ashamed. 'Oh, please don't bother,' she said eagerly. But instead of replying the fat man wrote something, glanced at her again. 'Do I remember this bright little face?' he said softly. 'Is it known to me of yore?' At that moment the band began playing; the fat man disappeared. He was tossed away on a great wave of music that came flying over the gleaming floor, breaking the groups up into couples, scattering them, sending them spinning ...

Leila had learned to dance at boarding school. Every Saturday afternoon the boarders were hurried off to a little corrugated iron mission hall where Miss Eccles (of London) held her 'select' classes. But the difference between that dusty-smelling hall — with calico texts on the walls, the poor terrified little woman in a brown velvet toque with rabbit's ears thumping the cold piano, Miss Eccles poking the girls' feet with her long white wand — and this was so tremendous that Leila was sure if her partner didn't come and she had to listen to that marvellous music and to watch the others sliding, gliding over the golden floor, she would die at least, or faint, or lift her arms and fly out of one of those dark windows that showed the stars.

'Ours, I think — ' Some one bowed, smiled, and offered her his arm; she hadn't to die after all. Some one's hand pressed her waist, and she floated away like a flower that is tossed into a pool.

'Quite a good floor, isn't it?' drawled a faint voice close to her ear.

'I think it's most beautifully slippery,' said Leila.

'Pardon!' The faint voice sounded surprised. Leila said it again. And there was a tiny pause before the voice echoed, 'Oh, quite!' and she was swung round again.

He steered so beautifully. That was the great difference between dancing with girls and men, Leila decided. Girls banged into each other, and stamped on each other's feet; the girl who was gentleman always clutched you so.

The azaleas were separate flowers no longer; they were pink and white flags steaming by.

'Were you at the Bells' last week?' the voice came again. It sounded tired. Leila wondered whether she ought to ask him if he would like to stop.

'No, this is my first dance,' said she.

Her partner gave a little gasping laugh. 'Oh, I say,' he protested.

'Yes, it is really the first dance I've ever been to.' Leila was most fervent. It was such a relief to be able to tell somebody. 'You see, I've lived in the country all my life up till now ... '

At that moment the music stopped, and they went to sit on two chairs against the wall. Leila tucked her pink satin feet under and fanned herself, while she blissfully watched the other couples passing and disappearing through the swing doors.

'Enjoying yourself, Leila?' asked Jose, nodding her golden head.

Laura passed and gave her the faintest little wink; it made Leila wonder for a moment whether she was quite grown up after all. Certainly her partner did not say very much. He coughed, tucked his handkerchief away, pulled down his waistcoat, took a minute thread off his sleeve. But it didn't matter. Almost immediately the band started, and her second partner seemed to spring from the ceiling.

'Floor's not bad,' said the new voice. Did one always begin with the floor? And then, 'Were you at the Neaves' on Tuesday?' And again Leila explained. Perhaps it was a little strange that her partners were not more interested. For it was thrilling. Her first ball! She was only at the beginning of everything. It seemed to her that she had never known what the night was like before. Up till now it had been dark, silent, beautiful very often — oh, yes — but mournful somehow. Solemn. And now it would never be like that again — it had opened dazzling bright.

'Care for an ice?' said her partner. And they went through the swing doors, down the passage, to the supper room. Her cheeks burned, she was fearfully thirsty. How sweet the ices looked on little glass plates, and how cold the frosted spoon was, iced too!

And when they came back to the hall there was the fat man waiting for her by the door. It gave her quite a shock again to see how old he was; he ought to have been on the stage with the fathers and mothers. And when Leila compared him with her other partners he looked shabby. His waistcoat was creased, there was a button off his glove, his coat looked as if it was dusty with French chalk.

'Come along, little lady,' said the fat man. He scarcely troubled to clasp her, and they moved away so gently, it was more like walking than dancing. But he said not a word about the floor. 'Your first dance, isn't it?' he murmured.

'How *did* you know?'

'Ah,' said the fat man, 'that's what it is to be old!' He wheezed faintly as he steered her past an awkward couple. 'You see, I've been doing this kind of thing for the last thirty years.'

'Thirty years?' cried Leila. Twelve years before she was born!

'It hardly bears thinking about, does it?' said the fat man gloomily. Leila looked at his bald head, and she felt quite sorry for him.

'I think it's marvellous to be still going on,' she said kindly.

'Kind little lady,' said the fat man, and he pressed her a little closer, and hummed a bar of the waltz. 'Of course,' he said, 'you can't hope to last anything like as long as that. No-o,' said the fat man, 'long before that you'll be sitting up there on the stage, looking on, in your nice black velvet. And these pretty arms will have turned into little short fat ones, and you'll beat time with such a different kind of fan — a black bony one.' The fat man seemed to shudder. 'And you'll smile away like the poor old dears up there, and point to your daughter, and tell the elderly lady next to you how some dreadful man tried to kiss her at the club ball. And your heart will ache, ache' — the fat man squeezed her closer still, as if he really was sorry for that poor heart — 'because no one wants to kiss you now. And you'll say how unpleasant these polished floors are to walk on, how dangerous they are. Eh, Mademoiselle Twinkletoes?' said the fat man softly.

Leila gave a light little laugh, but she did not feel like laughing. Was it — could it all be true? It sounded terribly true. Was this first ball only the beginning of her last ball after all? At that the music seemed to change; it sounded sad, sad; it rose upon a great sigh. Oh, how quickly things changed! Why didn't happiness last for ever? For ever wasn't a bit too long.

'I want to stop,' she said in a breathless voice. The fat man led her to the door.

'No,' she said, 'I won't go outside. I won't sit down. I'll just stand here, thank you.' She leaned against the wall, tapping with her foot, pulling up her gloves and trying to smile. But deep inside her a little girl threw her pinafore over her head and sobbed. Why had he spoiled it all?

'I say, you know,' said the fat man, 'you musn't take me seriously, little lady.'

'As if I should!' said Leila, tossing her small dark head and sucking her underlip ...

Again the couples paraded. The swing doors opened and shut. Now new music was given out by the bandmaster. But Leila didn't want to dance any more. She wanted to be home, or sitting on the verandah listening to those baby owls. When she looked through the dark windows at the stars, they had long beams like wings ...

But presently a soft, melting, ravishing tune began, and a young man with curly hair bowed before her. She would have to dance, out of politeness, until she could find Meg. Very stiffly she walked into the middle; very haughtily she put her hand on his sleeve. But in one minute, in one turn, her feet glided, glided. The lights, the azaleas, the dresses, the pink faces, the velvet chairs, all became one beautiful flying wheel. And when her next partner bumped into the fat man and he said, 'Par*don*,' she smiled at him more radiantly than ever. She didn't even recognize him again.

At the Bay

I

Very early morning. The sun was not yet risen, and the whole of Crescent Bay was hidden under a white sea-mist. The big bush-covered hills at the back were smothered. You could not see where they ended and the paddocks and bungalows began. The sandy road was gone and the paddocks and bungalows the other side of it; there were no white dunes covered with reddish grass beyond them; there was nothing to mark which was beach and where was the sea. A heavy dew had fallen. The grass was blue. Big drops hung on the bushes and just did not fall; the silvery, fluffy toi-toi was limp on its long stalks, and all the marigolds and the pinks in the bungalow gardens were bowed to the earth with wetness. Drenched were the cold fuchsias, round pearls of dew lay on the flat nasturtium leaves. It looked as though the sea had beaten up softly in the darkness, as though one immense wave had come rippling, rippling — how far? Perhaps if you had waked up in the middle of the night you might have seen a big fish flicking in at the window and gone again ...

Ah-Aah! sounded the sleepy sea. And from the bush there came the sound of little streams flowing, quickly, lightly, slipping between the smooth stones, gushing into ferny basins and out again; and there was the splashing of big drops on large leaves, and something else — what was it? — a faint stirring and shaking, the snapping of a twig and then such silence that it seemed some one was listening.

Round the corner of Crescent Bay, between the piled-up masses of broken rock, a flock of sheep came pattering. They were huddled together, a small, tossing, woolly mass, and their thin, stick-like legs trotted along quickly as if the cold and the quiet had frightened them. Behind them an old sheep-dog, his soaking paws covered with sand, ran along with his nose to the ground, but carelessly, as if thinking of something else. And then in the rocky gateway the shepherd himself appeared. He was a lean, upright old man, in a frieze coat that was covered with a web of tiny drops, velvet trousers tied under the knee, and a wide-awake with a folded blue handkerchief round the brim. One hand was crammed into his belt, the other grasped a beautifully smooth yellow stick. And as he walked, taking his time, he kept up a very soft light whistling, an airy, far-away fluting that sounded mournful and tender. The old dog cut an ancient caper or two and then drew up sharp, ashamed of his levity, and walked a few dignified paces by his master's side. The sheep ran forward in little pattering rushes; they began to bleat, and ghostly flocks and herds answered them from under the sea. 'Baa! Baa!' For a time they seemed to be always on the same piece of ground. There ahead was stretched the sandy road with shallow puddles, the same soaking bushes showed on either side and the same shadowy palings. Then something immense came into view; an enormous shock-haired giant with his arms stretched out. It was the big gum-tree outside Mrs Stubbs's shop, and as they passed by there was a strong whiff of eucalyptus. And now big spots of light gleamed in the mist. The shepherd stopped whistling; he rubbed his red nose and wet beard on his wet sleeve and, screwing up his eyes, glanced in the direction of the sea. The sun was rising. It was marvellous how quickly the mist thinned, sped away, dissolved from the shallow plain, rolled up from the bush and was gone as if in a hurry to escape; big twists and curls jostled and shouldered each other as the silvery beams broadened. The far-away sky — a bright, pure blue — was reflected in the puddles, and the drops, swimming along the telegraph wires, flashed into points of light. Now the leaping, glittering sea was so bright it made one's eyes ache to look at it. The shepherd drew a pipe, the bowl as small as an acorn, out of his breast pocket, fumbled for a chunk of speckled tobacco, pared off a few shavings and stuffed the bowl. He was a grave, fine-looking old man. As he lit up and the blue smoke wreathed his head, the dog, watching, looked proud of him.

'Baa! Baaa!' The sheep spread out into a fan. They were just clear of the summer colony before the first sleeper turned over and lifted a drowsy head; their cry sounded in the dreams of little children ... who lifted their arms to drag down, to cuddle the darling little woolly lambs of sleep. Then the first inhabitant appeared; it was the Burnells' cat Florrie, sitting on the gatepost, far too early as usual, looking for their milk-girl. When she saw the old sheep-dog she sprang up quickly, arched her back, drew in her tabby head, and seemed to give a little fastidious shiver. 'Ugh! What a coarse, revolting creature!' said Florrie. But the old sheepdog, not looking up, waggled past, flinging out his legs from side to side. Only one of his ears twitched to prove that he saw, and thought her a silly young female.

The breeze of morning lifted in the bush and the smell of leaves and wet black earth mingled with the sharp smell of the sea. Myriads of birds were singing. A goldfinch flew over the shepherd's head and, perching on the tiptop of a spray, it turned to the sun, ruffling its small breast feathers. And now they had passed the fisherman's hut, passed the charred-looking little *whare* where Leila the milk-girl lived with her old Gran. The sheep strayed over a yellow swamp and Wag, the sheep-dog, padded after, rounded them up and headed them for the steeper, narrower rocky pass that led out of Crescent Bay and towards Daylight Cove. 'Baa! Baaa!' Faint the cry came as they rocked along the fast-drying road. The shepherd put away his pipe, dropping it into his breast-pocket so that the little bowl hung over. And straightway the soft airy whistling began again. Wag ran out along a ledge of rock after something that smelled, and ran back again disgusted. Then pushing, nudging, hurrying, the sheep rounded the bend and the shepherd followed after out of sight.

II

A few moments later the back door of one of the bungalows opened, and a figure in a broad-striped bathing suit flung down the paddock, cleared the stile, rushed through the tussock grass into the hollow, staggered up the sandy hillock, and raced for dear life over the big porous stones, over the cold, wet pebbles, on to the hard sand that gleamed like oil. Splish-Splosh! Splish-Splosh! The water bubbled round his legs as Stanley Burnell waded out exulting. First man in as usual! He'd beaten them all again. And he swooped down to souse his head and neck.

'Hail, brother! All hail, Thou Mighty One!' A velvety bass voice came booming over the water.

Great Scott! Damnation take it! Stanley lifted up to see a dark head bobbing far out and an arm lifted. It was Jonathan Trout — there before him! 'Glorious morning!' sang the voice.

'Yes, very fine!' said Stanley briefly. Why the dickens didn't the fellow stick to his part of the sea? Why should he come barging over to this exact spot? Stanley gave a kick, a lunge and struck out, swimming overarm. But Jonathan was a match for him. Up he came, his black hair sleek on his forehead, his short beard sleek.

'I had an extraordinary dream last night!' he shouted.

What was the matter with the man? This mania for conversation irritated Stanley beyond words. And it was always the same — always some piffle about a dream he'd had, or some cranky idea he'd got hold of, or some rot he'd been reading. Stanley turned over on his back and kicked with his legs till he was a living waterspout. But even then ... 'I dreamed I was hanging over a terrifically high cliff, shouting to some one below.' You would be! thought Stanley. He could stick no more of it. He stopped splashing. 'Look here, Trout,' he said, 'I'm in rather a hurry this morning.'

'You're WHAT?' Jonathan was so surprised — or pretended to be — that he sank under the water, then reappeared again blowing.

'All I mean is,' said Stanley, 'I've no time to — to — to fool about. I want to get this over. I'm in a hurry. I've work to do this morning — see?'

Jonathan was gone before Stanley had finished. 'Pass, friend!' said the bass voice gently, and he slid away through the water with scarcely a ripple. ... But curse the fellow! He'd ruined Stanley's bathe. What an unpractical idiot the man was! Stanley struck out to sea again, and then as quickly swam in again, and away he rushed up the beach. He felt cheated.

Jonathan stayed a little longer in the water. He floated, gently moving his hands like fins, and letting the sea rock his long, skinny body. It was curious, but in spite of everything he was fond of Stanley Burnell. True, he had a fiendish desire to tease him sometimes, to poke fun at him, but at bottom he was sorry for the fellow. There was something pathetic in his determination to make a job of everything. You couldn't help feeling he'd be caught out one day, and then what an almighty cropper he'd come! At that moment an immense wave lifted Jonathan, rode past him, and broke along the beach with a joyful sound. What a beauty! And now there came another. That was the way to live — carelessly, recklessly, spending oneself. He got on to his feet and began to wade towards the shore, pressing his toes into the firm, wrinkled sand. To take things easy, not to fight against the ebb and flow of life, but to give way to it — that was what was needed. It was this tension that was all wrong. To live — to live! And the perfect morning, so fresh and fair, basking in the light, as though laughing at its own beauty, seemed to whisper, 'Why not?'

But now he was out of the water Jonathan turned blue with cold. He ached all over; it was as though some one was wringing the blood out of him. And stalking up the beach, shivering, all his muscles tight, he too felt his bathe was spoilt. He'd stayed in too long.

III

Beryl was alone in the living-room when Stanley appeared, wearing a blue serge suit, a stiff collar and a spotted tie. He looked almost uncannily clean and brushed; he was going to town for the day. Dropping into his chair, he pulled out his watch and put it beside his plate.

'I've just got twenty-five minutes,' he said. 'You might go and see if the porridge is ready, Beryl?'

'Mother's just gone for it,' said Beryl. She sat down at the table and poured out his tea.

'Thanks!' Stanley took a sip. 'Hallo!' he said in an astonished voice, 'you've forgotten the sugar.'

'Oh, sorry!' But even then Beryl didn't help him; she pushed the basin across. What did this mean? As Stanley helped himself his blue eyes widened; they seemed to quiver. He shot a quick glance at his sister-in-law and leaned back.

'Nothing wrong, is there?' he asked carelessly, fingering his collar.

Beryl's head was bent; she turned her plate in her fingers.

'Nothing,' said her light voice. Then she too looked up, and smiled at Stanley. 'Why should there be?'

'O-oh! No reason at all as far as I know. I thought you seemed rather — '

At that moment the door opened and the three little girls appeared, each carrying a porridge plate. They were dressed alike in blue jerseys and knickers; their brown legs were bare, and each had her hair plaited and pinned up in what was called a horse's tail. Behind them came Mrs Fairfield with the tray.

'Carefully, children,' she warned. But they were taking the very greatest care. They loved being allowed to carry things. 'Have you said good morning to your father?'

'Yes, grandma.' They settled themselves on the bench opposite Stanley and Beryl.

'Good morning, Stanley!' Old Mrs Fairfield gave him his plate.

'Morning, mother! How's the boy?'

'Splendid! He only woke up once last night. What a perfect morning!' The old woman paused, her hand on the loaf of bread, to gaze out of the open door into the garden. The sea sounded. Through the wide-open window streamed the sun on to the yellow varnished walls and bare floor. Everything on the table flashed and glittered. In the middle there was an old salad bowl filled with yellow and red nasturtiums. She smiled, and a look of deep content shone in her eyes.

'You might *cut* me a slice of that bread, mother,' said Stanley. 'I've only twelve and a half minutes before the coach passes. Has anyone given my shoes to the servant girl?'

'Yes, they're ready for you.' Mrs Fairfield was quite unruffled.

'Oh, Kezia! Why are you such a messy child!' cried Beryl despairingly.

'Me, Aunt Beryl?' Kezia stared at her. What had she done now? She had only dug a river down the middle of her porridge, filled it, and was eating the banks away. But she did that every single morning, and no one had said a word up till now.

'Why can't you eat your food properly like Isabel and Lottie?' How unfair grownups are!

'But Lottie always makes a floating island, don't you, Lottie?'

'I don't,' said Isabel smartly. 'I just sprinkle mine with sugar and put on the milk and finish it. Only babies play with their food.'

Stanley pushed back his chair and got up.

'Would you get me those shoes, mother? And, Beryl, if you've finished, I wish you'd cut down to the gate and stop the coach. Run in to your mother, Isabel, and ask her where my bowler hat's been put. Wait a minute — have you children been playing with my stick?'

'No, father!'

'But I put it here,' Stanley began to bluster. 'I remember distinctly putting it in this corner. Now, who's had it? There's no time to lose. Look sharp! The stick's got to be found.'

Even Alice, the servant-girl, was drawn into the chase. 'You haven't been using it to poke the kitchen fire with by any chance?'

Stanley dashed into the bedroom where Linda was lying. 'Most extraordinary thing. I can't keep a single possession to myself. They've made away with my stick, now!'

'Stick dear? What stick?' Linda's vagueness on these occasions could not be real, Stanley decided. Would nobody sympathize with him?

'Coach! Coach, Stanley!' Beryl's voice cried from the gate.

Stanley waved his arm to Linda. 'No time to say good-bye!' he cried. And he meant that as a punishment to her.

He snatched his bowler hat, dashed out of the house, and swung down the garden path. Yes, the coach was there waiting, and Beryl, leaning over the open gate, was laughing up at somebody or other just as if nothing had happened. The heartlessness of women! The way they took it for granted it was your job to slave away for them while they didn't even take the trouble to see that your walking-stick wasn't lost. Kelly trailed his whip across the horses.

'Good-bye, Stanley,' called Beryl, sweetly and gaily. It was easy enough to say good-bye! And there she stood, idle, shading her eyes with her hand. The worst of it was Stanley had to shout good-bye too, for the sake of appearances. Then he saw her turn, give a little skip and run back to the house. She was glad to be rid of him!

Yes, she was thankful. Into the living-room she ran and called 'He's gone!' Linda cried from her room: 'Beryl! Has Stanley gone?' Old Mrs Fairfield appeared, carrying the boy in his little flannel coatee.

'Gone?'

'Gone!'

Oh, the relief, the difference it made to have the man out of the house. Their very voices were changed as they called to one another; they sounded warm and loving and as if they shared a secret. Beryl went over to the table. 'Have another cup of tea, mother. It's still hot.' She wanted, somehow, to celebrate the fact that they could do what they liked now. There was no man to disturb them; the whole perfect day was theirs.

'No, thank you, child,' said old Mrs Fairfield, but the way at that moment she tossed the boy up and said 'a-goos-a-goos-a-ga!' to him meant that she felt the same. The little girls ran into the paddock like chickens let out of a coop.

Even Alice, the servant-girl, washing up the dishes in the kitchen, caught the infection and used the precious tank water in a perfectly reckless fashion.

'Oh, these men!' said she, and she plunged the teapot into the bowl and held it under the water even after it had stopped bubbling, as if it too was a man and drowning was too good for them.

IV

'Wait for me, Isa-bel! Kezia, wait for me!'

There was poor little Lottie, left behind again, because she found it so fearfully hard to get over the stile by herself. When she stood on the first step her knees began to wobble; she grasped the post. Then you had to put one leg over. But which leg? She never could decide. And when she did finally put one leg over with a sort of stamp of despair — then the feeling was awful. She was half in the paddock still and half in the tussock grass. She clutched the post desperately and lifted up her voice. 'Wait for me!'

'No, don't you wait for her, Kezia!' said Isabel. 'She's such a little silly. She's always making a fuss. Come on!' And she tugged

Kezia's jersey. 'You can use my bucket if you come with me,' she said kindly. 'It's bigger than yours.' But Kezia couldn't leave Lottie all by herself. She ran back to her. By this time Lottie was very red in the face and breathing heavily.

'Here, put your other foot over,' said Kezia.

'Where?'

Lottie looked down at Kezia as if from a mountain height.

'Here where my hand is.' Kezia patted the place.

'Oh, *there* do you mean?' Lottie gave a deep sigh and put the second foot over.

'Now — sort of turn round and sit down and slide,' said Kezia.

'But there's nothing to sit down *on*, Kezia,' said Lottie.

She managed it at last, and once it was over she shook herself and began to beam.

'I'm getting better at climbing over stiles, aren't I, Kezia?'

Lottie's was a very hopeful nature.

The pink and the blue sunbonnet followed Isabel's bright red sunbonnet up that sliding, slipping hill. At the top they paused to decide where to go and to have a good stare at who was there already. Seen from behind, standing against the skyline, gesticulating largely with their spades, they looked like minute puzzled explorers.

The whole family of Samuel Josephs was there already with their lady-help, who sat on a camp-stool and kept order with a whistle that she wore tied round her neck, and a small cane with which she directed operations. The Samuel Josephs never played by themselves or managed their own game. If they did, it ended in the boys pouring water down the girls' necks or the girls trying to put little black crabs into the boys' pockets. So Mrs S. J. and the poor lady-help drew up what she called a 'brogramme' every morning to keep them 'abused and out of bischief'. It was all competitions or races or round games. Everything began with a piercing blast of the lady-help's whistle and ended with another. There were even prizes — large, rather dirty paper parcels which the lady-help with a sour little smile drew out of a bulging string kit. The Samuel Josephs fought fearfully for the prizes and cheated and pinched one another's arms — they were all expert pinchers. The only time the Burnell children ever played with them Kezia had got a prize, and when she undid three bits of paper she found a very small rusty button-hook. She couldn't understand why they made such a fuss ...

But they never played with the Samuel Josephs now or even went to their parties. The Samuel Josephs were always giving children's parties at the Bay and there was always the same food. A big washhand basin of very brown fruit-salad, buns cut into four and a washhand jug full of something the lady-help called 'Limmonadear'. And you went away in the evening with half the frill torn off your frock or something spilled all down the front of your open-work pinafore, leaving the Samuel Josephs leaping like savages on their lawn. No. They were too awful.

On the other side of the beach, close down to the water, two little boys, their knickers rolled up, twinkled like spiders. One was digging, the other pattered in and out of the water, filling a small bucket. They were the Trout boys, Pip and Rags. But Pip was so busy digging and Rags was so busy helping that they didn't see their little cousins until they were quite close.

'Look!' said Pip. 'Look what I've discovered.' And he showed them an old, wet, squashed-looking boot. The three little girls stared.

'Whatever are you going to do with it?' asked Kezia.

'Keep it, of course!' Pip was very scornful. 'It's a find — see?'

Yes, Kezia saw that. All the same ...

'There's lots of things buried in the sand,' explained Pip. 'They get chucked up from wrecks. Treasure. Why — you might find — '

'But why does Rags have to keep on pouring water in?' asked Lottie.

'Oh, that's to moisten it,' said Pip, 'to make the work a bit easier. Keep it up, Rags.'

And good little Rags ran up and down, pouring in the water that turned brown like cocoa.

'Here, shall I show you what I found yesterday?' said Pip mysteriously, and he stuck his spade into the sand. 'Promise not to tell.'

They promised.

'Say, cross my heart straight dinkum.'

The little girls said it.

Pip took something out of his pocket, rubbed it a long time on the front of his jersey, then breathed on it and rubbed it again.

'Now turn round!' he ordered.

They turned round.

'All look the same way! Keep still! Now!'

And his hand opened; he held up to the light something that flashed, that winked, that was a most lovely green.

'It's a nemeral,' said Pip solemnly.

'Is it really, Pip?' Even Isabel was impressed.

The lovely green thing seemed to dance in Pip's fingers. Aunt Beryl had a nemeral in a ring, but it was a very small one. This one was as big as a star and far more beautiful.

V

As the morning lengthened whole parties appeared over the sandhills and came down on the beach to bathe. It was understood that at eleven o'clock the women and children of the summer colony had the sea to themselves. First the women undressed, pulled on their bathing dresses and covered their heads in hideous caps like sponge bags; then the children were unbuttoned. The beach was strewn with little heaps of clothes and shoes; the big summer hats, with stones on them to keep them from blowing away, looked like immense shells. It was strange that even the sea seemed to sound differently when all those leaping, laughing figures ran into the waves. Old Mrs Fairfield, in a lilac cotton dress and a black hat tied under the chin, gathered her little brood and got them ready. The little Trout boys whipped their shirts over their heads, and away the five sped, while their grandma sat with one hand in her knitting-bag ready to draw out the ball of wool when she was satisfied they were safely in.

The firm compact little girls were not half so brave as the tender, delicate-looking little boys. Pip and Rags, shivering, crouching down, slapping the water, never hesitated. But Isabel, who could swim twelve strokes, and Kezia, who could nearly swim eight, only followed on the strict understanding they were not be splashed. As for Lottie, she didn't follow at all. She liked to be left to go in her own way, please. And that way was to sit down at the edge of the water, her legs straight, her knees pressed together, and to make vague motions with her arms as if she expected to be wafted out to sea. But when a bigger wave than usual, an old whiskery one, came lolloping along in her direction, she scrambled to her feet with a face of horror and flew up the beach again.

'Here, mother, keep those for me, will you?'

Two rings and a thin gold chain were dropped into Mrs Fairfield's lap.

'Yes, dear. But aren't you going to bathe here?'

'No-o,' Beryl drawled. She sounded vague. 'I'm undressing farther along. I'm going to bathe with Mrs Harry Kember.'

'Very well.' But Mrs Fairfield's lips set. She disapproved of Mrs Harry Kember. Beryl knew it.

Poor old mother, she smiled as she skimmed over the stones. Poor old mother! Old! Oh, what joy, what bliss it was to be young ...

'You look very pleased,' said Mrs Harry Kember. She sat hunched up on the stones, her arms round her knees, smoking.

'It's such a lovely day,' said Beryl, smiling down at her.

'Oh, my *dear!*' Mrs Harry Kember's voice sounded as though she knew better than that. But then her voice always sounded as though she knew something more about you than you did yourself. She was a long, strange-looking woman with narrow hands and feet. Her face, too, was long and narrow and exhausted-looking; even her fair curled fringe looked burnt out and withered. She was the only woman at the Bay who smoked, and she smoked incessantly, keeping the cigarette between her lips while she talked, and only taking it out when the ash was so long you could not understand why it did not fall. When she was not playing bridge — she played bridge every day of her life — she spent her time lying in the full glare of the sun. She could stand any amount of it; she never had enough. All the same, it did not seem to warm her. Parched, withered, cold, she lay stretched on the stones like a piece of tossed-up driftwood. The women at the Bay thought she was very, very fast. Her lack of vanity, her slang, the way she treated men as though she was one of them, and the fact that she didn't care twopence about her house and called the servant Gladys 'Glad-eyes', was disgraceful. Standing on the veranda steps Mrs Kember would call in her indifferent, tired voice, 'I say, Glad-eyes, you might heave me a handkerchief if I've got one, will you?' And Glad-eyes, a red bow in her hair instead of a cap, and white shoes, came running with an impudent smile. It was an absolute scandal! True, she had no children, and her husband ... Here the voices were always raised; they became fervent. How can he have married her? How can he, how can he? It must have been money, of course, but even then!

Mrs Kember's husband was at least ten years younger than she was, and so incredibly handsome that he looked like a mask or a most perfect illustration in an American novel rather than a man. Black hair, dark blue eyes, red lips, a slow sleepy smile, a fine tennis player, a perfect dancer, and with it all a mystery. Harry Kember was like a man walking in his sleep. Men couldn't stand him, they couldn't get a word out of the chap; he ignored his wife just as she ignored him. How did he live? Of course there were stories, but such stories! They simply couldn't be told. The women he'd been seen with, the places he'd been seen in ... but nothing was ever certain, nothing definite. Some of the women at the Bay privately thought he'd commit a murder one day. Yes, even while they talked to Mrs Kember and took in the awful concoction she was wearing, they saw her, stretched as she lay on the beach; but cold, bloody, and still with a cigarette stuck in the corner of her mouth.

Mrs Kember rose, yawned, unsnapped her belt buckle, and tugged at the tape of her blouse. And Beryl stepped out of her skirt and shed her jersey, and stood up in her short white petticoat, and her camisole with ribbon bows on the shoulders.

'Mercy on us,' said Mrs Harry Kember, 'what a beauty you are!'

'Don't!' said Beryl softly; but, drawing off one stocking and then the other, she felt a little beauty.

'My dear — why not?' said Mrs Harry Kember, stamping on her own petticoat. Really — her underclothes! A pair of blue cotton knickers and a linen bodice that reminded one somehow of a pillow-case ... 'And you don't wear stays, do you?' She touched Beryl's waist, and Beryl sprang away with a small affected cry. Then 'Never!' she said firmly.

'Lucky little creature,' sighed Mrs Kember, unfastening her own.

Beryl turned her back and began the complicated movements of some one who is trying to take off her clothes and to pull on her bathing-dress all at one and the same time.

'Oh, my dear — don't mind me,' said Mrs Harry Kember. 'Why be shy? I shan't eat you. I shan't be shocked like those other ninnies.' And she gave her strange neighing laugh and grimaced at the other women.

But Beryl was shy. She never undressed in front of anybody. Was that silly? Mrs Harry Kember made her feel it was silly, even something to be ashamed of. Why be shy indeed! She glanced quickly at her friend standing so boldly in her torn chemise and lighting a fresh cigarette; and a quick, bold, evil feeling started up in her breast. Laughing recklessly, she drew on the limp, sandy-feeling bathing-dress that was not quite dry and fastened the twisted buttons.

'That's better,' said Mrs Harry Kember. They began to go down the beach together. 'Really, it's a sin for you to wear clothes, my dear. Somebody's got to tell you some day.'

The water was quite warm. It was that marvellous transparent blue, flecked with silver, but the sand at the bottom looked gold; when you kicked with your toes there rose a little puff of gold-dust. Now the waves just reached her breast. Beryl stood, her arms outstretched, gazing out, and as each wave came she gave the slightest little jump, so that it seemed it was the wave which lifted her so gently.

'I believe in pretty girls having a good time,' said Mrs Harry Kember. 'Why not? Don't you make a mistake, my dear. Enjoy yourself.' And suddenly she turned turtle, disappeared, and swam away quickly, quickly, like a rat. Then she flicked round and began swimming back. She was going to say something else. Beryl felt that she was being poisoned by this cold woman, but she longed to hear. But oh, how strange, how horrible! As Mrs Harry Kember came up close she looked, in her black waterproof bathing-cap, with her sleepy face lifted above the water, just her chin touching, like a horrible caricature of her husband.

V I

In a steamer chair, under a manuka tree that grew in the middle of the front grass patch, Linda Burnell dreamed the morning away. She did nothing. She looked up at the dark, close, dry leaves of the manuka, at the chinks of blue between, and now and again a tiny yellowish flower dropped on her. Pretty — yes, if you held one of those flowers on the palm of your hand and looked at it closely, it was an exquisite small thing. Each pale yellow petal shone as if each was the careful work of a loving hand. The tiny tongue in the centre gave it the shape of a bell. And when you turned it over the outside was a deep bronze colour. But as soon as they flowered, they fell and were scattered. You brushed them off your frock as you talked; the horrid little things got caught in one's hair. Why, then, flower at all? Who takes the trouble — or the joy — to make all these things that are wasted, wasted ... It was uncanny.

On the grass beside her, lying between two pillows, was the boy. Sound asleep he lay his head turned away from his mother. His fine dark hair looked more like a shadow than like real hair, but his ear was a bright, deep coral. Linda clasped her hands above her head and crossed her feet. It was very pleasant to know that all these bungalows were empty, that everybody was down on the beach, out of sight, out of hearing. She had the garden to herself; she was alone.

Dazzling white the picotees shone; the golden-eyed marigolds glittered; the nasturtiums wreathed the veranda poles in green and gold flame. If only one had time to look at these flowers long enough, time to get over the sense of novelty and strangeness, time to know them! But as soon as one paused to part the petals, to discover the under-side of the leaf, along came Life and one was swept away. And lying in her cane chair, Linda felt so light; she felt like a leaf. Along came Life like a wind and she was seized and shaken; she had to go. Oh dear, would it always be so? Was there no escape?

... Now she sat on the veranda of their Tasmanian home, leaning against her father's knee. And he promised, 'As soon as you and I are old enough, Linny, we'll put off somewhere, we'll escape. Two boys together. I have a fancy I'd like to sail up a river in China.' Linda saw that river, very wide, covered with little rafts and boats. She saw the yellow hats of the boatmen and she heard their high, thin voices as they called ...

'Yes, papa.'

But just then a very broad young man with bright ginger hair walked slowly past their house, and slowly, solemnly even, uncovered. Linda's father pulled her ear teasingly, in the way he had.

'Linny's beau,' he whispered.

'Oh, papa, fancy being married to Stanley Burnell!'

Well, she was married to him. And what was more she loved him. Not the Stanley whom every one saw, not the everyday one; but a timid, sensitive, innocent Stanley who knelt down every night to say his prayers, and who longed to be good. Stanley was simple. If he believed in people — as he believed in her, for instance — it was with his whole heart. He could not be disloyal; he could not tell a lie. And how terribly he suffered if he thought anyone — she — was not being dead straight, dead sincere with him! 'This is too subtle for me!' He flung out the words, but his open quivering, distraught look was like the look of a trapped beast.

But the trouble was — here Linda felt almost inclined to laugh, though Heaven knows it was no laughing matter — she saw *her* Stanley so seldom. There were glimpses, moments, breathing spaces of calm, but all the rest of the time it was like living in a house that couldn't be cured of the habit of catching on fire, on a ship that got wrecked every day. And it was always Stanley who was in the thick of the danger. Her whole time was spent in rescuing him, and restoring him, and calming him down, and listening to his story. And what was left of her time was spent in the dread of having children.

Linda frowned; she sat up quickly in her steamer chair and clasped her ankles. Yes, that was her real grudge against life; that was what she could not understand. That was the question she asked and asked, and listened in vain for the answer. It was all very well to say it was the common lot of women to bear children. It wasn't true. She, for one, could prove that wrong. She was broken, made weak, her courage was gone, through child-bearing. And what made it doubly hard to bear was, she did not love her children. It was useless pretending. Even if she had had the strength she never would have nursed and played with the little girls. No, it was as though a cold breath had chilled her through and through on each of those awful journeys; she had no warmth left to give them. As to the boy — well, thank Heaven, mother had taken him; he was mother's, or Beryl's, or anybody's who wanted him. She had hardly held him in her arms. She was so indifferent about him that as he lay there … Linda glanced down.

The boy had turned over. He lay facing her, and he was no longer asleep. His dark-blue, baby eyes were open; he looked as though he was peeping at his mother. And suddenly his face dimpled; it broke into a wide, toothless smile, a perfect beam, no less.

'I'm here!' that happy smile seemed to say. 'Why don't you like me?'

There was something so quaint, so unexpected about that smile that Linda smiled herself. But she checked herself and said to the boy coldly, 'I don't like babies.'

'Don't like babies?' The boy couldn't believe her. 'Don't like *me*?' He waved his arms foolishly at his mother.

Linda dropped off her chair on to the grass.

'Why do you keep on smiling?' she said severely. 'If you knew what I was thinking about, you wouldn't.'

But he only squeezed up his eyes, slyly, and rolled his head on the pillow. He didn't believe a word she said.

'We know all about that!' smiled the boy.

Linda was so astonished at the confidence of this little creature … Ah no, be sincere. That was not what she felt; it was
something far different, it was something so new, so … The tears
danced in her eyes; she breathed in a small whisper to the boy,
'Hallo, my funny!'

But by now the boy had forgotten his mother. He was serious again. Something pink, something soft waved in front of
him. He made a grab at it and it immediately disappeared. But
when he lay back, another, like the first, appeared. This time he
determined to catch it. He made a tremendous effort and rolled
right over.

VII

The tide was out; the beach was deserted; lazily flopped the
warm sea. The sun beat down, beat down hot and fiery on the fine
sand, baking the grey and blue and black and white-veined pebbles. It sucked up the little drop of water that lay in the hollow of
the curved shells; it bleached the pink convolvulus that threaded
through and through the sand-hills. Nothing seemed to move but
the small sand-hoppers. Pit-pit-pit! They were never still.

Over there on the weed-hung rocks that looked at low tide
like shaggy beasts come down to the water to drink, the sunlight
seemed to spin like a silver coin dropped into each of the small
rock pools. They danced, they quivered, and minute ripples laved
the porous shores. Looking down, bending over, each pool was
like a lake with pink and blue houses clustered on the shores; and
oh! the vast mountainous country behind those houses — the
ravines, the passes, the dangerous creeks and fearful tracks that
led to the water's edge. Underneath waved the sea-forest —
pink thread-like trees, velvet anemones, and orange berry-
spotted weeds. Now a stone on the bottom moved, rocked, and
there was a glimpse of a black feeler; now a thread-like creature
wavered by and was lost. Something was happening to the pink

waving trees; they were changing to a cold moonlight blue. And now there sounded the faintest 'plop'. Who made that sound? What was going on down there? And how strong, how damp the seaweed smelt in the hot sun …

The green blinds were drawn in the bungalows of the summer colony. Over the verandahs, prone on the paddock, flung over the fences, there were exhausted-looking bathing-dresses and rough striped towels. Each back window seemed to have a pair of sand-shoes on the sill and some lumps of rock or a bucket or a collection of pawa shells. The bush quivered in a haze of heat; the sandy road was empty except for the Trouts' dog Snooker, who lay stretched in the very middle of it. His blue eye was turned up, his legs stuck out stiffly, and he gave an occasional desperate-sounding puff, as much as to say he had decided to make an end of it and was only waiting for some kind cart to come along.

'What are you looking at, my grandma? Why do you keep stopping and sort of staring at the wall?'

Kezia and her grandmother were taking their siesta together. The little girl, wearing only her short drawers and her under-bodice, her arms and legs bare, lay on one of the puffed-up pillows of her grandma's bed, and the old woman, in a white ruf-fled dressing-gown, sat in a rocker at the window, with a long piece of pink knitting on her lap. This room that they shared, like the other rooms of the bungalow, was of light varnished wood and the floor was bare. The furniture was of the shabbiest, the simplest. The dressing-table, for instance, was a packing-case in a sprigged muslin petticoat, and the mirror above was very strange; it was as though a little piece of forked lightning was imprisoned in it. On the table there stood a jar of sea-pinks, pressed so tightly together they looked more like a velvet pin-cushion, and a special shell which Kezia had given her grandma for a pin-tray, and another even more special which she had thought would make a very nice place for a watch to curl up in.

'Tell me, grandma,' said Kezia.

The old woman sighed, whipped the wool twice round her thumb, and drew the bone needle through. She was casting on.

'I was thinking of your Uncle William, darling,' she said quietly.

'My Australian Uncle William?' said Kezia. She had another.

'Yes, of course.'

'The one I never saw?'

'That was the one.'

'Well, what happened to him?' Kezia knew perfectly well, but she wanted to be told again.

'He went to the mines, and he got a sunstroke there and died,' said old Mrs Fairfield.

Kezia blinked and considered the picture again … A little man fallen over like a tin soldier by the side of a big black hole.

'Does it make you sad to think about him, grandma?' She hated her grandma to be sad.

It was the old woman's turn to consider. Did it make her sad? To look back, back. To stare down the years, as Kezia had seen her doing. To look after *them* as a woman does, long after *they* were out of sight. Did it make her sad? No, life was like that.

'No, Kezia.'

'But why?' asked Kezia. She lifted one bare arm and began to draw things in the air. 'Why did Uncle William have to die? He wasn't old.'

Mrs Fairfield began counting the stitches in threes. 'It just happened,' she said in an absorbed voice.

'Does everybody have to die?' asked Kezia.

'Everybody!'

'*Me*?' Kezia sounded fearfully incredulous.

'Some day, my darling.'

'But, grandma.' Kezia waved her left leg and waggled her toes. They felt sandy. 'What if I just won't?'

The old woman sighed again and drew a long thread from the ball.

'We're not asked, Kezia,' she said sadly. 'It happens to all of us sooner or later.'

Kezia lay still thinking this over. She didn't want to die. It meant she would have to leave here, leave everywhere, for ever, leave — leave her grandma. She rolled over quickly.

'Grandma,' she said in a startled voice.

'What, my pet!'

'*You're* not to die.' Kezia was very decided.

'Ah, Kezia' — her grandma looked up and smiled and shook her head — 'don't let's talk about it.'

'But you're not to. You couldn't leave me. You couldn't not be there.' This was awful. 'Promise me you won't ever do it, grandma,' pleaded Kezia.

The old woman went on knitting.

'Promise me! Say never!'

But still her grandma was silent.

Kezia rolled off the bed; she couldn't bear it any longer, and lightly she leapt on to her grandma's knees, clasped her hands round the old woman's throat and began kissing her, under the chin, behind the ear, and blowing down her neck.

'Say never ... say never ... say never — ' She gasped between the kisses. And then she began, very softly and lightly, to tickle her grandma.

'Kezia!' The old woman dropped her knitting. She swung back in the rocker. She began to tickle Kezia. 'Say never, say never, say never,' gurgled Kezia, while they lay there laughing in each other's arms. 'Come, that's enough, my squirrel! That's enough, my wild pony!' said old Mrs Fairfield, setting her cap straight. 'Pick up my knitting.'

Both of them had forgotten what the 'never' was about.

VIII

The sun was still full on the garden when the back door of the Burnells' shut with a bang, and a very gay figure walked down the path to the gate. It was Alice, the servant-girl, dressed for her afternoon out. She wore a white cotton dress with such large red spots on it, and so many that they made you shudder, white shoes and a leghorn turned up under the brim with poppies. Of course she wore gloves, white ones, stained at the fastenings with iron-mould, and in one hand she carried a very dashed-looking sun-shade which she referred to as her *perishall*.

Beryl, sitting in the window, fanning her freshly washed hair, thought she had never seen such a guy. If Alice had only blacked her face with a piece of cork before she started out, the picture would have been complete. And where did a girl like that go to in a place like this? The heart-shaped Fijian fan beat scornfully at that lovely bright mane. She supposed Alice had picked up some horrible common larrikin and they'd go off into the bush to-gether. Pity to make herself so conspicuous; they'd have hard work to hide with Alice in that rig-out.

But no, Beryl was unfair. Alice was going to tea with Mrs Stubbs, who'd sent her an 'invite' by the little boy who called for orders. She had taken ever such a liking to Mrs Stubbs ever since the first time she went to the shop to get something for her mos-quitoes.

'Dear heart!' Mrs Stubbs had clapped her hand to her side. 'I never seen anyone so eaten. You might have been attacked by canningbals.'

Alice did wish there'd been a bit of life on the road though. Made her feel so queer, having nobody behind her. Made her feel all weak in the spine. She couldn't believe that some one wasn't watching her. And yet it was silly to turn round; it gave you away. She pulled up her gloves, hummed to herself and said to the dis-tant gum-tree, 'Shan't be long now.' But that was hardly company.

I X

Mrs Stubbs's shop was perched on a little hillock just off the road. It had two big windows for eyes. A broad veranda for a hat, and the sign on the roof, scrawled MRS STUBBS'S, was like a little card stuck rakishly in the hat crown.

On the verandah there hung a long string of bathing-dresses, clinging together as though they'd just been rescued from the sea rather than waiting to go in, and beside them there hung a cluster of sand-shoes so extraordinarily mixed that to get at one pair you had to tear apart and forcibly separate at least fifty. Even then it was the rarest thing to find the left that belonged to the right. So many people had lost patience and gone off with one shoe that fitted and one that was a little too big ... Mrs Stubbs prided herself on keeping something of everything. The two windows, arranged in the form of precarious pyramids, were crammed so tight, piled so high, that it seemed only a conjurer could prevent them from toppling over. In the left-hand corner of one window, glued to the pane by four gelatine lozenges, there was — and there had been from time immemorial — a notice.

LOST! HANSOME GOLE BROOCH
SOLID GOLD
ON OR NEAR BEACH
REWARD OFFERED

Alice pressed open the door. The bell jangled, the red serge curtains parted, and Mrs Stubbs appeared. With her broad smile and the long bacon knife in her hand, she looked like a friendly brigand. Alice was welcomed so warmly that she found it quite difficult to keep up her 'manners'. They consisted of persistent little coughs and hems, pulls at her gloves, tweaks at her skirt, and a curious difficulty in seeing what was set before her or understanding what was said.

Tea was laid on the parlour table — ham, sardines, a whole pound of butter, and such a large johnny cake that it looked like an advertisement for somebody's baking-powder. But the Primus stove roared so loudly that it was useless to try to talk above it. Alice sat down on the edge of a basket-chair while Mrs Stubbs pumped the stove still higher. Suddenly Mrs Stubbs whipped the cushion off a chair and disclosed a large brown-paper parcel.

'I've just had some new photers taken, my dear,' she shouted cheerfully to Alice. 'Tell me what you think of them.'

In a very dainty, refined way Alice wet her finger and put the tissue back from the first one. Life! How many there were! There were three dozzing at least. And she held hers up to the light.

Mrs Stubbs sat in an arm-chair, leaning very much to one side. There was a look of mild astonishment on her large face, and well there might be. For though the arm-chair stood on a carpet, to the left of it, miraculously skirting the carpet-border, there was a dashing water-fall. On her right stood a Grecian pillar with a giant fern-tree on either side of it, and in the background towered a gaunt mountain, pale with snow.

'It is a nice style, isn't it?' shouted Mrs Stubbs; and Alice had just screamed 'Sweetly' when the roaring of the Primus stove died down, fizzled out, ceased, and she said 'Pretty' in a silence that was frightening.

'Draw up your chair, my dear,' said Mrs Stubbs, beginning to pour out. 'Yes,' she said thoughtfully, as she handed the tea, 'but I don't care about the size. I'm having an enlargemint. All very well for Christmas cards, but I never was the one for small photers myself. You get no comfort out of them. To say the truth, I find them dis'eartening.'

Alice quite saw what she meant.

'Size,' said Mrs Stubbs. 'Give me size. That was what my poor dear husband was always saying. He couldn't stand anything small. Gave him the creeps. And, strange as it may seem, my dear' — here Mrs Stubbs creaked and seemed to expand herself at the memory — 'it was dropsy that carried him off at the larst.

Many's the time they drawn one and a half pints from 'im at the 'ospital ... It seemed like a judgmint.'

Alice burned to know exactly what it was that was drawn from him. She ventured, 'I suppose it was water.'

But Mrs Stubbs fixed Alice with her eyes and replied meaningly, 'It was *liquid*, my dear.'

Liquid! Alice jumped away from the word like a cat and came back to it, nosing and wary.

'That's 'im!' said Mrs Stubbs, and she pointed dramatically to the life-size head and shoulders of a burly man with a dead white rose in the button-hole of his coat that made you think of a curl of cold mutting fat. Just below, in silver letters on a red cardboard ground, were the words, 'Be not afraid, it is I.'

'It's ever such a fine face,' said Alice faintly.

The pale-blue bow on the top of Mrs Stubbs's fair frizzy hair quivered. She arched her plump neck. What a neck she had! It was bright pink where it began and then it changed to warm apricot, and that faded to the colour of a brown egg and then to a deep creamy.

'All the same, my dear,' she said surprisingly, 'freedom's best!' Her soft, fat chuckle sounded like a purr. 'Freedom's best,' said Mrs Stubbs again.

Freedom! Alice gave a loud, silly little titter. She felt awkward. Her mind flew back to her own kitching. Ever so queer! She wanted to be back in it again.

X

A strange company assembled in the Burnells' washhouse after tea. Round the table there sat a bull, a rooster, a donkey that kept forgetting it was a donkey, a sheep and a bee. The washhouse was the perfect place for such a meeting because they could make as much noise as they liked, and nobody ever interrupted. It was a small tin shed standing apart from the bungalow. Against the wall there was a deep trough and in the corner a copper with a basket of clothes-pegs on top of it. The little window, spun over the cobwebs, had a piece of candle and a mouse-trap on the dusty sill. There were clothes-lines criss-crossed overhead and, hanging from a peg on the wall, a very big, a huge, rusty horseshoe. The table was in the middle with a form at either side.

'You can't be a bee, Kezia. A bee's not an animal. It's a ninseck.'

'Oh, but I do want to be a bee frightfully,' wailed Kezia … A tiny bee, all yellow-furry, with striped legs. She drew her legs up under her and leaned over the table. She felt she was a bee.

'A ninseck must be an animal,' she said stoutly. 'It makes a noise. It's not like a fish.'

'I'm a bull, I'm a bull!' cried Pip. And he gave such a tremendous bellow — how did he make that noise? — that Lottie looked quite alarmed.

'I'll be a sheep,' said little Rags. 'A whole lot of sheep went past this morning.'

'How do you know?'

'Dad heard them. Baa!' He sounded like the little lamb that trots behind and seems to wait to be carried.

'Cock-a-doodle-do!' shrilled Isabel. With her red cheeks and bright eyes she looked like a rooster.

'What'll I be?' Lottie asked everybody, and she sat there smiling, waiting for them to decide for her. It had to be an easy one.

'Be a donkey, Lottie.' It was Kezia's suggestion. 'Hee-haw! You can't forget that.'

'Hee-haw!' said Lottie solemnly. 'When do I have to say it?'

'I'll explain, I'll explain,' said the bull. It was he who had the cards. He waved them round his head. 'All be quiet! All listen!' And he waited for them. 'Look here, Lottie.' He turned up a card. 'It's got two spots on it — see? Now, if you put that card in the middle and somebody else has one with two spots as well, you say "Hee-haw," and the card's yours.'

'Mine?' Lottie was round-eyed. 'To keep?'

'No, silly. Just for the game, see? Just while we're playing.' The bull was very cross with her.

'Oh, Lottie, you *are* a silly,' said the proud rooster.

Lottie looked at both of them. Then she hung her head; her lip quivered. 'I don't want to play,' she whispered. The others glanced at one another like conspirators. All of them knew what that meant. She would go away and be discovered somewhere standing with her pinny thrown over her head, in a corner, or against a wall, or even behind a chair.

'Yes, you *do*, Lottie. It's quite easy,' said Kezia.

And Isabel, repentant, said exactly like a grown-up, 'Watch *me*, Lottie, and you'll soon learn.'

'Cheer up, Lot,' said Pip. 'There, I know what I'll do. I'll give you the first one. It's mine, really, but I'll give it to you. Here you are.' And he slammed the card down in front of Lottie.

Lottie revived at that. But now she was in another difficulty. 'I haven't got a hanky,' she said; 'I want one badly, too.'

'Here, Lottie, you can use mine.' Rags dipped into his sailor blouse and brought up a very wet-looking one, knotted together. 'Be very careful,' he warned her. 'Only use that corner. Don't undo it. I've got a little starfish inside I'm going to try and tame.'

'Oh, come on, you girls,' said the bull. 'And mind — you're not to look at your cards. You've got to keep your hands under the table till I say "Go." '

Smack went the cards round the table. They tried with all their might to see, but Pip was too quick for them. It was very exciting, sitting there in the washhouse; it was all they could do not to burst into a little chorus of animals before Pip had finished dealing.

'Now, Lottie, you begin.'

Timidly Lottie stretched out a hand, took the top card off her pack, had a good look at it — it was plain she was counting the spots — and put it down.

'Now, Lottie, you can't do that. You mustn't look first. You must turn it the other way over.'

'But then everybody will see it the same time as me,' said Lottie.

The game proceeded. Mooe-ooo-er! The bull was terrible. He charged over the table and seemed to eat the cards up.

Bss-ss! said the bee.

Cock-a-doodle-do! Isabel stood up in her excitement and moved her elbows like wings.

Baa! Little Rags put down the King of Diamonds and Lottie put down the one they called the King of Spain. She had hardly any cards left.

'Why don't you call out, Lottie?'

'I've forgotten what I am,' said the donkey woefully.

'Well, change! Be a dog instead! Bow-wow!'

'Oh yes. That's *much* easier.' Lottie smiled again. But when she and Kezia both had a one Kezia waited on purpose. The others made signs to Lottie and pointed. Lottie turned very red; she looked bewildered, and at last she said, 'Hee-haw! Ke-zia.'

'Ss! Wait a minute!' They were in the very thick of it when the bull stopped them, holding up his hand. 'What's that? What's that noise?'

'What noise? What do you mean?' asked the rooster.

'Ss! Shut up! Listen!' They were mouse-still. 'I thought I heard a — a sort of knocking,' said the bull.

'What was it like?' asked the sheep faintly.

No answer.

The bee gave a shudder. 'Whatever did we shut the door for?' she said softly. Oh, why, why had they shut the door?

While they were playing, the day had faded; the gorgeous sunset had blazed and died. And now the quick dark came racing over the sea, over the sand-hills, up the paddock. You were frightened to look in the corners of the washhouse, and yet you had to look with all your might. And somewhere, far away, grandma was lighting a lamp. The blinds were being pulled down; the kitchen fire leapt in the tins on the mantelpiece.

'It would be awful now,' said the bull, 'if a spider was to fall from the ceiling on to the table, wouldn't it?'

'Spiders don't fall from ceilings.'

'Yes, they do. Our Min told us she's seen a spider as big as a saucer, with long hairs on it like a gooseberry.'

Quickly all the little heads were jerked up; all the little bodies drew together, pressed together.

'Why doesn't somebody come and call us?' cried the rooster.

Oh, those grown-ups, laughing and snug, sitting in the lamp-light, drinking out of cups! They'd forgotten about them. No, not really forgotten. That was what their smile meant. They had decided to leave them there all by themselves.

Suddenly Lottie gave such a piercing scream that all of them jumped off the forms, all of them screamed too. 'A face — a face looking!' shrieked Lottie.

It was true, it was real. Pressed against the window was a pale face, black eyes, a black beard.

'Grandma! Mother! Somebody!'

But they had not got to the door, tumbling over one another, before it opened for Uncle Jonathan. He had come to take the little boys home.

X I

He had meant to be there before, but in the front garden he had come upon Linda walking up and down the grass, stopping to pick off a dead pink or give a top-heavy carnation something to lean against, or to take a deep breath of something, and then walking on again, with her little air of remoteness. Over her white frock she wore a yellow, pink-fringed shawl from the Chinaman's shop.

'Hallo, Jonathan!' called Linda. And Jonathan whipped off his shabby panama, pressed it against his breast, dropped on one knee, and kissed Linda's hand.

'Greeting, my Fair One! Greeting, my Celestial Peach Blossom!' boomed the bass voice gently. 'Where are the other noble dames?'

'Beryl's out playing bridge and mother's giving the boy his bath ... Have you come to borrow something?'

The Trouts were for ever running out of things and sending across to the Burnells' at the last moment.

But Jonathan only answered, 'A little love, a little kindness'; and he walked by his sister-in-law's side.

Linda dropped into Beryl's hammock under the manuka tree, and Jonathan stretched himself on the grass beside her, pulled a long stalk and began chewing it. They knew each other well. The voices of children cried from the other gardens. A fisherman's light cart shook along the sandy road, and from far away they heard a dog barking; it was muffled as though the dog had its head in a sack. If you listened you could just hear the soft swish of the sea at full tide sweeping the pebbles. The sun was sinking.

'And so you go back to the office on Monday, do you, Jonathan?' asked Linda.

'On Monday the cage door opens and clangs to upon the victim for another eleven months and a week,' answered Jonathan.

Linda swung a little. 'It must be awful,' she said slowly.

'Would ye have me laugh, my fair sister? Would ye have me weep?'

Linda was so accustomed to Jonathan's way of talking that she paid no attention to it.

'I suppose,' she said vaguely, 'one gets used to it. One gets used to anything.'

'Does one? Hum!' The 'Hum' was so deep it seemed to

boom from underneath the ground. 'I wonder how it's done,' brooded Jonathan; 'I've never managed it.'

Looking at him as he lay there, Linda thought again how attractive he was. It was strange to think that he was only an ordinary clerk, that Stanley earned twice as much money as he. What was the matter with Jonathan? He had no ambition; she supposed that was it. And yet one felt he was gifted, exceptional. He was passionately fond of music; every spare penny he had went on books. He was always full of new ideas, schemes, plans. But nothing came of it all. The new fire blazed in Jonathan; you almost heard it roaring softly as he explained, described and dilated on the new thing; but a moment later it had fallen in and there was nothing but ashes, and Jonathan went about with a look like hunger in his black eyes. At these times he exaggerated his absurd manner of speaking, and he sang in church — he was the leader of the choir — with such fearful dramatic intensity that the meanest hymn put on an unholy splendour.

'It seems to me just as imbecile, just as infernal, to have to go to the office on Monday,' said Jonathan, 'as it always has done and always will do. To spend all the best years of one's life sitting on a stool from nine to five, scratching in somebody's ledger! It's a queer use to make of one's ... one and only life, isn't it? Or do I fondly dream?' He rolled over on the grass and looked up at Linda. 'Tell me, what is the difference between my life and that of an ordinary prisoner. The only difference I can see is that I put myself in jail and nobody's ever going to let me out. That's a more intolerable situation than the other. For if I'd been — pushed in, against my will — kicking, even — once the door was locked, or at any rate in five years or so, I might have accepted the fact and begun to take an interest in the flight of flies or counting the warder's steps along the passage with particular attention to variations of tread and so on. But as it is, I'm like an insect that's flown into a room of its own accord. I dash against the walls, dash against the windows, flop against the ceiling, do everything on God's earth, in fact, except fly out again. And all the while I'm thinking, like that moth, or that butterfly, or whatever it is, "The shortness of life! The shortness of life!" I've only one night or one day, and there's this vast dangerous garden, waiting out there, undiscovered, unexplored.'

'But, if you feel like that, why — ' began Linda quickly.

'*Ah!*' cried Jonathan. And that 'Ah!' was somehow almost exultant. 'There you have me. Why? Why indeed? There's the maddening, mysterious question. Why don't I fly out again? There's the window or the door or whatever it was I came in by. It's not hopelessly shut — is it? Why don't I find it and be off? Answer me that, little sister.' But he gave her no time to answer.

'I'm exactly like that insect again. For some reason' — Jonathan paused between the words — 'it's not allowed, it's forbidden, it's against the insect law, to stop banging and flopping and crawling up the pane even for an instant. Why don't I leave the office? Why don't I seriously consider, this moment, for instance, what it is that prevents me leaving? It's not as though I'm tremendously tied. I've two boys to provide for, but, after all, they're boys. I could cut off to sea, or get a job up-country, or — ' Suddenly he smiled at Linda and said in a changed voice, as if he were confiding a secret, 'Weak ... weak. No stamina. No anchor. No guiding principle, let us call it.' But then the dark velvety voice rolled out:

> Would ye hear the story
> How it unfolds itself ...

and they were silent.

The sun had set. In the western sky there were great masses of crushed-up rose-coloured clouds. Broad beams of light shone through the clouds and beyond them as if they would cover the whole sky. Overhead the blue faded; it turned a pale gold, and the bush outlined against it gleamed dark and brilliant like metal. Sometimes when those beams of light show in the sky they are very awful. They remind you that up there sits Jehovah, the jealous God, the Almighty, Whose eye is upon you, ever watchful, never weary. You remember that at His coming the whole earth will shake into one ruined graveyard; the cold, bright angels will drive you this way and that, and there will be no time to explain what could be explained so simply ... But to-night it seemed to Linda there was something infinitely joyful in those silver beams. And now no sound came from the sea. It breathed softly as if it would draw that tender, joyful beauty into its own bosom.

'It's all wrong, it's all wrong,' came the shadowy voice of Jonathan. 'It's not the scene, it's not the setting for ... three stools, three desks, three inkpots and a wire blind.'

Linda knew that he would never change, but she said, 'Is it too late, even now?'

'I'm old — I'm old,' intoned Jonathan. He bent towards her, he passed his hand over his head. 'Look!' His black hair was speckled all over with silver, like the breast plumage of a black fowl.

Linda was surprised. She had no idea that he was grey. And yet, as he stood up beside her and sighed and stretched, she saw him, for the first time, not resolute, not gallant, not careless, but touched already with age. He looked very tall on the darkening grass, and the thought crossed her mind, 'He is like a weed.'

Jonathan stooped again and kissed her fingers.

'Heaven reward thy sweet patience, lady mine,' he murmured. 'I must go seek those heirs to my fame and fortune ...' He was gone.

XII

Light shone in the windows of the bungalow. Two square patches of gold fell upon the pinks and the peaked marigolds. Florrie, the cat, came out on to the veranda, and sat on the top step, her white paws close together, her tail curled round. She looked content, as though she had been waiting for this moment all day.

'Thank goodness, it's getting late,' said Florrie. 'Thank goodness, the long day is over.' Her greengage eyes opened.

Presently there sounded the rumble of the coach, the crack of Kelly's whip. It came near enough for one to hear the voices of the men from town, talking loudly together. It stopped at the Burnells' gate.

Stanley was half-way up the path before he saw Linda. 'Is that you, darling?'

'Yes, Stanley.'

He leapt across the flower-bed and seized her in his arms. She was enfolded in that familiar, eager, strong embrace.

'Forgive me, darling, forgive me,' stammered Stanley, and he put his hand under her chin and lifted her face to him.

'Forgive you?' smiled Linda. 'But whatever for?'

'Good God! You can't have forgotten,' cried Stanley Burnell. 'I've thought of nothing else all day. I've had the hell of a day. I made up my mind to dash out and telegraph, and then I thought the wire mightn't reach you before I did. I've been in tortures, Linda.'

'But, Stanley,' said Linda, 'what must I forgive you for?'

'Linda!' — Stanley was very hurt — 'didn't you realize — you must have realized — I went away without saying good-bye to you this morning? I can't imagine how I can have done such a thing. My confounded temper, of course. But — well' — and he sighed and took her in his arms again — 'I've suffered for it enough to-day.'

'What's that you've got in your hand?' asked Linda. 'New gloves? Let me see.'

'Oh, just a cheap pair of wash-leather ones,' said Stanley humbly. 'I noticed Bell was wearing some in the coach this morning, so, as I was passing the shop, I dashed in and got myself a pair. What are you smiling at? You don't think it was wrong of me, do you?'

'On the *con*-trary, darling,' said Linda. 'It think it was most sensible.'

She pulled one of the large, pale gloves on her own fingers and looked at her hand, turning it this way and that. She was still smiling.

Stanley wanted to say, 'I was thinking of you the whole time I bought them.' It was true, but for some reason he couldn't say it. 'Let's go in,' said he.

XIII

Why does one feel so different at night? Why is it so exciting to be awake when everybody else is asleep? Late — it is very late! And yet every moment you feel more and more wakeful, as though you were slowly, almost with every breath, waking up into a new, wonderful, far more thrilling and exciting world than the daylight one. And what is this queer sensation that you're a conspirator? Lightly, stealthily you move about your room. You take something off the dressing-table and put it down again without a sound. And everything, even the bed-post, knows you, responds, shares your secret …

You're not very fond of your room by day. You never think about it. You're in and out, the door opens and slams, the cupboard creaks. You sit down on the side of your bed, change your shoes and dash out again. A dive down to the glass, two pins in your hair, powder your nose and off again. But now — it's suddenly dear to you. It's a darling little funny room. It's yours. Oh, what a joy it is to own things! Mine — my own!

'My very own for ever?'

'Yes.' Their lips met.

No, of course, that had nothing to do with it. That was all nonsense and rubbish. But, in spite of herself, Beryl saw so plainly two people standing in the middle of her room. Her arms were round his neck; he held her. And now he whispered, 'My beauty, my little beauty!' She jumped off her bed, ran over to the window and kneeled on the window-seat, with her elbows on the sill. But the beautiful night, the garden, every bush, every leaf, even the white palings, even the stars, were conspirators too. So bright was the moon that the flowers were bright as by day; the shadow of the nasturtiums, exquisite lily-like leaves and wide-open flowers, lay across the silvery veranda. The manuka tree, bent by the southerly winds, was like a bird on one leg stretching out a wing.

But when Beryl looked at the bush, it seemed to her the bush was sad.

'We are dumb trees, reaching up in the night, imploring we know not what,' said the sorrowful bush.

It is true when you are by yourself and you think about life, it is always sad. All that excitement and so on has a way of suddenly leaving you, and it's as though, in the silence, somebody called your name, and you heard your name for the first time. 'Beryl!'

'Yes, I'm here. I'm Beryl. Who wants me?'

'Beryl!'

'Let me come.'

It is lonely living by oneself. Of course, there are relations, friends, heaps of them; but that's not what she means. She wants some one who will find the Beryl they none of them know, who will expect her to be that Beryl always. She wants a lover.

'Take me away from all these other people, my love. Let us go far away. Let us live our life, all new, all ours, from the very beginning. Let us make our fire. Let us sit down to eat together. Let us have long talks at night.'

And the thought was almost, 'Save me, my love. Save me!'

... 'Oh, go on! Don't be a prude, my dear. You enjoy yourself while you're young. That's my advice.' And a high rush of silly laughter joined Mrs Harry Kember's loud, indifferent neigh.

You see, it's so frightfully difficult when you've nobody. You're so at the mercy of things. You can't just be rude. And you've always this horror of seeming inexperienced and stuffy like the other ninnies at the Bay. And — and it's fascinating to know you've power over people. Yes, that is fascinating ...

Oh why, oh why doesn't 'he' come soon?

If I go on living here, thought Beryl, anything may happen to me.

'But how do you know he is coming at all?' mocked a small voice within her.

But Beryl dismissed it. She couldn't be left. Other people, perhaps, but not she. It wasn't possible to think that Beryl Fairfield never married, that lovely fascinating girl.

'Do you remember Beryl Fairfield?'

'Remember her! As if I could forget her! It was one summer at the Bay that I saw her. She was standing on the beach in a blue' — no, pink — 'muslin frock holding on a big cream' — no, black — 'straw hat. But it's years ago now.'

'She's as lovely as ever, more so if anything.'

Beryl smiled, bit her lip, and gazed over the garden. As she gazed, she saw somebody, a man, leave the road, step along the paddock beside their palings as if he was coming straight towards her. Her heart beat. Who was it? Who could it be? It couldn't be a burglar, certainly not a burglar, for he was smoking and he strolled lightly. Beryl's heart leapt; it seemed to turn right over, and then to stop. She recognized him.

'Good evening, Miss Beryl,' said the voice softly.

'Good evening.'

'Won't you come for a little walk?' it drawled.

Come for a walk — at that time of night! 'I couldn't. Everybody's in bed. Everybody's asleep.'

'Oh,' said the voice lightly, and a whiff of sweet smoke

reached her. 'What does everybody matter? Do come! It's such a fine night. There's not a soul about.'

Beryl shook her head. But already something stirred in her, something reared its head.

The voice said, 'Frightened?' It mocked, 'Poor little girl!'

'Not in the least,' said she. As she spoke that weak thing within her seemed to uncoil, to grow suddenly tremendously strong; she longed to go!

And just as if this was quite understood by the other, the voice said, gently and softly, but finally, 'Come along!'

Beryl stepped over her low window, crossed the veranda, ran down the grass to the gate. He was there before her.

'That's right,' breathed the voice, and it teased, 'You're not frightened, are you? You're not frightened?'

She was; now she was here she was terrified, and it seemed to her everything was different. The moonlight stared and glittered; the shadows were like bars of iron. Her hand was taken.

'Not in the least,' she said lightly. 'Why should I be?'

Her hand was pulled gently, tugged. She held back.

'No, I'm not coming any farther,' said Beryl.

'Oh, rot!' Harry Kember didn't believe her. 'Come along! We'll just go as far as that fuchsia bush. Come along!'

The fuchsia bush was tall. It fell over the fence in a shower. There was a little pit of darkness beneath.

'No, really, I don't want to,' said Beryl.

For a moment Harry Kember didn't answer. Then he came close to her, turned to her, smiled and said quickly, 'Don't be silly! Don't be silly!'

His smile was something she'd never seen before. Was he drunk? That bright, blind, terrifying smile froze her with horror. What was she doing? How had she got here? The stern garden asked her as the gate pushed open, and quick as a cat Harry Kember came through and snatched her to him.

'Cold little devil! Cold little devil!' said the hateful voice.

But Beryl was strong. She slipped, ducked, wrenched free.

'You are vile, vile,' said she.

'Then why in God's name did you come?' stammered Harry Kember.

Nobody answered him.

XIV

A cloud, small, serene, floated across the moon. In that moment of darkness the sea sounded deep, troubled. Then the cloud sailed away, and the sound of the sea was a vague murmur, as though it waked out of a dark dream. All was still.

The Voyage

The Picton boat was due to leave at half-past eleven. It was a beautiful night, mild, starry, only when they got out of the cab and started to walk down the Old Wharf that jutted out into the harbour, a faint wind blowing off the water ruffled under Fenella's hat, and she put up her hand to keep it on. It was dark on the Old Wharf, very dark; the wool sheds, the cattle trucks, the cranes standing up so high, the little squat railway engine, all seemed carved out of solid darkness. Here and there on a rounded wood-pile, that was like the stalk of a huge black mushroom, there hung a lantern, but it seemed afraid to unfurl its timid, quivering light in all that blackness; it burned softly, as if for itself.

Fenella's father pushed on with quick, nervous strides. Beside him her grandma bustled along in her crackling black ulster; they went so fast that she had now and again to give an undignified little skip to keep up with them. As well as her luggage strapped into a neat sausage, Fenella carried clasped to her

her grandma's umbrella, and the handle, which was a swan's head, kept giving her shoulder a sharp little peck as if it too wanted her to hurry ... Men, their caps pulled down, their collars turned up, swung by; a few women all muffled scurried along; and one tiny boy, only his little black arms and legs showing out of a white woolly shawl, was jerked along angrily between his father and mother; he looked like a baby fly that had fallen into the cream.

Then suddenly, so suddenly that Fenella and her grandma both leapt, there sounded from behind the largest wool shed, that had a trail of smoke hanging over it, *Mia-oo-oo-O-O!*

'First whistle,' said her father briefly, and at that moment they came in sight of the Picton boat. Lying beside the dark wharf, all strung, all beaded with round golden lights, the Picton boat looked as if she was more ready to sail among stars than out into the cold sea. People pressed along the gangway. First went her grandma, then her father, then Fenella. There was a high step down on to the deck, and an old sailor in a jersey standing by gave her his dry, hard hand. They were there; they stepped out of the way of the hurrying people, and standing under a little iron stairway that led to the upper deck they began to say good-bye.

'There, mother, there's your luggage!' said Fenella's father, giving grandma another strapped-up sausage.

'Thank you, Frank.'

'And you've got your cabin tickets safe?'

'Yes, dear.'

'And your other tickets?'

Grandma felt for them inside her glove and showed him the tips. 'That's right.'

He sounded stern, but Fenella, eagerly watching him, saw that he looked tired and sad. *Mia-oo-oo-O-O!* The second whistle blared just above their heads, and a voice like a cry shouted, 'Any more for the gangway?'

'You'll give my love to father,' Fenella saw her father's lips say. And her grandma, very agitated, answered. 'Of course I will, dear. Go now. You'll be left. Go now, Frank. Go now.'

'It's all right, mother. I've got another three minutes.' To her surprise Fenella saw her father take off his hat. He clasped grandma in his arms and pressed her to him. 'God bless you, mother!' she heard him say.

And grandma put her hand, with the black thread glove that was worn through on her ring finger, against his cheek, and she sobbed, 'God bless you, my own brave son!'

This was so awful that Fenella quickly turned her back on them, swallowed once, twice, and frowned terribly at a little green star on a mast head. But she had to turn round again; her father was going.

'Good-bye, Fenella. Be a good girl.' His cold, wet moustache brushed her cheek. But Fenella caught hold of the lapels of his coat.

'How long am I going to stay?' she whispered anxiously. He wouldn't look at her. He shook her off gently, and gently said, 'We'll see about that. Here! Where's your hand?' He pressed something into her palm. 'Here's a shilling in case you should need it.'

A shilling! She must be going away for ever! 'Father!' cried Fenella. But he was gone. He was the last off the ship. The sailors put their shoulders to the gangway. A huge coil of dark rope went flying through the air and fell 'thump' on the wharf. A bell rang; a whistle shrilled. Silently the dark wharf began to slip, to slide, to edge away from them. Now there was a rush of water between. Fenella strained to see with all her might. 'Was that father turning round?' — or waving? — or standing alone? — or walking off by himself? The strip of water grew broader, darker. Now the Picton boat began to swing round steady, pointing out to sea. It was no good looking any longer. There was nothing to be seen but a few lights, the face of the town clock hanging in the air, and more lights, little patches of them, on the dark hills.

The freshening wind tugged at Fenella's skirts; she went back to her grandma. To her relief grandma seemed no longer sad. She had put the two sausages of luggage one on top of the other, and she was sitting on them, her hands folded, her head a little on one side. There was an intent, bright look on her face. Then Fenella saw that her lips were moving and guessed that she was praying. But the old woman gave her a bright nod as if to say the prayer was nearly over. She unclasped her hands, sighed, clasped them again, bent forward, and at last gave herself a soft shake.

'And now, child,' she said fingering the bow of her bonnet-strings, 'I think we ought to see about our cabins. Keep close to me, and mind you don't slip.'

'Yes, grandma!'

'And be careful the umbrellas aren't caught in the stair rail. I saw a beautiful umbrella broken in half like that on my way over.'

'Yes, grandma.'

Dark figures of men lounged against the rails. In the glow of their pipes a nose shone out, or the peak of a cap, or a pair of surprised-looking eyebrows. Fenella glanced up. High in the air, a little figure, his hands thrust in his short jacket pockets, stood staring out to sea. The ship rocked ever so little, and she thought the stars rocked too. And now a pale steward in a linen coat, holding a tray high in the palm of his hand, stepped out of a lighted doorway and skimmed past them. They went through that doorway. Carefully over the high brass-bound step on to the rubber mat and then down such a terribly steep flight of stairs that grandma had to put both feet on each step, and Fenella clutched the clammy brass rail and forgot all about the swan-necked umbrella.

At the bottom grandma stopped; Fenella was rather afraid she was going to pray again. But no, it was only to get out the cabin tickets. They were in the saloon. It was glaring bright and stifling; the air smelled of paint and burnt chop-bones and india-rubber. Fenella wished her grandma would go on, but the old woman was not to be hurried. An immense basket of ham sand-wiches caught her eye. She went up to them and touched the top one delicately with her finger.

'How much are the sandwiches?' she asked.

'Tuppence!' bawled a rude steward, slamming down a knife and fork.

Grandma could hardly believe it.

'Twopence *each*?' she asked.

'That's right,' said the steward, and he winked at his companion.

Grandma made a small, astonished face. Then she whispered primly to Fenella. 'What wickedness!' And they sailed out at the further door and along a passage that had cabins on either side. Such a very nice stewardess came to meet them. She was dressed all in blue, and her collar and cuffs were fastened with large brass buttons. She seemed to know grandma well.

'Well, Mrs Crane,' said she, unlocking their washstand. 'We've got you back again. It's not often you give yourself a cabin.'

'No,' said grandma. 'But this time my dear son's thoughtful-ness — '

'I hope — ' began the stewardess. Then she turned round and took a long mournful look at grandma's blackness and at Fenella's black coat and skirt, black blouse, and hat with a crêpe rose.

Grandma nodded. 'It was God's will,' said she.

The stewardess shut her lips and, taking a deep breath, she seemed to expand.

'What I always say is,' she said, as though it was her own dis-covery, 'sooner or later each of us has to go, and that's a certingty.' She paused. 'Now, can I bring you anything, Mrs Crane? A cup of tea? I know it's no good offering you a little something to keep the cold out.'

Grandma shook her head. 'Nothing, thank you. We've got a few wine biscuits, and Fenella has a very nice banana.'

'Then I'll give you a look later on,' said the stewardess, and she went out, shutting the door.

What a very small cabin it was! It was like being shut up in a box with grandma. The dark round eye above the washstand gleamed at them dully. Fenella felt shy. She stood against the door, still clasping her luggage and the umbrella. Were they going to get undressed in here? Already her grandma had taken off her bonnet, and, rolling up the strings, she fixed each with a pin to the lining before she hung the bonnet up. Her white hair shone like silk; the little bun at the back was covered with a black net. Fenella hardly ever saw her grandma with her head uncovered; she looked strange.

'I shall put on the woollen fascinator your dear mother crocheted for me,' said grandma, and, unstrapping the sausage, she took it out and wound it round her head; the fringe of grey bobbles danced at her eyebrows and she smiled tenderly and mournfully at Fenella. Then she undid her bodice, and something under that, and something else underneath that. Then there seemed a short, sharp tussle, and grandma flushed faintly. Snip! Snap! She had undone her stays. She breathed a sigh of relief, and sitting on the plush couch, she slowly and carefully pulled off her elastic-sided boots and stood them side by side.

By the time Fenella had taken off her coat and skirt and put on her flannel dressing-down grandma was quite ready.

'Must I take off my boots, grandma? They're lace.'

Grandma gave them a moment's deep consideration. 'You'd feel a great deal more comfortable if you did, child,' said she. She kissed Fenella. 'Don't forget to say your prayers. Our dear Lord is with us when we are at sea even more than when we are on dry land. And because I am an experienced traveller,' said grandma briskly, 'I shall take the upper berth.'

'But, grandma, however will you get up there?'

Three little spider-like steps were all Fenella saw. The old woman gave a small silent laugh before she mounted them nimbly, and she peered over the high bunk at the astonished Fenella.

'You didn't think your grandma could do that, did you?' said she. And as she sank back Fenella heard her light laugh again.

The hard square of brown soap would not lather, and the water in the bottle was like a kind of blue jelly. How hard it was, too, to turn down those stiff sheets; you simply had to tear your way in. If everything had been different, Fenella might have got the giggles ... At last she was inside, and while she lay there panting, there sounded from above a long, soft whispering, as though some one was gently, gently rustling among tissue paper to find something. It was grandma saying her prayers ...

A long time passed. Then the stewardess came in; she trod softly and leaned her hand on grandma's bunk.

'We're just entering the Straits,' she said.

'Oh!'

'It's fine night, but we're rather empty. We may pitch a little.'

And indeed at that moment the Picton boat rose and rose and hung in the air just long enough to give a shiver before she swung down again, and there was the sound of heavy water slapping against her sides. Fenella remembered she had left that swan-necked umbrella standing up on the little couch. If it fell over, would it break? But grandma remembered too, at the same time.

'I wonder if you'd mind, stewardess, laying down my umbrella,' she whispered.

'Not at all, Mrs Crane.' And the stewardess, coming back to grandma, breathed, 'Your little granddaughter's in such a beautiful sleep.'

'God be praised for that!' said grandma.

'Poor little motherless mite!' said the stewardess. And

grandma was still telling the stewardess all about what happened when Fenella fell asleep.

But she hadn't been asleep long enough to dream before she woke up again to see something waving in the air above her head. What was it? What could it be? It was a small grey foot. Now another joined it. They seemed to be feeling about for something; there came a sigh.

'I'm awake, grandma,' said Fenella.

'Oh, dear, am I near the ladder?' asked grandma. 'I thought it was this end.'

'No, grandma, it's the other. I'll put your foot on it. Are we there?' asked Fenella.

'In the harbour,' said grandma. 'We must get up, child. You'd better have a biscuit to steady yourself before you move.'

But Fenella had hopped out of her bunk. The lamp was still burning, but night was over, and it was cold. Peering through that round eye, she could see far off some rocks. Now they were scattered over with foam; now a gull slipped by; and now there came a long piece of real land.

'It's land, grandma,' said Fenella, wonderingly, as though they had been at sea for weeks together. She hugged herself; she stood on one leg and rubbed it with the toes of the other foot; she was trembling. Oh, it had all been so sad lately. Was it going to change? But all her grandma said was, 'Make haste, child. I should leave your nice banana for the stewardess as you haven't eaten it.' And Fenella put on her black clothes again, and a button sprang off one of her gloves and rolled to where she couldn't reach it. They went up on deck.

But if it had been cold in the cabin, on deck it was like ice. The sun was not up yet, but the stars were dim, and the cold pale sky was the same colour as the cold pale sea. On the land a white mist rose and fell. Now they could see quite plainly dark bush. Even the shapes of the umbrella ferns showed, and those strange silvery withered trees that are like skeletons … Now they could see the landing-stage and some little houses, pale too, clustered together, like shells on the lid of a box. The other passengers tramped up and down, but more slowly than they had the night before, and they looked gloomy.

And now the landing-stage came out to meet them. Slowly it swam towards the Picton boat, and a man holding a coil of rope, and a cart with a small drooping horse and another man sitting on the step, came too.

'It's Mr Penreddy, Fenella, come for us,' said grandma. She sounded pleased. Her white waxen cheeks were blue with cold, her chin trembled, and she had to keep wiping her eyes and her little pink nose.

'You've got my — '

'Yes, grandma.' Fenella showed it to her.

The rope came flying through the air, and 'smack' it fell on to the deck. The gangway was lowered. Again Fenella followed her grandma on to the wharf over to the little cart, and a moment later they were bowling away. The hooves of the little horse drummed over the wooden piles, then sank softly into the sandy road. Not a soul was to be seen; there was not even a feather of smoke. The mist rose and fell, and the sea still sounded asleep as slowly it turned on the beach.

'I seen Mr Crane yestiddy,' said Mr Penreddy. 'He looked himself then. Missus knocked him up a batch of scones last week.'

And now the little horse pulled up before one of the shell-like houses. They got down. Fenella put her hand on the gate, and the big, trembling dew-drops soaked through her glove-tips. Up a little path of round white pebbles they went, with drenched sleeping flowers on either side. Grandma's delicate white picotees were so heavy with dew that they were fallen, but their sweet smell was part of the cold morning. The blinds were down in the little house; they mounted the steps on to the verandah. A pair of old bluchers was on one side of the door, and a large red watering-can on the other.

'Tut! tut! Your grandpa,' said grandma. She turned the handle. Not a sound. She called, 'Walter!' And immediately a deep voice that sounded half stifled called back, 'Is that you, Mary?'

'Wait, dear,' said grandma. 'Go in there.' She pushed Fenella gently into a small dusky sitting-room.

On the table a white cat, that had been folded up like a camel, rose, stretched itself, yawned, and then sprang on to the tips of its toes. Fenella buried one cold little hand in the white, warm fur, and smiled timidly while she stroked and listened to grandma's gentle voice and the rolling tones of grandpa.

A door creaked. 'Come in, dear.' The old woman beckoned, Fenella followed. There, lying to one side of an immense bed, lay grandpa. Just his head with a white tuft, and his rosy face and long silver beard showed over the quilt. He was like a very old wide-awake bird.

'Well, my girl!' said grandpa. 'Give us a kiss!' Fenella kissed him. 'Ugh!' said grandpa. 'Her little nose is as cold as a button. What's that she's holding? Her grandma's umbrella?'

Fenella smiled again, and crooked the swan neck over the bed-rail. Above the bed there was a big text in a deep-black frame: —

> *Lost! One Golden Hour*
> *Set with Sixty Diamond Minutes.*
> *No Reward is Offered*
> *For It Is* GONE FOR EVER!

'Yer grandma painted that,' said grandpa. And he ruffled his white tuft and looked at Fenella so merrily she almost thought he winked at her.

A Bad Idea

Something's happened to me — something bad. And I don't know what to do about it. I don't see any way out for the life of me. The worst of it is, I can't get this thing into focus — if you know what I mean. I just feel in a muddle — in the hell of a muddle. It ought to be plain to anyone that I'm not the kind of man to get mixed up in a thing like this. I'm not one of your actor Johnnies, or a chap in a book. I'm — well, I knew what I was all right until yesterday. But now — I feel helpless, yes, that's the world, helpless. Here I sit, chucking stones at the sea like a child that's missed its mother. And everybody else has cut along home hours ago and tea's over and it's getting on for time to light the lamp. I shall have to go home too, sooner or later. I see that, of course. In fact, would you believe it? at this very moment I wish I was there in spite of everything. What's she doing? My wife, I mean. Has she cleared away? Or has she stayed there staring at the table with the plates pushed back? My God! when I think that I could howl like a dog — if you know what I mean …

I should have realised it was all U.P. this morning when she didn't get up for breakfast. I did, in a way. But I couldn't face it. I had the feeling that if I said nothing special and just treated it as one of her bad headache days and went off to the office, by the time I got back this evening the whole affair would have blown over somehow. No, that wasn't it. I felt a bit like I do now, 'helpless'. What was I to do? Just go on. That was all I could think of. So I took her up a cup of tea and a couple of slices of thin bread and butter as per usual on her headache days. The blind was still down. She was lying on her back. I think she had a wet handkerchief on her forehead. I'm not sure, for I couldn't look at her. It was a beastly feeling. And she said in a weak kind of voice, 'Put the jug on the table, will you?' I put it down. I said, 'Can I do anything?' And she said, 'No. I'll be all right in half an hour.' But her voice, you know! It did for me. I barged out as quick as I could, snatched my hat and stick from the hall-stand and dashed off for the tram.

Here's a queer thing — you needn't believe me if you don't want to — the moment I got out of the house I forgot that about my wife. It was a splendid morning, soft, with the sun making silver ducks on the sea. The kind of morning when you know it's going to keep hot and fine all day. Even the tram bell sounded different, and the little school kids crammed between people's knees had bunches of flowers. I don't know — I can't understand why — I just felt happy, but happy in a way I'd never been before, happy to beat the band! That wind that had been so strong the night before was still blowing a bit. It felt like her — the other — touching me. Yes, it did. Brought it back, every bit of it. If I told you how it took me, you'd say I was mad. I felt reckless — didn't care if I was late for the office or not and I wanted to do every one a kindness. I helped the little kids out of the tram. One little chap dropped his cap, and when I picked it up for him and said, 'Here, sonny!'... well, it was all I could do not to make a fool of myself.

At the office it was just the same. It seemed to me I'd never known the fellows at the office before. When old Fisher came over to my desk and put down a couple of giant sweet peas as per usual with his 'Beat 'em, old man, beat 'em!' — I didn't feel annoyed. I didn't care that he was riddled with conceit about his garden. I just looked at them and I said quietly, 'Yes, you've done it this time.' He didn't know what to make of it. Came back in about five minutes and asked me if I had a headache.

And so it went on all day. In the evening I dashed home with the home-going crowd, pushed open the gate, saw the hall-door open as it always is and sat down on the little chair just inside to take off my boots. My slippers were there, of course. This seemed to me a good sign. I put my boots into the rack in the cupboard under the stairs, changed my office coat and made for the kitchen. I knew my wife was there. Wait a bit. The only thing I couldn't manage was my whistling as per usual, 'I often lie awake and think, What a dreadful thing is work ...' I had a try, but nothing came of it. Well, I opened the kitchen door and said, 'Hullo! How's everybody?' But as soon as I'd said that — even before — I knew the worst had happened. She was standing at the table beating the salad dressing. And when she looked up and gave a kind of smile and said 'Hullo!' you could have knocked me down! My wife looked dreadful — there's no other word for it. She must have been crying all day. She'd put some white flour stuff on her face to take away the marks — but it only made her look worse. She must have seen I spotted something, for she caught up the cup of cream and poured some into the salad bowl — like she always does, you know, so quick, so neat, in her own way — and began beating again. I said, 'Is your head better?' But she didn't seem to hear. She said, 'Are you going to water the garden before or after supper?' What could I say? I said, 'After,' and went off to the dining-room, opened the evening paper and sat by the open window — well, hiding behind that paper, I suppose.

I shall never forget sitting there. People passing by, going down the road, sounded so peaceful. And a man passed with some cows. I — I envied him. My wife came in and out. Then she called me to supper and we sat down. I suppose we ate some cold meat and salad. I don't remember. We must have. But neither of us spoke. It's like a dream now. Then she got up, changed the plates, and went to the larder for the pudding. Do you know what the pudding was? Well, of course, it wouldn't mean anything to you. It was my favourite — the kind she only made me on special occasions — honeycomb cream ...

A Married Man's Story

It is evening. Supper is over. We have left the small, cold dining room; we have come back to the sitting room where there is a fire. All is as usual. I am sitting at my writing table which is placed across a corner so that I am behind it, as it were, and facing the room. The lamp with the green shade is alight; I have before me two large books of reference, both open, a pile of papers ... All the paraphernalia, in fact, of an extremely occupied man. My wife, with our little boy on her lap, is in a low chair before the fire. She is about to put him to bed before she clears away the dishes and piles them up in the kitchen for the servant girl to-morrow morning. But the warmth, and quiet, and the sleepy baby, have made her dreamy. One of his red woollen boots is off; one is on. She sits, bent forward, clasping the little bare foot, staring into the glow, and as the fire quickens, falls, flares again, her shadow — an immense *Mother and Child* — is here and gone again upon the wall ...

Outside it is raining. I like to think of that cold drenched window behind the blind, and beyond, the dark bushes in the garden, their broad leaves bright with rain, and beyond the fence, the gleaming road with the two hoarse little gutters singing against each other, and the wavering reflections of the lamps, like fishes' tails ... While I am here, I am there, lifting my face to the dim sky, and it seems to me it must be raining all over the world — the whole earth is drenched, is sounding with a soft quick patter or hard steady drumming, or gurgling and something that is like sobbing and laughing mingled together, and that light playful splashing that is of water falling into still lakes and flowing rivers. And all at one and the same moment I am arriving in a strange city, slipping under the hood of the cab while the driver whips the cover off the breathing horse, running from shelter to shelter, dodging someone, swerving by someone else. I am conscious of tall houses, their doors and shutters sealed against the night, of dripping balconies and sodden flower pots, I am brushing through deserted gardens and peering into moist smelling summer-houses (you know how soft and almost crumbling the wood of a summer-house is in the rain), I am standing on the dark quayside, giving my ticket into the wet red hand of the old sailor in an oil-skin — How strong the sea smells! How loudly those tied-up boats knock against one another! I am crossing the wet stackyard, hooded in an old sack, carrying a lantern, while the house-dog, like a soaking doormat, springs, shakes himself over me. And now I am walking along a deserted road — it is impossible to miss the puddles and the trees are stirring — stirring ...

But one could go on with such a catalogue for ever — on and one — until one lifted the single arum lily leaf and discovered the tiny snails clinging, until one counted ... and what then? Aren't those just the signs, the traces of my feeling? The bright green streaks made by someone who walks over the dewy grass? Not the feeling itself. And as I think that, a mournful glorious voice begins to sing in my bosom. Yes, perhaps that is nearer what I mean. What a voice! What power! What velvety softness! Marvellous!

Suddenly my wife turns round quickly. She knows — how long has she known? — that I am not 'working'! It is strange that with her full, open gaze, she should smile so timidly — and that she should say in such a hesitating voice: 'What are you thinking?'

I smile and draw two fingers across my forehead in the way I have. 'Nothing,' I answer softly.

At that she stirs, and still trying not to make it sound impor-tant, she says: 'Oh, but you must have been thinking of some-thing!'

Then I really meet her gaze, meet it fully, and I fancy her face quivers. Will she never grow accustomed to these simple — one might say — everyday little lies? Will she never learn not to expose herself — or to build up defences?

'Truly, I was thinking of nothing!'

There! I seem to see it dart at her. She turns away, pulls the other red sock off the baby — sits him up, and begins to unbutton him behind. I wonder if that little soft rolling bundle sees anything, feels anything? Now she turns him over on her knee, and in this light, his soft arms and legs waving, he is extraordinarily like a young crab. A queer thing is I can't connect him with my wife and myself; I've never accepted him as ours. Each time when I come into the hall and see the perambulator, I catch myself thinking: 'H'm, someone has brought a baby.' Or, when his crying wakes me at night, I feel inclined to blame my wife for having brought the baby in from outside. The truth is, that though one might suspect her of strong maternal feelings, my wife doesn't seem to me the type of woman who bears children in her own body. There's an immense difference! Where is that … animal ease and playfulness, that quick kissing and cuddling one has been taught to expect of young mothers? She hasn't a sign of it. I believe that when she ties its bonnet she feels like an aunt and not a mother. But of course I may be wrong; she may be passionately devoted … I don't think so. At any rate, isn't it a trifle indecent to feel like this about one's own wife? Indecent or not, one has these feelings. And one other thing. How can I reasonably expect my wife, *a broken-hearted woman*, to spend her time tossing the baby? But that is beside the mark. She never even began to toss when her heart was whole.

And now she has carried the baby to bed. I hear her soft deliberate steps moving between the dining room and the kitchen, there and back again, to the tune of clattering dishes. And now all is quiet. What is happening now? Oh, I know just as surely as if I'd gone to see — she is standing in the middle of the kitchen, facing the rainy window. Her head is bent, with one finger she is tracing something — nothing — on the table. It is cold in the kitchen; the gas jumps; the tap drips; it's a forlorn picture.

And nobody is going to come behind her, to take her in his arms, to kiss her soft hair, to lead her to the fire and to rub [her] hands warm again. Nobody is going to call her or to wonder what she is doing out there. And she knows it. And yet, being a woman, deep down, deep down, she really does expect the miracle to happen; she really could embrace that dark, dark deceit, rather than live — like this.

To live like this ... I write those words, very carefully, very beautifully. For some reason I feel inclined to sign them, or to write underneath — Trying a New Pen. But seriously, isn't it staggering to think what may be contained in one innocent-looking little phrase? It temps me — it temps me terribly. Scene. The supper-table. My wife has just handed me my tea. I stir it, lift the spoon, idly chase and then carefully capture a speck of tea-leaf, and having brought it ashore, I murmur, quite gently, 'How long shall we continue to live — like — this?' And immediately there is that famous 'blinding flash and deafening roar. Huge pieces of débris (must say I like débris) are flung into the air ... and when the dark clouds of smoke have drifted away ...' But this will never happen; I shall never know it. It will be found upon me 'intact' as they say. 'Open my heart and you will see...'

Why? Ah, there you have me! There is the most difficult question of all to answer. Why do people stay together? Putting aside 'for the sake of the children', and 'the habit of years' and 'economic reasons' as lawyers' nonsense — it's not much more — if one really does try to find out why it is that people don't leave each other, one discovers a mystery. It is because they can't; they are bound. And nobody on earth knows what are the bands that bind them except those two. Am I being obscure? Well, the thing itself isn't so frightfully crystal clear, is it? Let me put it like this. Supposing you are taken, absolutely, first into his confidence and then into hers. Supposing you know all there is to know about the situation. And having given it not only your deepest sympathy but your most honest impartial criticism, you declare, very calmly (but not without the slightest suggestion of relish — for there is — I swear there is — in the very best of us — something that leaps up and cries 'A-ahh!' for joy at the thought of destroying), 'Well, my opinion is that you two people ought to part. You'll do no earthly good together. Indeed, it seems to me, it's the duty of either to set the other free.' What happens then? He — and she — agree. It is their conviction too. You are only saying what they have been thinking all last night. And away they go to act on your advice, immediately ... And the next time you hear of them they are still together. You see — you've reckoned without the unknown quantity — which is their secret relation to each other — and that they can't disclose even if they want to. Thus far you may tell and no further. Oh, don't misunderstand me! It need not necessarily have anything to do with their sleeping together ... But this brings me to a thought I've often half entertained. Which is, that human beings, as we know them, don't choose each other at all. It is the owner, the second self inhabiting them, who makes the choice for his own particular purposes, and — this may sound absurdly far-fetched — it's the second self in the other which responds. Dimly — dimly — or so it has seemed to me — we realise this, at any rate to the extent that we realise the hopelessness of trying to escape. So that, what it all amounts to is — if the impermanent selves of my wife and me are happy — *tant mieux pour nous* — if miserable — *tant pis* ... But I don't know, I don't know. And it may be that it's something entirely individual to me — this sensation (yes, it is even a sensation) of how extraordinarily *shell-like* we are as we are — little creatures, peering out of the sentry-box at the gate, ogling through our glass case at the entry, wan little servants, who never can say for certain, even, if the master is out or in ...

The door opens ... My wife. She says: 'I am going to bed.'

And I look up vaguely, and vaguely say: 'You are going to bed.'

'Yes.' A tiny pause. 'Don't forget — will you? — to turn out the gas in the hall.'

And again I repeat: 'The gas in the hall.'

There was a time — the time before — when this habit of mine (it really has become a habit now — it wasn't one then) was one of our sweetest jokes together. It began, of course, when, on several occasions, I really was deeply engaged and I didn't hear. I emerged only to see her shaking her head and laughing at me, 'You haven't heard a word!'

'No. What did you say?'

Why should she think that so funny and charming? She did; it delighted her. 'Oh, my darling, it's so like you! It's so — so — .' And I knew she loved me for it — knew she positively looked forward to coming in and disturbing me, and so — as one does — I played up. I was guaranteed to be wrapped away every evening at 10.30 p.m. But now? For some reason I feel it would be crude to stop my performance. It's simplest to play on. But what is she waiting for to-night? Why doesn't she go? Why prolong this? She is going. No, her hand on the door-knob, she turns round again, and she says in the most curious, small, breathless voice, 'You're not cold?'

Oh, it's not fair to be as pathetic as that! That was simply damnable. I shudder all over before I manage to bring out a slow 'No-o', while my left hand ruffles the reference pages.

She is gone; she will not come back again to-night. It is not only I who recognise that; the room changes, too. It relaxes, like an old actor. Slowly the mask is rubbed off; the look of strained attention changes to an air of heavy, sullen brooding. Every line, every fold breathes fatigue. The mirror is quenched; the ash whitens; only my shy lamp burns on ... But what a cynical indifference to me it all shows! Or should I perhaps be flattered? No, we understand each other. You know those stories of little children who are suckled by wolves and accepted by the tribe, and how for ever after they move freely among their fleet grey brothers? Something like that has happened to me. But wait — that about the wolves won't do. Curious! Before I wrote it down, while it was still in my head, I was delighted with it. It seemed to express, and more, to suggest, just what I wanted to say. But written, I can smell the falseness immediately and the ... source of the smell is in that word fleet. Don't you agree? Fleet, grey brothers! 'Fleet.' A word I never use. When I wrote 'wolves' it skimmed across my mind like a shadow and I couldn't resist it. Tell me! Tell me! Why it is so difficult to write simply — and not only simply but *sotto voce*, if you know what I mean? That is how I long to write. No fine effects — no bravuras. But just the plain truth, as only a liar can tell it.

I light a cigarette, lean back, inhale deeply — and find myself wondering if my wife is asleep. Or is she lying in her cold bed, staring into the dark with those trustful, bewildered eyes? Her eyes are like the eyes of a cow that is being driven along a road. 'Why am I being driven — what harm have I done?' But I really am not responsible for that look; it's her natural expression. One day, when she was turning out a cupboard, she found a little old photograph of herself, taken when she was a girl at school. In her confirmation dress, she explained. And there were the eyes, even then. I remember saying to her: 'Did you always look so sad?' Leaning over my shoulder, she laughed lightly. 'Do I look sad? I think it's just ... me.' And she waited for me to say something about it. But I was marvelling at her courage at having shown it to me at all. It was a hideous photograph! And I wondered again if she realised how plain she was, and comforted herself with the idea that people who loved each other didn't criticise but accepted everything, or if she really rather liked her appearance and expected me to say something complimentary. Oh, that was base of me! How could I have forgotten all the countless times when I have known her turn away, avoid the light, press her face into my shoulders. And above all, how could I have forgotten the afternoon of our wedding day, when we sat on the green bench in the Botanical Gardens and listened to the band, how, in an interval between two pieces, she suddenly turned to me and said in the voice in which one says: 'Do you think the grass is damp?' or 'Do you think it's time for tea?' … 'Tell me — do you think physical beauty is so very important?' I don't like to think how often she had rehearsed that question. And do you know what I answered? At that moment, as if at my command, there came a great gush of hard bright sound from the band. And I managed to shout above it — cheerfully — 'I didn't hear what you said.' Devilish! Wasn't it? Perhaps not wholly. She looked like the poor patient who hears the surgeon say, 'It will certainly be necessary to perform the operation — but not now!'

But all this conveys the impression that my wife and I were never really happy together. Not true! Not true! We were marvellously, radiantly happy. We were a model couple. If you had seen us together, any time, any place, if you had followed us, tracked us down, spied, taken us off our guard, you still would have been forced to confess, 'I have never seen a more ideally suited pair.' Until last autumn.

But really to explain what happened then I should have to go back and back, I should have to dwindle until my tiny hands clutched the banisters, the stair-rail was higher than my head, and I peered through to watch my father padding softly up and down. There were coloured windows on the landings. As he came up, first his bald head was scarlet; then it was yellow. How frightened I was! And when they put me to bed, it was to dream that we were living inside one of my father's big coloured bottles. For he was a chemist. I was born nine years after my parents were married; I was an only child, and the effort to produce even me — small, withered bud I must have been — sapped all my mother's strength. She never left her room again. Bed, sofa, window, she moved between the three. Well I can see her, on the window days, sitting, her cheek in her hand, staring out. Her room looked over the street. Opposite there was a wall plastered with advertisements for travelling shows and circuses and so on. I stand beside her, and we gaze at the slim lady in a red dress hitting a dark gentleman over the head with her parasol, or at the tiger purring through the jungle while the clown, close by, balances a bottle on his nose, or at a little golden-haired girl sitting on the knee of an old black man in a broad cotton hat ... She says nothing. On the sofa days there is a flannel dressing-gown that I loathe, and a cushion that keeps on slipping off the hard sofa. I pick it up. It has flowers and writing sewn on. I ask what the writing says, and she whispers, 'Sweet Repose!' In bed her fingers plait, in tight little plaits, the fringe of the quilt, and her lips are thin. And that is all there is of my mother, except the last queer 'episode' that comes later ...

My father — curled up on the corner on the lid of a round box that held sponges, I stared at my father so long it's as though his image, cut off at the waist by the counter, has remained solid in my memory. Perfectly bald, polished head, shaped like a thin egg, creased creamy cheeks, little bags under the eyes, large pale ears like handles. His manner was discreet, sly, faintly amused and tinged with impudence. Long before I could appreciate it I knew the mixture ... I even used to copy him in my corner, bending forward, with a small reproduction of his faint sneer. In the evening his customers were, chiefly, young women; some of them came in every day for his famous fivepenny pick-me-up. Their gaudy looks, their voices, their free ways, fascinated me. I longed to be my father, handing them across the counter the little glass of bluish stuff they tossed off so greedily. God knows what it was made of. Years after I drank some, just to see what it tasted like, and I felt as though someone had given me a terrific blow on the head; I felt stunned. One of those evenings I remember vividly. It was cold; it must have been autumn, for the flaring gas was lighted after my tea. I sat in my corner and my father was mixing something; the shop was empty. Suddenly the bell jangled and a young woman rushed in, crying so loud, sobbing so hard, that it didn't sound real. She wore a green cape trimmed with fur and a hat with cherries dangling. My father came from behind the screen. But she couldn't stop herself at first. She stood in the middle of the shop and wrung her hands, and moaned. I've never heard such crying since. Presently she managed to gasp out, 'Give me a pick-me-up.' Then she drew a long breath, trembled away from him and quavered: 'I've had *bad news!*' And in the flaring gaslight I saw the whole side of her face was puffed up and purple; her lip was cut, and her eyelid looked as though it was gummed fast over the wet eye. My father pushed the glass across the counter, and she took her purse out of her stocking and paid him. But she couldn't drink; clutching the glass, she stared in front of her as if she could not believe what she saw. Each time she put her head back the tears spurted out again. Finally she put the glass down. It was no use. Holding the cape with one hand, she ran in the same way out of the shop again. My father gave no sign. But long after she had gone I crouched in my corner, and when I think back it's as though I felt my whole body vibrating — 'So that's what it is outside,' I thought. 'That's what it's like out there.'

Do you remember your childhood? I am always coming across these marvellous accounts by writers who declare that they remember 'everything, everything'. I certainly don't. The dark stretches, the blanks, are much bigger than the bright glimpses.

I seem to have spent most of my time like a plant in a cupboard. Now and again, when the sun shone, a careless hand thrust me out on to the window-sill, and a careless hand whipped me in again — and that was all. But what happened in the darkness — I wonder? Did one grow? Pale stem ... timid leaves ... white, reluctant bud. No wonder I was hated at school. Even the masters shrank from me. I somehow knew that my soft hesitating voice disgusted them. I knew, too, how they turned away from my shocked, staring eyes. I was small and thin, and I smelled of the shop; my nickname was Gregory Powder. School was a tin building stuck on the raw hillside. There were dark red streaks like blood in the oozing clay banks of the playground. I hide in the dark passage, where the coats hang, and am discovered there by one of the masters. 'What are you doing there in the dark?' His terrible voice kills me; I die before his eyes. I am standing in a ring of thrust-out heads; some are grinning, some look greedy, some are sitting. And it is always cold. Big crushed up clouds press across the sky; the rusty water in the school tank is frozen; the bell sounds numb. One day they put a dead bird in my over-coat pocket. I found it just when I reached home. Oh, what a strange flutter there was at my heart, when I drew out that ter-ribly soft, cold little body, with the legs thin as pins and the claws wrung. I sat on the back door step in the yard and put the bird in my cap. The feathers round the neck looked wet and there was a tiny tuft just above the closed eyes that stood up too. How tightly the beak was shut; I could not see the mark where it was divided. I stretched out one wing and touched the soft, secret down underneath; I tried to make the claws curl round my little finger. But I didn't feel sorry for it — no! I wondered. The smoke from our kitchen chimney poured downwards, and flakes of soot floated — soft, light in the air. Through a big crack in the cement yard a poor-looking plant with dull reddish flowers had pushed its way. I looked at the dead bird again ... And that is the first time that I remember singing, rather ... listening to a silent voice inside a little cage that was me.

But what has all this to do with my married happiness? How can all this affect my wife and me? Why — to tell what happened last autumn — do I run all this way back into the Past? The Past — what is the Past? I might say the star-shaped flake of soot on the leaf of the poor-looking plant, and the bird lying on the quilted lining of my cap, and my father's pestle and my mother's cushion, belong to it. But that is not to say they are any less mine than they were when I looked upon them with my very eyes, and touched them with these fingers. No, they are more; they are a living part of me. Who am I, in fact, as I sit here at this table, but my own past? If I deny that, I am nothing. And if I were to try and divide my life into childhood, youth, early manhood and so on, it would be a kind of affectation; I should know I was doing it just because of the pleasantly important sensation it gives one to rule lines, and to use green ink for childhood, red for the next stage, and purple for the period of adolescence. For one, thing I have learnt, one thing I do believe is, Nothing Happens Suddenly. Yes, that is my religion, I suppose ...

My mother's death, for instance. Is it more distant from me to-day than it was then? It is just as close, as strange, as puzzling, and in spite of all the countless time I have recalled the circumstances, I know no more now than I did then whether I dreamed them or whether they really occurred. It happened when I was thirteen and I slept in a little strip of a room on what was called the Half Landing. One night I woke up with a start to see my mother, in her nightgown, without even the hated flannel dressing-gown, sitting on my bed. But the strange thing which frightened me was, she wasn't looking at me. Her head was bent; the short thin tail of hair lay between her shoulders; her hands were pressed between her knees, and my bed shook; she was shivering. It was the first time I had ever seen her out of her own room. I said, or I think I said, 'Is that you, mother?' And as she turned round I saw in the moonlight how queer she looked. Her face looked small — quite different. She looked like one of the boys at the school baths, who sits on a step, shivering just like that, and wants to go in and yet is frightened.

'Are you awake?' she said. Her eyes opened; I think she smiled. She leaned towards me. 'I've been poisoned,' she whispered. 'Your father's poisoned me.' And she nodded. Then, before I could say a word, she was gone, and I thought I heard the door shut. I sat quite still; I couldn't move. I think I expected something else to happen. For a long time I listened for something; there wasn't a sound. The candle was by my bed, but I was too frightened to stretch out my hand for the matches. But even while I wondered what I ought to do, even while my heart thumped — everything became confused. I lay down and pulled the blankets round me. I fell asleep, and the next morning my mother was found dead of failure of the heart.

Did that visit happen? Was it a dream? Why did she come to tell me? Or why, if she came, did she go away so quickly? And her expression — so joyous under the frightened look — was that real? I believed it fully the afternoon of the funeral, when I saw my father dressed up for his part, hat and all. That tall hat so gleaming black and round was like a cork covered with black sealing-wax, and the rest of my father was awfully like a bottle, with his face for the label — *Deadly Poison*. It flashed into my mind as I stood opposite him in the hall. And Deadly Poison, or old D.P., was my private name for him from that day.

Late, it grows late. I love the night. I love to feel the tide of darkness rising slowly and slowly washing, turning over and over, lifting, floating, all that lies strewn upon the dark beach, all that lies hid in rocky hollows. I love, I love this strange feeling of drifting

— whither? After my mother's death I hated to go to bed. I used to sit on the window-sill, folded up, and watch the sky. It seemed to me the moon moved much faster than the sun. And one big, bright green star I chose for my own. My star! But I never thought of it beckoning to me or twinkling merrily for my sake. Cruel, indifferent, splendid — it burned in the airy night. No matter — it was mine! But growing close up against the window there was a creeper with small, bunched up pink and purple flowers. These did know me. These, when I touched them at night, welcomed my fingers; the little tendrils, so weak, so delicate, knew I would not hurt them. When the wind moved the leaves I felt I understood their shaking. When I came to the window, it seemed to me the flowers said among themselves, 'The boy is here.'

As the months passed, there was often a light in my father's room below. And I heard voices and laughter. 'He's got some woman with him,' I thought. But it meant nothing to me. Then the gay voice, the sound of the laughter, gave me the idea it was one of the girls who used to come to the shop in the evenings — and gradually I began to imagine which girl it was. It was the dark one in the red coat and skirt, who once had given me a penny. A merry face stooped over me — warm breath tickled my neck — there were little beads of black on her long lashes, and when she opened her arms to kiss me, there came a marvellous wave of scent! Yes, that was the one. Time passed, and I forgot the moon and my green star and my shy creeper — I came to the window to wait for the light in my father's window, to listen for the laughing voice, until one night I dozed and I dreamed she came again — again she drew me to her, something soft, scented, warm and merry hung over me like a cloud. But when I tried to see, her eyes only mocked me, her red lips opened and she hissed, 'Little sneak! Little sneak!' But not as if she were angry, as if she understood, and her smile somehow was like a rat … hateful!

The night after, I lighted the candle and sat down at the table instead. By and by, as the flame steadied, there was a small lake of liquid wax, surrounded by a white, smooth wall. I took a pin and made little holes in this wall and then sealed them up faster than the wax could escape. After a time I fancied the candle flame joined in the game; it leapt up, quivered, wagged; it even seemed to laugh. But while I played with the candle and smiled and broke off the tiny white peaks of wax that rose above the wall and floated them on my lake, a feeling of awful dreariness fastened on me — yes, that is the word. It crept up from my knees to my thighs, into my arms; I ached all over with misery. And I felt so strangely that I couldn't move. Something bound me there by the table — I couldn't even let the pin drop that I held between my finger and thumb. For a moment I came to a stop, as it were.

Then the shrivelled case of the bud split and fell, the plant in the cupboard came into flower. 'Who am I?' I thought. 'What is all this?' And I looked at my room, at the broken bust of the man called Hahnemann on top of the cupboard, at my little bed with the pillow like an envelope. I saw it all, but not as I had seen before ... Everything lived, but everything. But that was not all. I was equally alive and — it's the only way I can express it — the barriers were down between us — I had come into my own world!

The barriers were down. I had been all my life a little outcast; but until that moment no one had 'accepted' me; I had lain in the cupboard — or the cave forlorn. But now — I was taken, I was accepted, claimed. I did not consciously turn away from the world of human beings; I had never known it; but I from that night did beyond words consciously turn towards my silent brothers ...

The Garden Party

And after all the weather was ideal. They could not have had a more perfect day for a garden party if they had ordered it. Windless, warm, the sky without a cloud. Only the blue was veiled with a haze of light gold, as it is sometimes in early summer. The gardener had been up since dawn, mowing the lawns and sweeping them, until the grass and the dark flat rosettes where the daisy plants had been seemed to shine. As for the roses, you could not help feeling they understood that roses are the only flowers that impress people at garden parties; the only flowers that everybody is certain of knowing. Hundreds, yes, literally hundreds, had come out in a single night; the green bushes bowed down as though they had been visited by archangels.

Breakfast was not yet over before the men came to put up the marquee.

'Where do you want the marquee put, mother?'

'My dear child, it's no use asking me. I'm determined to leave everything to you children this year. Forget I am your mother. Treat me as an honoured guest.'

But Meg could not possibly go and supervise the men. She had washed her hair before breakfast, and she sat drinking her coffee in a green turban, with a dark wet curl stamped on each cheek. Jose, the butterfly, always came down in a silk petticoat and a kimono jacket.

'You'll have to go, Laura, you're the artistic one.'

Away Laura flew, still holding her piece of bread-and-butter. It's so delicious to have an excuse for eating out of doors, and besides, she loved having to arrange things; she always felt she could do it so much better than anybody else.

Four men in their shirt-sleeves stood grouped together on the garden path. They carried staves covered with rolls of canvas, and they had big tool-bags slung on their backs. They looked impressive. Laura wished now that she was not holding that piece of bread-and-butter, but there was nowhere to put it, and she couldn't possibly throw it away. She blushed and tried to look severe and even a little bit short-sighted as she came up to them.

'Good morning,' she said, copying her mother's voice. But that sounded so fearfully affected that she was ashamed, and stammered like a little girl, 'Oh — er — have you come — is it about the marquee?'

'That's right, miss,' said the tallest of the men, a lanky, freck-led fellow, and he shifted his tool-bag, knocked back his straw hat and smiled down at her. 'That's about it.'

His smile was so easy, so friendly, that Laura recovered. What nice eyes he had, small, but such a dark blue! And now she looked at the others, they were smiling too. 'Cheer up, we won't bite,' their smile seemed to say. How very nice workmen were! And what a beautiful morning! She musn't mention the morning; she must be business-like. The marquee.

'Well, what about the lily-lawn? Would that do?'

And she pointed to the lily-lawn with the hand that didn't hold the bread-and-butter. They turned, they stared in the direction. A little fat chap thrust out his under-lip, and the tall fellow frowned.

'I don't fancy it,' said he. 'Not conspicuous enough. You see, with a thing like a marquee,' and he turned to Laura in his easy way, 'you want to put it somewhere where it'll give you a bang slap in the eye, if you follow me.'

Laura's upbringing made her wonder for a moment whether it was quite respectful of a workman to talk to her of bangs slap in the eye. But she did quite follow him.

'A corner of the tennis-court,' she suggested. 'But the band's going to be in one corner.'

'H'm, going to have a band, are you?' said another of the workmen. He was pale. He had a haggard look as his dark eyes scanned the tennis-court. What was he thinking?

'Only a very small band,' said Laura gently. Perhaps he wouldn't mind so much if the band was quite small. But the tall fellow interrupted.

'Look here, miss, that's the place. Against those trees. Over there. That'll do fine.'

Against the karakas. Then the karaka-trees would be hidden. And they were so lovely, with their broad, gleaming leaves, and their clusters of yellow fruit. They were like trees you imagined growing on a desert island, proud, solitary, lifting their leaves and fruits to the sun in a kind of silent splendour. Must they be hidden by a marquee?

They must. Already the men had shouldered their staves and were making for the place. Only the tall fellow was left. He bent down, pinched a sprig of lavender, put his thumb and forefinger to his nose and snuffed up the smell. When Laura saw the gesture she forgot all about the karakas in her wonder at him caring for things like that — caring for the smell of lavender. How many men that she knew would have done such a thing. Oh, how extraordinarily nice workmen were, she thought. Why couldn't she have workmen for friends rather than the silly boys she danced with and who came to Sunday night supper? She would get on much better with men like these.

It's all the fault, she decided, as the tall fellow drew something on the back of an envelope, something that was to be looped up or left to hang, of these absurd class distinctions. Well, for her part, she didn't feel them. Not a bit, not an atom ... And now there came the chock-chock of wooden hammers. Some one whistled, some one sang out, 'Are you right there, matey?' 'Matey!' The friendliness of it, the — the — Just to prove how happy she was, just to show the tall fellow how at home she felt, and how she despised stupid conventions, Laura took a big bite of her bread-and-butter as she stared at the little drawing. She felt just like a work-girl.

'Laura, Laura, where are you? Telephone, Laura!' a voice cried from the house.

'Coming!' Away she skimmed, over the lawn, up the path, up the steps, across the veranda, and into the porch. In the hall her father and Laurie were brushing their hats ready to go to the office.

'I say, Laura,' said Laurie very fast, 'you might just give a squiz at my coat before this afternoon. See if it wants pressing.'

'I will,' said she. Suddenly she couldn't stop herself. She ran at Laurie and gave him a small, quick squeeze. 'Oh, I do love parties, don't you?' gasped Laura.

'Ra-ther,' said Laurie's warm, boyish voice, and he squeezed his sister too, and gave her a gentle push. 'Dash off to the telephone, old girl.'

The telephone. 'Yes, yes; oh yes. Kitty? Good morning, dear. Come to lunch? Do, dear. Delighted of course. It will only be a very scratch meal — just the sandwich crusts and broken meringue-shells and what's left over. Yes, isn't it a perfect morning? Your white? Oh, I certainly should. One moment — hold the line. Mother's calling.' And Laura sat back. 'What, mother? Can't hear.'

Mrs Sheridan's voice floated down the stairs. 'Tell her to wear that sweet hat she had on last Sunday.'

'Mother says you're to wear that *sweet* hat you had on last Sunday. Good. One o'clock. Bye-bye.'

Laura put back the receiver, flung her arms over her head, took a deep breath, stretched and let them fall. 'Huh,' she sighed, and the moment after the sigh she sat up quickly. She was still, listening. All the doors in the house seemed to be open. The house was alive with soft, quick steps and running voices. The green baize door that led to the kitchen regions swung open and shut with a muffled thud. And now there came a long, chuckling absurd sound. It was the heavy piano being moved on its stiff castors. But the air! If you stopped to notice, was the air always like this? Little faint winds were playing chase in at the tops of the windows, out at the doors. And there were two tiny spots of sun, one on the inkpot. Especially the one on the inkpot lid. It was quite warm. A warm little silver star. She could have kissed it.

The front door bell pealed, and there sounded the rustle of Sadie's print skirt on the stairs. A man's voice murmured; Sadie answered, careless, 'I'm sure I don't know. Wait. I'll ask Mrs Sheridan.'

'What is it, Sadie?' Laura came into the hall.

'It's the florist, Miss Laura.'

It was, indeed. There, just inside the door, stood a wide, shallow tray full of pots of pink lilies. No other kind. Nothing but lilies — canna lilies, big pink flowers, wide open, radiant, almost frighteningly alive on bright crimson stems.

'O-oh, Sadie!' said Laura, and the sound was like a little moan. She crouched down as if to warm herself at that blaze of lilies; she felt they were in her fingers, on her lips, growing in her breast.

'It's some mistake,' she said faintly. 'Nobody ever ordered so many. Sadie, go and find mother.'

But at that moment Mrs Sheridan joined them.

'It's quite right,' she said calmly. 'Yes, I ordered them. Aren't they lovely?' She pressed Laura's arm. 'I was passing the shop yesterday, and I saw them in the window. and I suddenly thought for once in my life I shall have enough canna lilies. The garden party will be a good excuse.'

'But I thought you said you didn't mean to interfere,' said Laura. Sadie had gone. The florist's man was still outside at his van. She put her arm round her mother's neck and gently, very gently, she bit her mother's ear.

'My darling child, you wouldn't like a logical mother, would you? Don't do that. Here's the man.'

He carried more lilies still, another whole tray.

'Bank them up, just inside the door, on both sides of the porch, please,' said Mrs Sheridan. 'Don't you agree, Laura?'

'Oh, I *do*, mother.'

In the drawing-room Meg, Jose and good little Hans had at last succeeded in moving the piano.

'Now, if we put this chesterfield against the wall and move everything out of the room except the chairs, don't you think?'

'Quite.'

'Hans, move these tables into the smoking-room, and bring a sweeper to take these marks off the carpet and — one moment, Hans — ' Jose loved giving orders to the servants, and they loved obeying her. She always made them feel they were taking part in some drama. 'Tell Mother and Miss Laura to come here at once.'

'Very good, Miss Jose.'

She turned to Meg. 'I want to hear what the piano sounds like, just in case I'm asked to sing this afternoon. Let's try over "This life is Weary".'

Pom! Ta-ta-ta *Tee*-ta! The piano burst out so passionately that Jose's face changed. She clasped her hands. She looked mournfully and enigmatically at her mother and Laura as they came in.

> This Life is *Wee*-ary,
> A Tear — a Sigh.
> A Love that *Chan*-ges,
>   This Life is *Wee*-ary,
> A Tear — a Sigh.
> A Love that *Chan*-ges,
> And then … Good-bye!

But at the word 'Good-bye', and although the piano sounded more desperate than ever, her face broke into a brilliant, dreadfully unsympathetic smile.

'Aren't I in good voice, mummy?' she beamed.

> This Life is *Wee*-ary,
> Hope comes to Die.
> A Dream — a *Wa*-kening.

But now Sadie interrupted them. 'What is it, Sadie?'

'If you please, m'm, cook says have you got the flags for the sandwiches?'

'The flags for the sandwiches, Sadie?' echoed Mrs Sheridan dreamily. And the children knew by her face that she hadn't got them. 'Let me see.' And she said to Sadie firmly, 'Tell cook I'll let her have them in ten minutes.'

Sadie went.

'Now, Laura,' said her mother quickly, 'come with me into the smoking-room. I've got the names somewhere on the back of an envelope. You'll have to write them out for me. Meg, go upstairs this minute and take that wet thing off your head. Jose, run and finish dressing this instant. Do you hear me, children, or shall I have to tell your father when he comes home to-night? And — and, Jose, pacify cook if you do go into the kitchen, will you? I'm terrified of her this morning.'

The envelope was found at last behind the dining-room clock, though how it had got there Mrs Sheridan could not imagine.

'One of you children must have stolen it out of my bag, because I remember vividly — cream-cheese and lemon-curd. Have you done that?'

'Yes.'

'Egg and — ' Mrs Sheridan held the envelope away from her. 'It looks like mice. It can't be mice, can it?'

'Olive, pet,' said Laura, looking over her shoulder.

'Yes, of course, olive. What a horrible combination it sounds. Egg and olive.'

They were finished at last, and Laura took them off to the kitchen. She found Jose there pacifying the cook, who did not look at all terrifying. 'I have never seen such exquisite sandwiches,' said Jose's rapturous voice. 'How many kinds did you say there were, cook? Fifteen?'

'Fifteen, Miss Jose.'

'Well, cook, I congratulate you.'

Cook swept up crusts with the long sandwich knife, and smiled broadly.

'Godber's has come,' announced Sadie, issuing out of the pantry. She had seen the man pass the window.

That meant that cream puffs had come. Godber's were famous for their cream puffs. Nobody ever thought of making them at home.

'Bring them in and put them on the table, my girl,' ordered cook.

Sadie brought them in and went back to the door. Of course Laura and Jose were far too grown-up to really care about such things. All the same they couldn't help agreeing that the puffs looked very attractive. Very. Cook began arranging them, shaking off the extra icing sugar.

'Don't they carry one back to all one's parties?' said Laura.

'I suppose they do,' said practical Jose, who never liked to be carried back. 'They look beautifully light and feathery, I must say.'

'Have one each, my dears,' said cook in her comfortable voice. 'Yer ma won't know.'

Oh, impossible. Fancy cream puffs so soon after breakfast. The very idea made one shudder. All the same, two minutes later Jose and Laura were licking their fingers with that absorbed inward look that only comes from whipped cream.

'Let's go into the garden, out by the back way,' suggested Laura. 'I want to see how the men are getting on with the marquee. They're such awfully nice men.'

But the back door was blocked by cook, Sadie, Godber's man and Hans.

Something had happened.

'Tuk-tuk-tuk,' clucked cook like an agitated hen. Sadie had her hand clapped to her cheek as though she had toothache. Hans's face was screwed up in the effort to understand. Only Godber's man seemed to be enjoying himself; it was his story.

'What's the matter? What happened?'

'There's been a horrible accident,' said cook. 'A man killed.'

'A man killed! Where? How? When?'

But Godber's man wasn't going to have his story snatched from under his very nose.

'Know those little cottages just below here, miss?' Know them? Of course, she knew them. 'Well, there's a young chap living there, name of Scott, a carter. His horse shied at a traction-engine, corner of Hawke Street this morning, and he was thrown out on the back of his head. Killed.'

'Dead!' Laura stared at Godber's man.

'Dead when they picked him up,' said Godber's man with relish. 'They were taking the body home as I come up here.' And he said to the cook, 'He's left a wife and five little ones.'

'Jose, come here.' Laura caught hold of her sister's sleeve and dragged her through the kitchen to the other side of the green baize door. There she paused and leaned against it. 'Jose!' she said, horrified, 'however are we going to stop everything?'

'Stop everything, Laura!' cried Jose in astonishment. 'What do you mean?'

'Stop the garden party, of course.' Why did Jose pretend?

But Jose was still more amazed. 'Stop the garden party? My dear Laura, don't be so absurd. Of course we can't do anything of the kind. Nobody expects us to. Don't be so extravagant.'

'But we can't possibly have a garden party with a man dead just outside the front gate.'

That really was extravagant, for the little cottages were in a lane to themselves at the very bottom of a steep rise that led up to the house. A broad road ran between them. True, they were far too near. They were the greatest possible eyesore, and they had no right to be in that neighbourhood at all. They were little mean dwellings painted a chocolate brown. In the garden patches there was nothing but cabbage stalks, sick hens and tomato cans. The very smoke coming out of their chimneys was poverty-stricken. Little rags and shreds of smoke, so unlike the great silvery plumes that uncurled from the Sheridans' chimneys. Washer-women lived in the lane and sweeps and a cobbler, and a man whose house-front was studded all over with minute bird-cages. Children swarmed. When the Sheridans were little they were forbidden to set foot there because of the revolting language and of what they might catch. But since they were grown up, Laura and Laurie on their prowls sometimes walked through. It was disgusting and sordid. They came out with a shudder. But still one must go every-where; one must see everything. So through they went.

'And just think of what the band would sound like to that poor woman,' said Laura.

'Oh, Laura!' Jose began to be seriously annoyed. 'If you're going to stop a band playing every time some one has an acci-dent, you'll lead a very strenuous life. I'm every bit as sorry about it as you. I feel just as sympathetic.' Her eyes hardened. She looked at her sister just as she used to when they were little and fighting together. 'You won't bring a drunken workman back to life by being sentimental,' she said softly.

'Drunk! Who said he was drunk?' Laura turned furiously on Jose. She said just as they had used to say on those occasions, 'I'm going straight up to tell mother.'

'Do, dear,' cooed Jose.

'Mother, can I come into your room?' Laura turned the big glass door-knob.

'Of course, child. Why, what's the matter? What's given you such a colour?' And Mrs Sheridan turned round from her dressing-table. She was trying on a new hat.

'Mother, a man's been killed,' began Laura.

'*Not* in the garden?' interrupted her mother.

'No, no!'

'Oh, what a fright you gave me!' Mrs Sheridan sighed with relief, and took off the big hat and held it on her knees.

'But listen, mother,' said Laura. Breathless, half-choking, she told the dreadful story. 'Of course, we can't have our party, can we?' she pleaded. 'The band and everybody arriving. They'd hear us, mother; they're nearly neighbours!'

To Laura's astonishment her mother behaved just like Jose; it was harder to bear because she seemed amused. She refused to take Laura seriously.

'But, my dear child, use your common sense. It's only by accident we've heard of it. If some one had died there normally — and I can't understand how they keep alive in those poky little holes — we should still be having our party, shouldn't we?'

Laura had to say 'yes' to that, but she felt it was all wrong. She sat down on her mother's sofa and pinched the cushion frill.

'Mother, isn't it really terribly heartless of us?' she asked.

'Darling!' Mrs Sheridan got up and came over to her, carrying the hat. Before Laura could stop her she had popped it on. 'My child!' said her mother, 'the hat is yours. It's made for you. It's much too young for me. I have never seen you look such a picture. Look at yourself!' And she held up her hand-mirror.

'But, mother,' Laura began again. She couldn't look at herself; she turned aside.

This time Mrs Sheridan lost patience just as Jose had done.

'You are being very absurd, Laura,' she said coldly. 'People like that don't expect sacrifices from us. And it's not very sympathetic to spoil everybody's enjoyment as you're doing now.'

'I don't understand,' said Laura, and she walked quickly out of the room into her own bedroom. There, quite by chance, the first thing she saw was this charming girl in the mirror, in her black hat trimmed with gold daisies, and a long black velvet ribbon. Never had she imagined she could look like that. Is mother right? she thought. And now she hoped her mother was right. Am I being extravagant? Perhaps it was extravagant. Just for a moment she had another glimpse of that poor woman and those little children, and the body being carried into the house. But it all seemed blurred, unreal, like a picture in the newspaper. I'll remember it again after the party's over, she decided. And somehow that seemed quite the best plan ...

Lunch was over by half-past one. By half-past two they were all ready for the fray. The green-coated band had arrived and was established in a corner of the tennis-court.

'My dear!' trilled Kitty Maitland, 'aren't they too like frogs for words? You ought to have arranged them round the pond with the conductor in the middle on a leaf.'

Laurie arrived and hailed them on his way to dress. At the sight of him Laura remembered the accident again. She wanted to tell him. If Laurie agreed with the others, then it was bound to be all right. And she followed him into the hall.

'Laurie!'

'Hallo!' He was half-way upstairs, but when he turned round and saw Laura he suddenly puffed out his cheeks and goggled his eyes at her. 'My word, Laura! You do look stunning,' said Laurie. 'What an absolutely topping hat!'

Laura said faintly 'Is it?' and smiled up at Laurie, and didn't tell him after all.

Soon after that people began coming in streams. The band struck up; the hired waiters ran from the house to the marquee.

Wherever you looked there were couples strolling, bending to the flowers, greeting, moving on over the lawn. They were like bright birds that had alighted in the Sheridans' garden for this one afternoon, on their way to — where? Ah, what happiness it is to be with people who all are happy, to press hands, press cheeks, smile into eyes.

'Darling Laura, how well you look!'

'What a becoming hat, child!'

'Laura, you look quite Spanish. I've never seen you look so striking.'

And Laura, glowing, answered softly, 'Have you had tea? Won't you have an ice? The passion-fruit ices really are rather special.' She ran to her father and begged him. 'Daddy darling, can't the band have something to drink?'

And the perfect afternoon slowly ripened, slowly faded, slowly its petals closed.

'Never a more delightful garden party ...' 'The greatest success ...' 'Quite the most ...'

Laura helped her mother with the good-byes. They stood side by side in the porch till it was all over.

'All over, all over, thank heaven,' said Mrs Sheridan. 'Round up the others, Laura. Let's go and have some fresh coffee. I'm exhausted. Yes, it's been very successful. But oh, these parties, these parties! Why will you children insist on giving parties!' And they all of them sat down in the deserted marquee.

'Have a sandwich, daddy dear. I wrote the flag.'

'Thanks.' Mr Sheridan took a bite and the sandwich was gone. He took another. 'I suppose you didn't hear of a beastly accident that happened to-day?' he said.

'My dear,' said Mrs Sheridan, holding up her hand, 'we did. It nearly ruined the party. Laura insisted we should put it off.'

'Oh, mother!' Laura didn't want to be teased about it.

'It was a horrible affair all the same,' said Mr Sheridan. 'The chap was married too. Lived just below in the lane, and leaves a wife and half a dozen kiddies, so they say.'

An awkward little silence fell. Mrs Sheridan fidgeted with her cup. Really, it was very tactless of father ...

Suddenly she looked up. There on the table were all those sandwiches, cakes, puffs, all un-eaten, all going to be wasted. She had one of her brilliant ideas.

'I know,' she said. 'Let's make up a basket. Let's send that poor creature some of this perfectly good food. At any rate, it will be the greatest treat for the children. Don't you agree? And she's sure to have neighbours calling in and so on. What a point to have it all ready prepared. Laura!' She jumped up. 'Get me the big basket out of the stairs cupboard.'

'But, mother, do you really think it's a good idea?' said Laura.

Again, how curious, she seemed to be different from them all. To take scraps from their party. Would the poor woman really like that?

'Of course! What's the matter with you to-day? An hour or two ago you were insisting on us being sympathetic, and now — '

Oh well! Laura ran for the basket. It was filled, it was heaped by her mother.

'Take it yourself, darling,' said she. 'Run down just as you are. No, wait, take the arum lilies too. People of that class are so impressed by arum lilies.'

'The stems will ruin her lace frock,' said practical Jose.

So they would. Just in time. 'Only the basket, then. And, Laura!' — her mother followed her out of the marquee — 'don't on any account — '

'What, mother?'

No, better not put such ideas into the child's head! 'Nothing! Run along.'

It was just growing dusky as Laura shut their garden gates. A big dog ran by like a shadow. The road gleamed white, and down below in the hollow the little cottages were in deep shade. How quiet it seemed after the afternoon. Here she was going down the hill to somewhere where a man lay dead, and she couldn't realize it. Why couldn't she? She stopped a minute. And it seemed to her that kisses, voices, tinkling spoons, laughter, the smell of crushed grass were somehow inside her. She had no room for anything else. How strange! She looked up at the pale sky, and all she thought was, 'Yes, it was the most successful party.'

Now the broad road was crossed. The lane began, smoky and dark. Women in shawls and men's tweed caps hurried by. Men hung over the palings; the children played in the doorways. A low hum came from the mean little cottages. In some of them there was a flicker of light, and a shadow, crab-like, moved across the window. Laura bent her head and hurried on. She wished now she had put on a coat. How her frock shone! And the big hat with the velvet streamer — if only it was another hat! Were the people looking at her? They must be. It was a mistake to have come; she knew all along it was a mistake. Should she go back even now?

No, too late. This was the house. It must be. A dark knot of people stood outside. Beside the gate an old, old woman with a crutch sat in a chair, watching. She had her feet on a newspaper. The voices stopped as Laura drew near. The group parted. It was as though she was expected, as though they had known she was coming here.

Laura was terribly nervous. Tossing the velvet ribbon over her shoulder, she said to a woman standing by, 'Is this Mrs Scott's house?' and the woman, smiling queerly, said, 'It is, my lass.'

Oh, to be away from this! She actually said, 'Help me, God,' as she walked up the tiny path and knocked. To be away from those staring eyes, or to be covered up in anything, one of those women's shawls even. I'll just leave the basket and go, she decided. I shan't even wait for it to be emptied.

Then the door opened. A little woman in black showed in the gloom.

Laura said, 'Are you Mrs Scott?' But to her horror the woman answered, 'Walk in, please, miss,' and she was shut in the passage.

'No,' said Laura, 'I don't want to come in. I only want to leave this basket. Mother sent — '

The little woman in the gloomy passage seemed not to have heard her. 'Step this way, please, miss,' she said in an oily voice, and Laura followed her.

She found herself in a wretched little low kitchen, lighted by a smoky lamp. There was a woman sitting before the fire.

'Em,' said the little creature who had let her in. 'Em! It's a young lady.' She turned to Laura. She said meaningly, 'I'm 'er sister, miss. You'll excuse 'er, won't you?'

'Oh, but of course!' said Laura. 'Please, please don't disturb her. I — I only want to leave — '

But at that moment the woman at the fire turned round. Her face, puffed up, red, with swollen eyes and swollen lips, looked terrible. She seemed as though she couldn't understand why Laura was there. What did it mean? Why was this stranger standing in the kitchen with a basket? What was it all about? And the poor face puckered up again.

'All right, my dear,' said the other. 'I'll thenk the young lady.'

And again she began, 'You'll excuse her, miss, I'm sure,' and her face, swollen too, tried an oily smile.

Laura only wanted to get out, to get away. She was back in the passage. The door opened. She walked straight through into the bedroom where the dead man was lying.

'You'd like a look at 'im, wouldn't you?' said Em's sister, and she brushed past Laura over to the bed. 'Don't be afraid, my lass,' — and now her voice sounded fond and sly, and fondly she drew down the sheet — ' 'e looks a picture. There's nothing to show. Come along, my dear.'

Laura came.

There lay a young man, fast asleep — sleeping so soundly, so deeply, that he was far, far away from them both. Oh, so remote, so peaceful. He was dreaming. Never wake him up again. His head was sunk in the pillow, his eyes were closed; they were blind under the closed eyelids. He was given up to his dream. What did garden parties and baskets and lace frocks matter to him? He was far from all those things. He was wonderful, beautiful. While they were laughing and while the band was playing, this marvel had come to the lane. Happy … happy … All is well, said that sleeping face. This is just as it should be. I am content.

But all the same you had to cry, and she couldn't go out of the room without saying something to him. Laura gave a loud childish sob.

'Forgive my hat,' she said.

And this time she didn't wait for Em's sister. She found her way out of the door, down the path, past all those dark people. At the corner of the lane she met Laurie.

He stepped out of the shadow. 'Is that you, Laura?'

'Yes.'

'Mother was getting anxious. Was it all right?'

'Yes, quite. Oh, Laurie!' She took his arm, she pressed up against him.

'I say, you're not crying, are you?' asked her brother.

Laura shook her head. She was.

Laurie put his arm round her shoulder. 'Don't cry,' he said in his warm, loving voice. 'Was it awful?'

'No,' sobbed Laura. 'It was simply marvellous. But, Laurie —' She stopped, she looked at her brother. 'Isn't life,' she stammered, 'isn't life — ' But what life was she couldn't explain. No matter. He quite understood.

'*Isn't* it, darling?' said Laurie.

The Doll's House

When dear old Mrs Hay went back to town after staying with the
Burnells she sent the children a doll's house. It was so big that the
carter and Pat carried it into the courtyard, and there it stayed,
propped up on two wooden boxes beside the feed-room door.
No harm could come to it; it was summer. And perhaps the smell
of paint would have gone off by the time it had to be taken in.
For, really, the smell of paint coming from that doll's house
('Sweet of old Mrs Hay, of course; most sweet and generous!')
— but the smell of paint was quite enough to make anyone seriously ill, in Aunt Beryl's opinion. Even before the sacking was
taken off. And when it was . . .

There stood the doll's house, a dark, oily, spinach green,
picked out with bright yellow. Its two solid little chimneys,
glued on to the roof, were painted red and white, and the door,
gleaming with yellow varnish, was like a little slab of toffee.
Four windows, real windows, were divided into panes by a
broad streak of green. There was actually a tiny porch, too,
painted yellow, with big lumps of congealed paint hanging along
the edge.

But perfect, perfect little house! Who could possibly mind
the smell? It was part of the joy, part of the newness.

'Open it quickly, someone!'

The hook at the side was stuck fast. Pat prised it open with
his penknife, and the whole house-front swung back, and —
there you were, gazing at one and the same moment into the
drawing-room and dining-room, the kitchen and two bedrooms.
This is the way for a house to open! Why don't all houses open
like that? How much more exciting than peering through the slit
of a door into a mean little hall with a hatstand and two umbrellas! That is — isn't it? — what you long to know about a house
when you put your hand on the knocker. Perhaps it is the way

God opens houses at dead of night when He is taking a quiet turn with an angel …

'O-oh!' The Burnell children sounded as though they were in despair. It was too marvellous; it was too much for them. They had never seen anything like it in their lives. All the rooms were papered. There were pictures on the walls, painted on the paper, with gold frames complete. Red carpet covered all the floors except the kitchen; red plush chairs in the drawing-room, green in the dining-room; tables, beds with real bedclothes, a cradle, a stove, a dresser with tiny plates and one big jug. But what Kezia liked more than anything, what she liked frightfully, was the lamp. It stood in the middle of the dining-room table, an exquisite little amber lamp with a white globe. It was even filled all ready for lighting, though of course you couldn't light it. But there was something inside that looked like oil and that moved when you shook it.

The father and mother dolls, who sprawled very stiff as though they had fainted in the drawing-room, and their two little children asleep upstairs, were really too big for the doll's house. They didn't look as though they belonged. But the lamp was perfect. It seemed to smile at Kezia, to say, 'I live here.' The lamp was real.

The Burnell children could hardly walk to school fast enough the next morning. They burned to tell everybody, to describe, to — well — to boast about their doll's house before the school-bell rang.

'I'm to tell,' said Isabel, 'because I'm the eldest. And you two can join in after. But I'm to tell first.'

There was nothing to answer. Isabel was bossy, but she was always right, and Lottie and Kezia knew too well the powers that went with being eldest. They brushed through the thick butter-cups at the road edge and said nothing.

'And I'm to choose who's to come and see it first. Mother said I might.'

For it had been arranged that while the doll's house stood in the courtyard they might ask the girls at school, two at a time, to come and look. Not to stay to tea, of course, or to come traipsing through the house. But just to stand quietly in the courtyard while Isabel pointed out the beauties, and Lottie and Kezia looked pleased …

But hurry as they might, by the time they had reached the tarred palings of the boys' playground the bell had begun to jangle. They only just had time to whip off their hats and fall into line before the roll was called. Never mind. Isabel tried to make up for it by looking very important and mysterious and by whispering behind her hand to the girls near her, 'Got something to tell you at playtime.'

Playtime came and Isabel was surrounded. The girls of her class nearly fought to put their arms round her, to walk away with her, to beam flatteringly, to be her special friend. She held quite a court under the huge pine trees at the side of the playground. Nudging, giggling together, the little girls pressed up close. And the only two who stayed outside the ring were the two who were always outside, the little Kelveys. They knew better than to come anywhere near the Burnells.

For the fact was, the school the Burnell children went to was not at all the kind of place their parents would have chosen if there had been any choice. But there was none. It was the only school for miles. And the consequence was all the children of the neighbourhood, the Judge's little girls, the doctor's daughters, the store-keeper's children, the milkman's, were forced to mix together. Not to speak of their being an equal number of rude, rough little boys as well. But the line had to be drawn somewhere. It was drawn at the Kelveys. Many of the children, including the Burnells, were not allowed even to speak to them. They walked past the Kelveys with their heads in the air, and as they set the fashion in all matters of behaviour, the Kelveys were shunned by everybody. Even the teacher had a special voice for them, and a special smile for the other children when Lil Kelvey came up to her desk with a bunch of dreadfully common-looking flowers.

They were the daughters of a spry, hard-working little washerwoman, who went about from house to house by the day. This was awful enough. But where was Mr Kelvey? Nobody knew for certain. But everybody said he was in prison. So they were the daughters of a washerwoman and a jailbird. Very nice company for other people's children! And they looked it. Why Mrs Kelvey made them so conspicuous was hard to understand. The truth was they were dressed in 'bits' given to her by the people for whom she worked. Lil, for instance, who was a stout, plain child, with big freckles, came to school in a dress made from a green art-serge table-cloth of the Burnells', with red plush sleeves from the Logans' curtains. Her hat, perched on top of her high forehead, was a grown-up woman's hat, once the property of Miss Lecky, the postmistress. It was turned up at the back and trimmed with a large scarlet quill. What a little guy she looked! It was impossible not to laugh. And her little sister, our Else, wore a long white dress, rather like a nightgown, and a pair of little boy's boots. But whatever our Else wore she would have looked strange. She was a tiny wishbone of a child, with cropped hair and enormous solemn eyes — a little white owl. Nobody had ever seen her smile; she scarcely ever spoke. She went through life holding on to Lil, with a piece of Lil's skirt screwed up in her hand. Where Lil went, our Else followed. In the playground, on the road going to and from school, there was Lil marching in front and our Else holding on behind. Only when she wanted anything, or when she was out of breath, our Else gave Lil a tug, a twitch, and Lil stopped and turned around. The Kelveys never failed to understand each other.

Now they hovered at the edge; you couldn't stop them

listening. When the little girls turned round and sneered, Lil, as usual, gave her silly shamefaced smile, but our Else only looked.

And Isabel's voice, so very proud, went on telling. The carpet made a great sensation, but so did the beds with real bedclothes, and the stove with an oven door.

When she finished Kezia broke in. 'You've forgotten the lamp, Isabel.'

'Oh, yes,' said Isabel, 'and there's a teeny little lamp, all made of yellow glass, with a white globe that stands on the dining-room table. You couldn't tell it from a real one.'

'The lamp's best of all,' cried Kezia. She thought Isabel wasn't making half enough of the little lamp. But nobody paid any attention. Isabel was choosing the two who were to come back with them that afternoon and see it. She chose Emmie Cole and Lena Logan. But when the others knew they were all to have a chance, they couldn't be nice enough to Isabel. One by one they put their arms round Isabel's waist and walked her off. They had something to whisper to her, a secret. 'Isabel's *my* friend.'

Only the little Kelveys moved away forgotten; there was nothing more for them to hear.

Days passed, and as more children saw the doll's house, the fame of it spread. It became the one subject, the rage. The one question was, 'Have you seen Burnells' doll's house? Oh, ain't it lovely!' 'Haven't you seen it? Oh, I say!'

Even the dinner hour was given up to talking about it. The little girls sat under the pines eating their thick mutton sandwiches and big slabs of johnny cake spread with butter. While always, as near as they could get, sat the Kelveys, our Else holding on to Lil, listening too, while they chewed their jam sandwiches out of a newspaper soaked with large red blobs ...

'Mother,' said Kezia, 'can't I ask the Kelveys just once?'

'Certainly not, Kezia.'

'But why not?'

'Run away, Kezia; you know quite well why not.'

At last everybody had seen it except them. On that day the subject rather flagged. It was the dinner hour. The children stood together under the pine trees, and suddenly, as they looked at the Kelveys eating out of their paper, always by themselves, always listening, they wanted to be horrid to them. Emmie Cole started the whisper.

'Lil Kelvey's going to be a servant when she grows up.'

'O-oh, how awful!' said Isabel Burnell, and she made eyes at Emmie.

Emmie swallowed in a very meaning way and nodded to Isabel as she'd seen her mother do on those occasions.

'It's true — it's true — it's true,' she said.

Then Lena Logan's little eyes snapped. 'Shall I ask her?' she whispered.

'Bet you don't,' said Jessie May.

'Pooh, I'm not frightened,' said Lena. Suddenly she gave a little squeal and danced in front of the other girls. 'Watch! Watch me! Watch me now!' said Lena. And sliding, gliding, dragging one foot, giggling behind her hand, Lena went over to the Kelveys.

Lil looked up from her dinner. She wrapped the rest quickly away. Our Else stopped chewing. What was coming now?

'Is it true you're going to be a servant when you grow up, Lil Kelvey?' shrilled Lena.

Dead silence. But instead of answering, Lil only gave her silly shamefaced smile. She didn't seem to mind the question at all. What a sell for Lena! The girls began to titter.

Lena couldn't stand that. She put her hands on her hips; she shot forward. 'Yah, yer father's in prison!' she hissed, spitefully.

This was such a marvellous thing to have said that the little girls rushed away in a body, deeply, deeply excited, wild with joy.

Someone found a long rope, and they began skipping. And never did they skip so high, run in and out so fast, or do such daring things as on that morning.

In the afternoon Pat called for the Burnell children with the buggy and they drove home. There were visitors. Isabel and Lottie, who liked visitors, went upstairs to change their pinafores. But Kezia thieved out at the back. Nobody was about; she began to swing on the big white gates of the courtyard. Presently, looking along the road, she saw two little dots. They grew bigger, they were coming towards her. Now she could see that one was in front and one close behind. Now she could see that they were the Kelveys. Kezia stopped swinging. She slipped off the gate as if she was going to run away. Then she hesitated. The Kelveys came nearer, and beside them walked their shadows, very long, stretching right across the road with their heads in the buttercups. Kezia clambered back on the gate; she had made up her mind; she swung out.

'Hullo,' she said to the passing Kelveys.

They were so astounded that they stopped. Lil gave her silly smile. Our Else stared.

'You can come and see our doll's house if you want to,' said Kezia, and she dragged one toe on the ground. But at that Lil turned red and shook her head quickly.

'Why not?' asked Kezia.

Lil gasped, then she said, 'Your ma told our ma you wasn't to speak to us.'

'Oh, well,' said Kezia. She didn't know what to reply. 'It doesn't matter. You can come and see our doll's house all the same. Come on. Nobody's looking.'

But Lil shook her head still harder.

'Don't you want to?' asked Kezia.

Suddenly there was a twitch, a tug at Lil's skirt. She turned round. Our Else was looking at her with big imploring eyes; she was frowning; she wanted to go. For a moment Lil looked at our Else very doubtfully. But then our Else twitched her skirt again. She started forward. Kezia led the way. Like two little stray cats they followed across the courtyard to where the doll's house stood.

'There it is,' said Kezia.

There was a pause. Lil breathed loudly, almost snorted; our Else was still as a stone.

'I'll open it for you,' said Kezia kindly. She undid the hook and they looked inside.

'There's the drawing-room and the dining-room, and that's the — '

'Kezia!'

Oh, what a start they gave!

'Kezia!'

It was Aunt Beryl's voice. They turned round. At the back door stood Aunt Beryl, staring as if she couldn't believe what she saw.

'How dare you ask the little Kelveys into the courtyard?' said her cold, furious voice. 'You know as well as I do you're not allowed to talk to them. Run away, children, run away at once. And don't come back again,' said Aunt Beryl. And she stepped into the yard and shooed them out as if they were chickens.

'Off you go immediately!' she called, cold and proud.

They did not need telling twice. Burning with shame, shrinking together, Lil huddling along like her mother, our Else dazed, somehow they crossed the big courtyard and squeezed through the white gate.

'Wicked, disobedient little girl!' said Aunt Beryl bitterly to Kezia, and she slammed the doll's house to.

The afternoon had been awful. A letter had come from Willie Brent, a terrifying, threatening letter, saying if she did not meet him that evening in Pulman's Bush, he'd come to the front door and ask the reason why! But now that she had frightened those little rats of Kelveys and given Kezia a good scolding, her heart felt lighter. That ghastly pressure was gone. She went back to the house humming.

When the Kelveys were well out of sight of Burnells', they sat down to rest on a big red drainpipe by the side of the road. Lil's cheeks were still burning; she took off the hat with the quill and held it on her knee. Dreamily they looked over the hay paddocks, past the creek, to the group of wattles where Logan's cows stood waiting to be milked. What were their thoughts?

Presently our Else nudged up close to her sister. By now she had forgotten the cross lady. She put out a finger and stroked her sister's quill; she smiled her rare smile.

'I seen the little lamp,' she said, softly.

Then both were silent once more.

Six Years After

It was not the afternoon to be on deck — on the contrary. It was exactly the afternoon when there is no snugger place than a warm cabin, a warm bunk. Tucked up with a rug, a hot-water bottle and a piping hot cup of tea she would not have minded the weather in the least. But he — hated cabins, hated to be inside anywhere more than was absolutely necessary. He had a passion for keeping, as he called it, above board, especially when he was travelling. And it wasn't surprising, considering the enormous amount of time he spent cooped up in the office. So, when he rushed away from her as soon as they got on board and came back five minutes later, to say he had secured two deck chairs on the lee side and the steward was undoing the rugs, her voice through the high sealskin collar murmured 'Good'; and because he was looking at her, she smiled with bright eyes and blinked quickly, as if to say, 'Yes, perfectly all right — absolutely.' And she meant it.

'Then we'd better — ' said he, and he tucked her hand inside his arm and began to rush her off to where their chairs stood. But she just had time to breathe, 'Not so fast, Daddy, please,' when he remembered too and slowed down.

Strange! They had been married twenty-eight years, and it still was an effort to him, each time, to adapt his pace to hers.

'Not cold, are you?' he asked, glancing sideways at her. Her little nose, geranium pink above the dark fur, was answer enough. But she thrust her free hand into the velvet pocket of her jacket and murmured gaily, 'I shall be glad of my rug.'

He pressed her tighter to his side — a quick nervous pressure. He knew, of course, that she ought to be down in the cabin; he knew that it was no afternoon for her to be sitting on deck, in this cold and raw mist, lee side or no lee side, rugs or no rugs, and he realised how she must be hating it. But he had come to believe that it really was easier for her to make these sacrifices than it was for him. Take their present case, for instance. If he had gone down to the cabin with her, he would have been miserable the whole time, and he couldn't have helped showing it. At any rate she would have found him out. Whereas, having made up her mind to fall in with his ideas, he would have betted anybody she would even go so far as to enjoy the experience. Not because she was without personality of her own. Good Lord! She was absolutely brimming with it. But because ... but here his thoughts always stopped. Here they always felt the need of a cigar, as it were. And, looking at the cigar-tip, his fine blue eyes narrowed: it was a law of marriage, he supposed ... All the same, he always felt guilty when he asked these sacrifices of her. That was what that quick pressure meant. His being said to her being: 'You do understand, don't you?' and there was an answering tremor of her fingers, 'I *understand*.'

Certainly, the steward — good little chap — had done all in his power to make them comfortable. He had put up their chairs in whatever warmth there was and out of the smell. She did hope he would be tipped adequately. It was on occasions like this (and her life seemed to be full of such occasions) that she wished it was the woman who controlled the purse.

'Thank you, steward. That will do beautifully.'

'Why are stewards so often delicate-looking?' she wondered, as her feet were tucked under. 'This poor little chap looks as though he'd got a chest, and yet one would have thought ... the sea air ...'

The button of the pigskin purse was undone. The tray was tilted. She saw sixpences, shillings, half-crowns.

'I should give him five shillings,' she decided, 'and tell him to buy himself a good nourishing — '

He was given a shilling, and he touched his cap and seemed genuinely grateful.

Well, it might have been worse. It might have been sixpence. It might, indeed. For at that moment Father turned towards her and said, half-apologetically, stuffing the purse back, 'I gave him a shilling. I think it was worth it, don't you?'

'Oh, quite! Every bit!' said she.

It is extraordinary how peaceful it feels on a little steamer once the bustle of leaving port is over. In a quarter of an hour one might have been at sea for days. There is something almost touching, childish, in the way people submit themselves to the new conditions. They go to bed in the early afternoon, they shut their eyes and 'it's night' like little children who turn the table upside down and cover themselves with the tablecloth. And those who remain on deck — they seem to be always the same, those few hardened men travellers — pause, light their pipes, stamp softly, gaze out to sea, and their voices are subdued as they walk up and down. The long-legged little girl chases after the red-cheeked boy, but soon both are captured; and the old sailor, swinging an unlighted lantern, passes and disappears ...

He lay back, the rug up to his chin and she saw he was breathing deeply. Sea air! If anyone believed in sea air, it was he. He had the strongest faith in its tonic qualities. But the great thing was, according to him, to fill the lungs with it the moment you came on board. Otherwise, the sheer strength of it was enough to give you a chill ...

She gave a small chuckle, and he turned to her quickly. 'What is it?'

'It's your cap,' she said. 'I never can get used to you in a cap. You look such a thorough burglar.'

'Well, what the deuce am I to wear?' He shot up one grey eyebrow and wrinkled his nose. 'It's a very good cap, too. Very fine specimen of its kind. It's got a very rich white satin lining.' He paused. He declaimed, as he had hundreds of times before at this stage, 'Rich and rare were the gems she wore.'

But she was thinking he really was childishly proud of the white satin lining. He would like to have taken off his cap and made her feel it. 'Feel the quality!' How often had she rubbed between finger and thumb his coat, his shirt cuff, tie, sock, linen handkerchief, while he said that.

She slipped down more deeply into her chair.

And the little steamer pressed on, pitching gently, over the grey, unbroken, gently-moving water, that was veiled with slanting rain.

Far out, as though idly, listlessly, gulls were flying. Now they settled on the waves, now they beat up into the rainy air, and shone against the pale sky like the lights within a pearl. They looked cold and lonely. How lonely it will be when we have passed by, she thought. There will be nothing but the waves and those birds and rain falling.

She gazed through the rust-spotted railing along which big drops trembled, until suddenly she shut her lips. It was as if a warning voice inside her had said, 'Don't look!'

'No, I won't,' she decided. 'It's too depressing, much too depressing.'

But immediately, she opened her eyes and looked again. Lonely birds, water lifting, white pale sky — how were they changed?

And it seemed to her there was a presence far out there, between the sky and the water; someone very desolate and longing watched them pass and cried as if to stop them — but cried to her alone.

'Mother!'

'Don't leave me,' sounded in the cry. 'Don't forget me! You are forgetting me, you know you are!' And it was as though from her own breast there came the sound of childish weeping.

'My son — my precious child — it isn't true!'

Sh! How was it possible that she was sitting there on that quiet steamer beside Father and at the same time she was hushing and holding a little slender boy — so pale — who had just waked out of a dreadful dream?

'I dreamed I was in a wood — somewhere far away from everybody — and I was lying down and a great blackberry vine grew over me. And I called and called to you — and you wouldn't come — you couldn't come — so I had to lie there for ever.'

What a terrible dream! He had always had terrible dreams. How often, years ago, when he was small, she had made some excuse and escaped from their friends in the dining-room or the drawing-room to come to the foot of the stairs and listen. 'Mother!' And when he was asleep, his dream had journeyed with her back into the circle of lamplight; it had taken its place there like a ghost. And now —

Far more often — at all times, in all places, like now, for instance — she never settled down, she was never off her guard for a moment but she heard him. He wanted her. 'I am coming as fast as I can! As fast as I can!' But the dark stairs have no ending, and the worst dream of all — the one that is always the same — goes for ever and ever uncomforted.

This is anguish! How is it to be borne? Still, it is not the idea of her suffering which is unbearable — it is his. Can one do nothing for the dead? And for a long time the answer had been — Nothing!

And then finally there is his first leave. She does not go to the station to meet him. Daddy goes alone. As a matter of fact she is frightened to go. The shock may upset her and spoil their joy. So she tries to bear it at home —

Late afternoon. The lights on. Gorgeous fires everywhere — in his bedroom too, of course. She goes to see it too often, but each time there is something to be done — the curtains to be drawn — or she makes sure he has enough blankets. For some reason there is no place for the girls in this memory; they might be unborn. She is alone in that warm breathing bright house except for the servants. Each time she comes into the hall she hears that distant twitter from the kitchen, or the face of steps down the area. *They* are on the lookout. And at this point she always remembers his favourite dinner: roast chicken — asparagus — meringues — champagne. And then — Oh God help me bear this moment! There's the taxi. It's turned into the square. Is it slowing now?

'Here it is 'm.'

'No, Nellie — I don't think so.'

Yes — yes — it is. Courage! Be brave. It's stopping. Is that Father's glove at the window? Oh, the door is open, she is on the step. Father's voice rings out, 'Here he is.' And all at one and the same moment the taxi stops, and bursts open. A young muffled figure bounds up the steps.

'Mummy!'

'My precious, precious son!'

But here it's no use. Here she must break down. Just a moment — just one. Pressing her head against the cold buttons of his British warm.

'Child!'

He holds her. And his father is behind him grabbing his shoulder, and his laugh rings out —

'Well, you've got him. Are you satisfied?'

The door is shut. He is pulling off his gloves, and scarf and coat, and pressing them on to the chest in the hall. The old familiar quick shot back of his head while he looks at her, laughing, while he describes how he spotted Daddy immediately — and Father absolutely refused to recognise *him*.

... But softly without a sound the dark curtain has rolled down. There is no more to come. That is the end of the play. But it can't end like that — so suddenly. There must be more. No, it's cold, it's still. There is nothing to be gained by waiting.

But — did he go back again? Or, when the war was over, did he come home for good? Surely, he will marry — later on — not for several years. Surely, one day I shall remember his wedding and my first grandchild — a beautiful dark-haired boy born in the early morning — a lovely morning — spring!

'Oh, Mother, it's not fair to me to put these ideas into my head! Stop, Mother, stop! When I think of all I have missed, I can't bear it.'

'I can't bear it!' She sits up breathing the words and tosses the dark rug away. It is colder than ever, and now the dusk is falling, falling like ash upon the pallid water.

And the little steamer, quietly determined, throbbed on, pressed on, as if at the end of the journey there waited ...

Weak Heart

I

Although it sounded all the year round, although it rang out sometimes as early as half-past six in the morning, sometimes as late as half-past ten at night, it was in the spring, when Bengel's violet patch just inside the gate was blue with flowers, that that piano ... made the passers-by not only stop talking, but slow down, pause, look suddenly — if they were men — grave, even stern, and if they were women — dreamy, even sorrowful.

Tarana Street was beautiful in the spring; there was not a single house without its garden and trees and a plot of grass big enough to be called 'the lawn'. Over the low painted fences, you could see, as you ran by, whose daffys were out, whose wild snowdrop border was over and who had the biggest hyacinths, so pink and white, the colour of coconut ice. But nobody had violets that grew, that smelled in the spring sun like Bengel's. Did they really smell like that? Or did you shut your eyes and lean over the fence because of Edie Bengel's piano?

A little wind ruffles among the leaves like a joyful hand looking for the finest flowers; and the piano sounds gay, tender, laughing. Now a cloud, like a swan, flies across the sun, the violets shine cold, like water, and a sudden questioning cry rings from Edie Bengel's piano.

... Ah, if life must pass so quickly, why is the breath of these flowers so sweet? What is the meaning of this feeling of longing, of sweet trouble — of flying joy? Goodbye! Farewell! The young bees lie half awake on the slender dandelions, silver are the pink tipped arrowy petals of the daisies; the new grass shakes in the light. Everything is beginning again, marvellous as ever, heavenly fair. 'Let us stay! Let us stay!' pleads Edie Bengel's piano.

II

It is the afternoon, sunny and still. The blinds are down in the front to save the carpets, but upstairs the slats are open and in the golden light little Mrs Bengel is feeling under her bed for the square bonnet box. She is flushed. She feels timid, excited, like a girl. And now the tissue paper is parted, her best bonnet, the one trimmed with a jet butterfly, which reposes on top, is lifted out and solemnly blown upon.

Dipping down to the glass she tries it with fingers that tremble. She twitches her dolman round her slender shoulders, clasps her purse and before leaving the bedroom kneels down a moment to ask God's blessing on her 'goings out'. And as she kneels there quivering, she is rather like a butterfly herself, fanning her wings before her Lord. When the door is open the sound of the piano coming up through the silent house is almost frightening, so bold, so defiant, so reckless it rolls under Edie's fingers. And just for a moment the thought comes to Mrs Bengel and is gone again, that there is a stranger with Edie in the drawing-room, but a fantastic person, out of a book, a — a — villain. It's very absurd. She flits across the hall, turns the door handle and confronts her flushed daughter. Edie's hands drop from the keys. She squeezes them between her knees, her head is bent, her curls are fallen forward. She gazes at her mother with brilliant eyes. There is something painful in that glance, something very strange. It is dusky in the drawing-room, the top of the piano is open. Edie has been playing from memory; it's as though the air still tingles.

'I'm going, dear,' said Mrs Bengel softly, so softly it is like a sigh.

'Yes, Mother,' came from Edie.

'I don't expect I shall be long.'

Mrs Bengel lingers. She would very much like just a word, of sympathy, of understanding, even from Edie, to cheer her on her way.

But Edie murmurs, 'I'll put the kettle on in half an hour.'

'Do, dear!' Mrs Bengel grasped at that even. A nervous little smile touched her lips. 'I expect I shall want my tea.'

But to that Edie makes no reply; she frowns, she stretches out a hand, quickly unscrews one of the piano candle-sticks, lifts off a pink china ring and screws all tight again. The ring has been rattling. As the front door bangs softly after her mother Edie and the piano seem to plunge together into deep dark water, into waves that flow over both, relentless. She plays on desperately until her nose is white and her heart beats. It is her way of getting over her nervousness and her way too of praying. Would they accept her? Would she be allowed to go? Was it possible that in a week's time she would be one of Miss Farmer's girls, wearing a red and blue hat band, running up the broad steps leading to the big grey painted house that buzzed, that hummed as you went by? Their pew in Church faced Miss Farmer's boarders. Would she at last know the names of the girls she had looked at so often? The pretty pale one with red hair, the dark one with a fringe, the fair one who held Miss Farmer's hand during the sermon? ... But after all ...

It was Edie's fourteenth birthday. Her father gave her a silver brooch with a bar of music, two crotchets, two quavers and a minim headed by a very twisted treble clef. Her mother gave her blue satin gloves and two boxes for gloves and handkerchiefs, hand-painted the glove box with a sprig of gold roses tying up the capital G and the handkerchief box with a marvellously lifelike butterfly quivering on the capital H. From the aunts in ...

There was a tree at the corner of Tarana Street and May Street. It grew so close to the pavement that the heavy boughs stretched over, and on that part of the pavement there was always a fine sifting of minute twigs.

But in the dusk, lovers parading came into its shade as into a tent. There, however long they had been together, they greeted each other again with long kisses, with embraces that were sweet torture, agony to bear, agony to end.

Edie never knew that Roddie 'loved' it, Roddie never knew that it meant anything to Edie.

Roddie, spruce, sleek with water, bumped his new bike down the wooden steps, through the gate. He was off for a spin, and looking at that tree, dark in the glow of evening, he felt the tree was watching him. He wanted to do marvels, to astonish, to shock, to amaze it …

Roddie had a complete new outfit for the occasion. A black serge suit, a black tie, a straw hat so white it was almost silver, a dazzling white straw hat with a broad black band. Attached to the hat there was a thick guard that somehow reminded one of a fishing line and the little clasp on the brim was like a fly … He stood at the graveside, his legs apart, his hands loosely clasped, and watched Edie being lowered into the grave — as a half-grown boy watches anything, a man at work, or a bicycle accident, or a chap cleaning a spring-carriage wheel — but suddenly as the men drew back he gave a violent start, turned, muttered something to his father and dashed away, so fast that people looked positively frightened, through the cemetery, down the avenue of dripping clay banks into Tarana Road, and started pelting for home. His suit was very tight and hot. It was like a dream. He kept his head down and his fists clenched, he couldn't look up, nothing could have made him look higher than the tops of the fences — What was he thinking of as he pressed along? On, on until the gate was reached, up the steps, in at the front door, through the hall, up to the drawing-room.

'Edie!' called Roddie. 'Edie, old girl!'

And he gave a low strange squawk and cried 'Edie!' and stared across at Edie's piano.

But cold, solemn, as if frozen, heavily the piano stared back at Roddie. Then it answered, but on its own behalf, on behalf of the house and the violet patch, the garden, the velvet tree at the corner of May Street, and all that was delightful: 'There is nobody here of that name, young man!'

Daphne

I had been in Port Willin six months when I decided to give a one-man show. Not that I was particularly keen, but little Field, the picture-shop man, had just started a gallery and he wanted me — begged me, rather — to kick off for him. He was a decent little chap; I hadn't the heart to refuse. And besides, as it happened, I had a good deal of stuff that I felt it would be rather fun to palm off on any one who was fool enough to buy it. So with these high aims I had the cards printed, the pictures framed in plain white frames, and God knows how many cups and saucers ordered for the Private View.

What was I doing in Port Willin? Oh well — why not? I'll own it does sound an unlikely spot, but when you are an impermanent movable, as I am, it's just those unlikely spots that have a trick of holding you. I arrived, intending to stay a week and go on to Fiji. But I had letters to one or two people, and the morning of my arrival, hanging over the side of the ship while we were waiting in the stream, with nothing on earth to do but stare, I took an extraordinary fancy to the shape — to the look of the place.

It's a small town, you know, planted at the edge of a fine deep harbour like a lake. Behind it, on either side, there are hills. The houses are built of light painted wood. They have iron roofs coloured red. And there are big dark plumy trees massed together, breaking up those light shapes, giving a depth — warmth — making a composition of it well worth looking at ... Well, we needn't go into that — But it had me that fine morning. And the first days after my arrival, walking, or driving out in one of the big swinging, rocking cabs, I took an equal fancy to the people.

Not to quite all of them. The men left me cold. Yes, I must say, colonial men are not the brightest specimens. But I never struck a place where the average of female attractiveness was so high. You can't help noticing it, for a peculiarity of Port Willin is the number of its teashops and the vast quantity of tea absorbed by its inhabitants. Not tea only — sandwiches, cream cakes, ices, fruit salad with fresh pine-apples. From eleven o'clock in the morning you meet with couples and groups of girls and young married women hurrying off to their first tea. It was a real eleven o'clock function. Even the business men knocked off and went to a café. And the same thing happened in the afternoon. From four until half-past six the streets were gay as a garden. Which reminds me, it was early spring when I arrived and the town smelled of moist earth and the first flowers. In fact, wherever one went one got a strong whiff, like the whiff of violets in a wood, which was enough in itself to make one feel like lingering ...

There was a theatre too, a big bare building plastered over with red and blue bills which gave it an oriental look in that blue air, and a touring company was playing 'San Toy'. I went my first evening. I found it, for some reason, fearfully exciting. The inside smelled of gas, of glue and burnt paper. Whistling draughts cut along the corridors — a strong wind among the orchestra kept the palms trembling, and now and again the curtain blew out and there was a glimpse of a pair of large feet walking rapidly away. But what women! What girls in muslin dresses with velvet sashes and little caps edged with swansdown! In the intervals long ripples of laughter sounded from the stalls, from the dress-circle. And I leaned against a pillar that looked as though it was made of wedding-cake icing — and fell in love with whole rows at a time ...

Then I presented my letters, I was asked out to dine, and I met these charmers in their own homes. That decided it. They were something I had never known before — so gay, so friendly, so impressed with the idea of one's being an artist! It was rather like finding oneself in the playground of an extremely attractive girls' school.

I painted the Premier's daughter, a dark beauty, against a tree hung with long, bell-like flowers as white as wax. I painted a girl with a pigtail curled up on a white sofa playing with a pale-red fan ... and a little blonde in a black jacket with pearl grey gloves ... I painted like fury.

I'm fond of women. As a matter of fact I'm a great deal more at my ease with women than I am with men. Because I've cultivated them, I suppose. You see, it's like this with me. I've always had enough money to live on, and the consequence is I have never had to mix with people more than I wished. And I've equally always had — well, I suppose you might call it — a passion for painting. Painting is far and away the most important thing in my life — as I see it. But — my work's my own affair. It's the separate compartment which is me. No strangers allowed in. I haven't the smallest desire to explain what it is I'm after — or to hear other men. If people like my work I'm pleased. If they don't — well, if I was a shrugging person, I'd shrug. This sounds arrogant. It isn't; I know my limitations. But the truth about oneself always sounds arrogant, as no doubt you've observed.

But women — well, I can only speak for myself — I find the presence of women, the consciousness of women, an absolute necessity. I know they are considered a distraction, that the very Big Pots seal themselves in their hives to keep away. All I can say is work without women would be to me like dancing without music or food without wine or a sailing boat without a breeze. They just give me that … what is it? Stimulus is not enough; inspiration is far too much. That — well, if I knew what it is, I should have solved a bigger problem than my own! And problems aren't in my line.

I expected a mob at my Private View, and I got it, too … What I hadn't reckoned on was that there would be no men. It was one thing to ask a painter fellow to knock you up something to the tune of fifty guineas or so, but it quite another to make an ass of yourself staring. The Port Willin men would as soon have gazed into shops. True, when you come to Europe, you visited the galleries, but then you shop-gazed too. It didn't matter what you did in Europe. You could walk about for a week without being recognised.

So there were little Field and I absolutely alone among all that loveliness; it frightened him out of his life, but I didn't mind, I thought it rather fun, especially as the sightseers didn't hesitate to find my pictures amusing. I'm by no means an out-and-out modern, as they say; people like violins and landscapes of telegraph poles leave me cold. But Port Willin is still trying to swallow Rossetti, and Hope by Watts is looked upon as very advanced. It was natural my pictures should surprise them. The fat old Lady Mayoress became quite hysterical. She drew me over to one drawing; she patted my arm with her fan.

'I don't wonder you drew her slipping out,' she gurgled. 'And how depressed she looks! The poor dear never could have sat down in it. It's much too small. There ought to be a little cake of Pears' Soap on the floor.' And overcome by her own joke, she flopped on the little double bench that ran down the middle of the room, and even her fan seemed to laugh.

At that moment two girls passed in front of us. One I knew, a big fair girl called May Pollock, pulled her companion by the sleeve. 'Daphne!' she said. 'Daphne!' And the other turned towards her, then towards us, smiled and was born, christened part of my world from that moment.

'Daphne!' Her quick, beautiful smile answered ...

Saturday morning was gloriously fine. When I woke up and saw the sun streaming over the polished floor I felt like a little boy who has been promised a picnic. It was all I could do not to telephone Daphne. Was she feeling the same? It seemed somehow such a terrific lark that we should be going off together like this, just with a couple of rucksacks and our bathing suits. I thought of other week-ends, the preparation, the emotional tension, the amount of managing they'd needed. But I couldn't really think of them; I couldn't be bothered, they belonged to another life ...

It seemed to me suddenly so preposterous that two people should be as happy as we were and not be happier. Here we were, alone, miles away from everybody, free as air, and in love with each other. I looked again at Daphne, at her slender shoulders, her throat, her bosom, and, passionately in love, I decided, with fervour: Wouldn't it be rather absurd, then, to behave like a couple of children? Wouldn't she even, in spite of all she had said, be disappointed if we did? ...

And I went off at a tremendous pace, not because I thought she'd run after me, but I did think she might call, or I might look round ...

It was one of those still, hushed days when the sea and the sky seem to melt into one another, and it is long before the moisture dries on the leaves and grasses. One of those days when the sea smells strong and there are gulls standing in a row on the sand. The smoke from our wood fire hung in the air and the smoke of my pipe mingled with it. I caught myself staring at nothing. I felt dull and angry. I couldn't get over the ridiculous affair. You see, my *amour propre* was wounded.

Monday morning was grey, cloudy, one of those mornings peculiar to the seaside when everything, the sea most of all, seems exhausted and sullen. There had been a very high tide, the road was wet — on the beach there stood a long line of sickly-looking gulls ...

When we got on board she sat down on one of the green benches and, muttering something about a pipe, I walked quickly away. It was intolerable that we should still be together after what had happened. It was indecent. I only asked — I only longed for one thing — to be free of this still, unsmiling and piti-ful — that was the worst of it — creature who had been my playful Daphne.

For answer I telephoned her at once and asked if I might come and see her that evening. Her voice sounded grave, unlike the voice I remembered, and she seemed to deliberate. There was a long pause before she said, 'Yes — perhaps that would be best.'

'Then I shall come at half-past six.'

'Very well.'

And we went into a room full of flowers and very large art photographs of the Harbour by Night, A Misty Day, Moonrise over the Water, and I know I wondered if she admired them.

'Why did you send me that letter?'

'Oh, but I had to,' said Daphne. 'I meant every word of it. I only let you come to-night to ... No, I know I shall disappoint you. I'm wiser than you are for all your experience. I shan't be able to live up to it. I'm not the person for you. Really I'm not!' ...

Taking the Veil

It seemed impossible that anyone should be unhappy on such a beautiful morning. Nobody was, decided Edna, except herself. The windows were flung wide in the houses. From within there came the sound of pianos, little hands chased after each other and ran away from each other, practising scales. The trees fluttered in the sunny gardens, all bright with spring flowers. Street boys whistled, a little dog barked; people passed by, walking so lightly, so swiftly, they looked as though they wanted to break into a run. Now she actually saw in the distance a parasol, peach-coloured, the first parasol of the year.

Perhaps even Edna did not look quite as unhappy as she felt. It is not easy to look tragic at eighteen, when you are extremely pretty, with the cheeks and lips and shining eyes of perfect health. Above all, when you are wearing a French blue frock and your new spring hat trimmed with cornflowers. True, she carried under her arm a book bound in horrid black leather. Perhaps the book provided a gloomy note, but only by accident; it was the ordinary Library binding. For Edna had made going to the Library an excuse for getting out of the house to think, to realise what had happened, to decide somehow what was to be done now.

An awful thing had happened. Quite suddenly, at the theatre last night, when she and Jimmy were seated side by side in the dress-circle, without a moment's warning — in fact, she had just finished a chocolate almond and passed the box to him again — she had fallen love with an actor. But — *fallen — in — love* ...

The feeling was unlike anything she had ever imagined before. It wasn't in the least pleasant. It was hardly thrilling. Unless you can call the most dreadful sensation of hopeless misery, despair, agony and wretchedness, thrilling. Combined with the certainty that if that actor met her on the pavement after, while Jimmy was fetching their cab, she would follow him to the ends of the earth, at a nod, at a sign, without giving another thought to Jimmy or her father and mother or her happy home and countless friends again ...

The play had begun fairly cheerfully. That was at the choco-late almond stage. Then the hero had gone blind. Terrible moment! Edna had cried so much she had to borrow Jimmy's folded, smooth-feeling handkerchief as well. Not that crying mattered. Whole rows were in tears. Even the men blew their noses with a loud trumpeting noise and tried to peer at the pro-gramme instead of looking at the stage. Jimmy, most mercifully dry-eyed — for what would she have done without his handker-chief? — squeezed her free hand, and whispered 'Cheer up, dar-ling girl!' And it was then she had taken a last chocolate almond to please him and passed the box again. Then there had been that ghastly scene with the hero alone on the stage in a deserted room at twilight, with a band playing outside and the sound of cheer-ing coming from the street. He had tried — ah, how painfully, how pitifully! — to grope his way to the window. He had suc-ceeded at last. There he stood holding the curtain while one beam of light, just one beam, shone full on his raised sightless face, and the band faded away into the distance ...

It was — really, it was absolutely — oh, the most — it was simply — in fact, from that moment Edna knew that life could never be the same. She drew her hand away from Jimmy's, leaned back, and shut the chocolate box for ever. This at last was love!

Edna and Jimmy were engaged. She had had her hair up for a year and a half; they had been publicly engaged for a year. But they had known they were going to marry each other ever since they walked in the Botanical Gardens with their nurses, and sat on the grass with a wine biscuit and a piece of barley-sugar each for their tea. It was so much an accepted thing that Edna had worn a wonderfully good imitation of an engagement-ring out of a cracker all the time she was at school. And up till now they had been devoted to each other.

But now it was over. It was so completely over that Edna found it difficult to believe that Jimmy did not realise it too. She smiled wisely, sadly, as she turned into the gardens of the Convent of the Sacred heart and mounted the path that led through them to Hill Street. How much better to know it now than to wait until after they were married! *Now* it was possible that Jimmy would get over it. No, it was no use deceiving herself; he would never get over it! His life was wrecked, was ruined; that was inevitable. But he was young ... Time, people always said, Time might make a little, just a little difference. In forty years when he was an old man, he might be able to think of her calmly — perhaps. But she — what did the future hold for her?

Edna had reached the top of the path. There under a new-leafed tree, hung with little bunches of white flowers, she sat down on a green bench and looked over the convent flower-beds. In the one nearest to her there grew tender stocks, with a border of blue, shell-like pansies, with at one corner a clump of creamy freezias, their light spears of green criss-crossed over the flowers. The Convent pigeons were tumbling high in the air, and she could hear the voice of Sister Agnes who was giving a singing lesson. Ah-me, sounded the deep tones of the nun, and Ah-me, they were echoed ...

If she did not marry Jimmy, of course she would marry nobody. The man she was in love with, the famous actor — Edna had far too much common-sense not to realise *that* would never be. It was very odd. She didn't even want it to be. Her love was too intense for that. It had to be endured, silently; it had to torment her. It was, she supposed, simply that kind of love.

'But, Edna,' cried Jimmy. 'Can you never change? Can I never hope again?'

Oh, what sorrow to have to say it, but it must be said. 'No, Jimmy, I will never change.'

Edna bowed her head and a little flower fell on her lap, and the voice of Sister Agnes cried suddenly Ah-no, and the echo came. Ah-no ...

At that moment the future was revealed. Edna saw it all. She was astonished; it took her breath away at first. But, after all, what could be more natural? She would go into a convent ... Her father and mother do everything to dissuade her, in vain. As for Jimmy, his state of mind hardly bears thinking about. Why can't they understand? How can they add to her suffering like this? The world is cruel, terribly cruel! After a last scene when she gives away her jewellery and so on to her best friends — she so calm, they so broken-hearted — into a convent she goes. No, one moment. The very evening of her going is the actor's last evening at Port Willin. He receives by a strange messenger a box. It is full of white flowers. But is there no name, no card, nothing? Yes, under the roses, wrapped in a white silk handkerchief, Edna's last photograph with, written underneath —

The world forgetting, by the world forgot.

Edna sat very still under the trees; she clasped the black book in her fingers as though it were her missal ... She takes the name of Sister Angela. Snip, snip! All her lovely hair is cut off. Will she be allowed to send one curl to Jimmy? It is contrived somehow. And in a blue gown with a white head-band Sister Angela goes from the convent to the chapel, from the chapel to the convent with something unearthly in her look, in her sorrowful eyes, and in the gentle smile with which she greets the little children who run to her. A saint! She hears it whispered as she paces the chill, wax-smelling corridors. A saint! And visitors to the chapel are told of the nun whose voice is heard above the other voices, of her youth, her beauty, of her tragic, tragic love. 'There is a man in this town whose life is ruined ...'

A big bee, a golden furry fellow, crept into a freezia, and the delicate flower leaned over, swung, shook; and when the bee flew away it fluttered still as though it were laughing. Happy, careless flower!

Sister Angela looked at it and said, 'Now it is winter.' One night, lying in her icy cell she hears a cry. Some stray animal is out there in the garden, a kitten or a lamb or — well, whatever little animal might be there. Up rises the sleepless nun. All in white, shivering but fearless, she goes and brings it in. But next morning, when the bell rings for matins, she is found tossing in high fever — in delirium — and she never recovers. In three days all is over. The service has been said in the chapel, and she is buried in the corner of the cemetery reserved for the nuns, where there are plain little crosses of wood. Rest in Peace, Sister Angela ...

Now it is evening. Two old people leaning on each other come slowly to the grave and kneel down sobbing, 'Our daughter! Our only daughter!' Now there comes another. He is all in black; he comes slowly. But when he is there and lifts his black hat, Edna sees to her horror his hair is snow-white. Jimmy! To late, too late! The tears are running down his face; he is crying *now*. Too late, too late! The wind shakes the leafless trees in the churchyard. He gives one awful bitter cry.

Edna's black book fell with a thud to the garden path. She jumped up, her heart beating. My darling! No, it's not too late. It's all been a mistake, a terrible dream. Oh, that white hair! How could she have done it? She has not done it. Oh, heavens! Oh, what happiness! She is free, young, and nobody knows her secret. Everything is still possible for her and Jimmy. The house they have planned may still be built, the little solemn boy with his hands behind his back watching them plant the standard roses may still be born. His baby sister ... But when Edna got as far as his baby sister, she stretched out her arms as though the little love came flying through the air to her, and gazing at the garden, at the white sprays on the tree, at those darling pigeons blue against the blue, and the Convent with its narrow windows, she realised that now at last for the first time in her life — she had never imagined any feeling like it before — she knew what it was to be in love, *but — in — love*!

The Canary

… You see that big nail to the right of the front door? I can scarcely look at it even now and yet I could not bear to take it out. I should like to think it was there always even after my time. I sometimes hear the next people saying, 'There must have been a cage hanging from there.' And it comforts me. I feel he is not quite forgotten.

… You cannot imagine how wonderfully he sang. It was not like the singing of other canaries. And that isn't just my fancy. Often, from the window I used to see people stop at the gate to listen, or they would lean over the fence by the mock-orange for quite a long time — carried away. I suppose it sounds absurd to you — it wouldn't if you had heard him — but it really seemed to me he sang whole songs, with a beginning and an end to them.

For instance, when I'd finished the house in the afternoon, and changed my blouse and brought my sewing on to the verandah here, he used to hop, hop, hop from one perch to the other, tap against the bars as if to attract my attention, sip a little water, just as a professional singer might, and then break into a song so exquisite that I had to put my needle down to listen to him. I can't describe it; I wish I could. But it was always the same, every afternoon, and I felt that I understood every note of it.

... I loved him. How I loved him! Perhaps it does not matter so very much what it is one loves in this world. But love something one must! Of course there was always my little house and the garden, but for some reason they were never enough. Flowers respond wonderfully, but they don't sympathise. Then I loved the evening star. Does that sound ridiculous? I used to go into the backyard, after sunset, and wait for it until it shone above the dark gum tree. I used to whisper, 'There you are, my darling.' And just in that first moment it seemed to be shining for me alone. It seemed to understand this ... something which is like longing, and yet it is not longing. Or regret — it is more like regret. And yet regret for what? I have much to be thankful for!

... But after he came into my life I forgot the evening star; I did not need it any more. But it was strange. When the Chinaman who came to the door with birds to sell held him up in his tiny cage, and instead of fluttering, fluttering, like the poor little goldfinches, he gave a faint, small chirp, I found myself saying, just as I had said to the star over the gum tree, 'There you are, my darling.' From that moment he was mine!

... It surprises even me now to remember how he and I shared each other's lives. The moment I came down in the morning and took the cloth off his cage he greeted me with a drowsy little note. I knew it meant 'Missus! Missus!' Then I hung him on the nail outside while I got my three young men their breakfasts, and I never brought him in, to do his cage, until we had the house to ourselves again. Then, when the washing-up was done, it was quite a little entertainment. I spread a newspaper over a corner of the table and when I put the cage on it he used to beat with his wings, despairingly, as if he didn't know what was coming. 'You're a regular little actor,' I used to scold him. I scraped the tray, dusted it with fresh sand, filled his seed and water tins, tucked a piece of chickweed and half a chilli between the bars. And I am perfectly certain he understood and appreciated every

item of this little performance. You see by nature he was exquisitely neat. There was never a speck on his perch. And you'd only
to see him enjoy his bath to realise he had a real small passion for
cleanliness. His bath was put in last. And the moment it was in
he positively leapt into it. First he fluttered one wing, then the
other, then he ducked his head and dabbled his breast feathers.
Drops of water were scattered all over the kitchen, but still he
would not get out. I used to say to him, 'Now that's quite
enough. You're only showing off.' And at last out he hopped and
standing on one leg he began to peck himself dry. Finally he gave
a shake, a flick, a twitter and he lifted his throat — Oh, I can
hardly bear to recall it. I was always cleaning the knives by then.
And it almost seemed to me the knives sang too, as I rubbed
them bright on the board.

... Company, you see, that was what he was. Perfect company. If you have lived alone you will realise how precious that is.
Of course there were my three young men who came in to
supper every evening, and sometimes they stayed in the dining-
room afterwards reading the paper. But I could not expect them
to be interested in the little things that made my day. Why should
they be? I was nothing to them. In fact, I overhead them one
evening talking about me on the stairs as 'the Scarecrow'. No
matter. It doesn't matter. Not in the least. I quite understand.
They are young. Why should I mind? But I remember feeling so
especially thankful that I was not quite alone that evening. I told
him, after they had gone. I said, 'Do you know what they call
Missus?' And he put his head on one side and looked at me with
his little bright eye until I could not help laughing. It seemed to
amuse him.

... Have you kept birds? If you haven't, all this must sound,
perhaps, exaggerated. People have the idea that birds are heartless, cold little creatures, not like dogs or cats. My washerwoman
used to say every Monday when she wondered why I didn't keep

'a nice fox terrier', 'There's no comfort, Miss, in a canary.'
Untrue! Dreadfully untrue! I remember one night. I had had a
very awful dream — dreams can be terribly cruel — even after
I had woken up I could not get over it. So I put on my dressing-
gown and came down to the kitchen for a glass of water. It was
a winter night and raining hard. I suppose I was half asleep still,
but through the kitchen window, that hadn't a blind, it seemed
to me the dark was staring in, spying. And suddenly I felt it was
unbearable that I had no one to whom I could say 'I've had such
a dreadful dream,' or — 'Hide me from the dark.' I even covered
my face for a minute. And then there came a little 'Sweet!
Sweet!' His cage was on the table, and the cloth had slipped so
that a chink of light shone through. 'Sweet! Sweet!' said the darling little fellow again, softly, as much as to say, 'I'm here, Missus.
I'm here!' That was so beautifully comforting that I nearly cried.

... And now he's gone. I shall never have another bird, another pet of any kind. How could I? When I found him, lying on
his back, with his eye dim and his claws wrung, when I realised
that never again should I hear my darling sing, something seemed
to die in me. My breast felt hollow, as if it was his cage. I shall get
over it. Of course I must. One can get over anything in time. And
people always say I have a cheerful disposition. They are quite
right. I thank God I have.

... All the same, without being morbid, or giving way to —
to memories and so on, I must confess that there does seem to
me something sad in life. It is hard to say what it is. I don't mean
the sorrow that we all know, like illness and poverty and death.
No, it is something different. It is there, deep down, deep down,
part of one, like one's breathing. However hard I work and tire
myself I have only to stop to know it is there, waiting. I often
wonder if everybody feels the same. One can never know. But
isn't it extraordinary that under his sweet, joyful little singing it
was just this — sadness? — Ah, what is it? — that I heard.

Notes

Of the twenty-five stories and unfinished sketches in this selection from the fiction Mansfield set in New Zealand, only nine were published in the volumes she put together herself — one *In a German Pension* in 1911, two in *Bliss and Other Stories* published in 1921, and six in *The Garden Party* the following year. Another eight were included by John Middleton Murry when he edited *The Doves' Nest and Other Stories* in 1921, soon after Mansfield's death, and five in *Something Childish and Other Stories* in 1924.

I have not included several New Zealand pieces Murry assembled in the posthumous volumes, on the grounds that they are too fragmentary to be described as 'stories'. Nor have I used a few completed stories that seem to me inferior work, or of a kind better represented by other stories that have been included.

Ian A. Gordon, in *Undiscovered Country* (1974), imaginatively brought together most of the available fragments, as well as most of the completed stories, of Mansfield's fictional New Zealand. (I disagree with Professor Gordon, however, on his regarding 'The Fly' as a New Zealand story.) The collection was arranged to suggest a kind of novel *manqué*, a clear arc from childhood, through adolescence, to family life and on to old age. To achieve this mosaic effect, pieces were arranged in order of subject, not date of composition. The intention of this volume now is quite different — to present the New Zealand stories in the order in which they were written, and as their different subjects or emphases variously engaged Mansfield's attention and developing skills.

The first publication date of the stories in this collection is given in the following notes and, where stories were not published before her death, their date of composition. The volume in which they were first collected is also given. Unless otherwise stated, the text for the stories is taken, with the late Antony Alpers' permission, from his superb edition of *The Stories of Katherine Mansfield* (Oxford University Press, 1984). Most of the information on dating and publication draws on the indispensable 'Commentary' at the end of that work. The reader is directed there for further details.

'About Pat', *Queen's College Magazine*, December 1905, Gordon, *Undiscovered Country*, 1974.

'In the Botanical Gardens', by 'Julian Mark', *Native Companion*, 2 December 1907, *Poems of Katherine Mansfield*, ed. Vincent O'Sullivan, Oxford University Press, 1988.

'Leves Amores', unpublished until *Poems*, 1988, from a typed copy in the Newberry Library, Chicago. The title means 'casual loves', which was taken from a poem in Arthur Symons' *London Nights*, 1896.

'A Birthday', *New Age*, 18 May 1911, *In a German Pension*, 1911.

'Love-Lies-Bleeding', text from the *Scrapbook of Katherine Mansfield*, ed. John Middleton Murry, 1939. Since the first edition of this volume, the appearance of Margaret Scott's transcription of *Katherine Mansfield's Notebooks* (1997) makes it clear that Mansfield was revising this story as late as 1917, although a strong case may still be made for regarding it as a work she began in the same period as *In a German Pension* and came back to much later. It is left next to 'A Birthday', which also used German names in a New Zealand setting, but my earlier claim for its dating must now be revised. The new edition of the *Notebooks* also makes clear that Mansfield did indeed call her character 'Muffi', and this has been restored to the present text.

'The Woman at the Store', *Rhythm*, Spring 1912, *Something Childish*, 1924.

'How Pearl Button was Kidnapped', by 'Lily Heron', *Rhythm*, September 1912, *Something Childish*, 1924.

'The Little Girl', *Rhythm*, October 1912, *Something Childish*, 1924.

'Ole Underwood', *Rhythm*, January 1913, *Something Childish*, 1924.

'Millie', *Blue Review*, June 1913, *Something Childish*, 1924.

'Old Tar', *Westminster Gazette*, 25 October 1913, text from Gordon, *Undiscovered Country*, 1974.

'The Wind Blows', as 'Autumn II', by 'Matilda Berry', *Signature*, 4 October 1915, *Bliss*, 1921.

'Kezia and Tui', text from *Scrapbook*, 1939.

'A Pic-Nic', *New Age*, 7 June 1917, *The Stories of Katherine Mansfield*, 1984.

'Prelude', *Prelude*, Hogarth Press, 1918, *Bliss*, 1921.

'The Stranger', *London Mercury*, January 1921, *The Garden Party*, 1922.

'An Ideal Family', dated July 1921, *The Garden Party*, 1922.

'Her First Ball', dated July 1921, *The Garden Party*, 1922.

'At the Bay', dated September 1921, *The Garden Party*, 1922.

'The Voyage', *Sphere*, 24 December 1921, *The Garden Party*, 1922.

'A Bad Idea', *Something Childish*, 1924. An undated draft survives. Because of its similarity in tone to 'A Married Man's Story', my guess has been to place the unfinished story in 1921.

'A Married Man's Story', unfinished, dated August 1921, *The Doves' Nest*, 1923.

'The Garden Party', dated September 1921, *The Garden Party*, 1922.

'The Doll's House', written in October 1921, *Nation and Athenaeum*, 4 February 1922, *The Doves' Nest*, 1923.

'Six Years After', unfinished, dated November 1921, *The Doves' Nest*, 1923.

'Weak Heart', unfinished, Alpers argues for September 1921, *The Doves' Nest*, 1923.

'Daphne', unfinished, dated November 1921, *The Doves' Nest*, 1923.

'Taking the Veil', *Sphere*, 22 February 1922, *The Doves' Nest*, 1923.

'The Canary', dated 7 July 1922, *The Doves' Nest*, 1923.

Katherine Mansfield Birthplace
Te Puakitanga
25 Tinakori Road, Thorndon, Wellington N.Z.
Tel/Fax: 04-473 7268
Email: kmbirthplace@xtra.co.nz